Visions

Of A Just and Reformed Union

by Russ Goodenough

Copyright, Content, Printing, Numbers & Donated Profits

Visions of a Just and Reformed Union

Copyrighted in 2023 by Russ Goodenough

Printed in the United States of America

Published and First Printed by Amazon in 2023

U.S. Copyright Office Case Number: In Process

Library of Congress Control Number: In Process

International Standard Book Number (ISBN): 9798387957710

CONTENT: Unless acknowledged within the book chapters, any photographs, drawings, or maps included herein are given attribution as to the source in a Credits document in the Documents Section at the end of this book. Cover designed by, and book formatted by Vincent Williams, Anaheim, California (vingraphics@gmail.com).

**All profits from book sales will be
donated to a non-profit organization**

About the Book Cover

The Statue of Liberty National Monument represents America to the entire world.
Thanks to Hotels.com *for the photo.*

The Statue of Liberty is a beautiful reminder to us all that America is a land of immigrants, whether those immigrants walked over the land bridge from Siberia over 50,000 years ago or on passenger ships from the Old World to the New. The Statue is a symbol of the United States that is perhaps better known worldwide than any other American symbol. It stands for the liberty for which all Americans can be grateful.

The California Golden Gate Bridge National Historic Landmark at the entrance to San Francisco Bay. Thanks to "Just Fun Facts" for the photo.

The iconic Golden Gate Bridge is also a beautiful structure that mainly stands for and reminds us of the Golden State of California and the western entrance to continental America. It is also an immigrant entry, just as the Statue is an eastern entrance.

Mount Rushmore National Memorial. Thanks to "Full Suitcase" for the photo.

However, the author has selected Mount Rushmore for the cover based on our current need for outstanding leadership. Rushmore honors four presidents who acted on cherished American values and who put the best interests of the United States above those of any individual. They were unique is that they became perhaps the most important presidents in the history of the American Republic, excepting FDB. America again craves for that type of moral guidance.

Carved out of granite, Mount Rushmore is in the Black Hills of the American State of South Dakota and has become one of the most popular of South Dakota travel destinations.

Thanks go to "Can Stock Photo/sframe" for providing the photo of Mount Rushmore on the front cover of this book. The Smithsonian photo on the back book cover shows a tattered American flag. It was an actual flag recovered from the ruins of the World Trade Center in New York City after the destructive attacks on September 11, 2001. It is an appropriate flag to include, in that it survived a horrendous external attack on America. It may again be symbolic of the resurrection of our country, only this time from the damages inflicted by internal conflict?

INTRODUCTION

Visions of a Just and Reformed Union

The national attack on Washington D.C. and New York City, on September 11, 2001,
brought us together. Our rallying cry was: "United We Stand."
Let us again stand together, united, as we did then.

From many perspectives, the United States is in crisis. The institutions that have been the backbone of our American democracy are no longer trusted by many Americans. Similar to the prelude to the Civil War, friends distrust friends and family members distrust other family members.

What are the causes and are there solutions?

The objective of this book is to offer America examples of what and how we can improve ourselves as a country. The author evaluates many different areas and discusses many diverse categories. The major premise of the book is that several of our problems are so deeply ingrained in our structure that the only possible answer to correct them is to again unite us in a convention to re-write our Constitution. In the process, we can attempt to solve the important, but lesser, problems that also need to be addressed.

The author grew up in small town America. He was a product of the ranches of Southern California. As most Americans from small towns, he grew up with a healthy amount of patriotism and an appreciation of what America is and how we got to where we are as a nation.

America is unique among nations and imbued with most of the qualities that sustained it through its development years and that propelled it from a relatively poor country with a strong industrial base to its greatest triumph, that of the defeat of Hitler and the Nazi menace during the colossally destructive World War II.

We emerged from WWII with the strongest economy in world history and the greatest military machine the world had ever seen. From that triumph over fascism, we then fought a still-to-be-won battle against the forces of totalitarianism. Our accomplishments to many are larger than life. We did what most thought impossible: in less than a decade, we landed Americans on the moon and claimed it for all of mankind. A listing of our accomplishments is in two documents in the Supporting Documents section at the end of this book. It is amazingly long and should be a source of pride for all of us.

Six photo gallery sections show, in photos, all 63 of our American National Parks. We have a beautiful park system that reveals our unique diversity from a physical standpoint that mirrors our unique diversity as a people. The photos and documents are meant to remind us all of who we are and what we have.

We have faced crises before and we will again. However, this crisis is the most severe internal one we have seen since our Civil War. With the defeat of Communism, we have been behaving as though we are rudderless. Prior to 1991, our nation always seemed to have a goal, a direction. Perhaps that is why we face the challenges that confronts us today?

No nation is perfect and our recent divisions have highlighted some of our imperfections. My criticisms included herein are not meant to denigrate us, but are meant to help identify areas where we can improve. Some of the facts are rather glaring and might be disturbing for the reader. When that happens, take time to view some of the park photos. Go to the back of the book and read about our accomplishments. The reader is asked not lose faith in the goodness of our people or the strength of our union.

THE AUTHOR:

The author feels that his experiences have prepared him to offer a perspective and his observations over a lifetime have given him ideas on how we might improve. Growing up on a ranch provided an education on agriculture and a glimpse into our labor concerns. Attending one of our national military service academies enlarged his perspective. Fighting in a clandestine air war in Asia illuminated the strength of our military and the dedication of our officer corps, as well as a graphic example of the horror, brutality, and destruction of warfare.

Flying for 15 years for one of our national airlines gave him insight into corporate America. Running a small business for 34 years introduced him, not only to the strengths of business, but also its weaknesses.

His travels around the world were instructive on areas and peoples. Flying over the Pacific while in the military and flying in the South and Central Pacific for Continental Airlines as well as its affiliate Air Micronesia, allowed additional insights.

He has lived in Southern California, Colorado, Texas, Florida, and Hawaii. Overseas he called Okinawa, Vietnam, and England home as well as living briefly in Libya. He has visited more than 40 Pacific islands as well as most of Europe, every American state, Vermont excepted, and all of North and Central America plus the Caribbean. Two years living in Europe plus extensive travels covering most of Europe, Asia, North Africa, and Oceania provided a global perspective.

For 15 years he served locally on many board of directors, committees, and commissions, including sitting on the boards of two chambers of commerce, that provided a deep understanding of local issues and the inner workings of city and county government. For several years, he chaired a business group that met weekly with the city mayor and city manager. He founded three businesses (an equipment and truck rental company, a propane tank exchange company, and an underground fuel tank pressure testing company) and helped found two retail business organizations. In Florida, he purchased vacant farmland and developed it into housing. In California, he developed, owned, and operated rental housing.

Educationally, he earned a BS in physics and engineering plus enough additional undergraduate units that would now qualify him for a master's in public affairs. Another year in college provided a certificate and license in real estate, and two years in a graduate MBA program answered questions needed in the running of a business.

With that background, he feels qualified to write this book.

News is usually always negative and today's media is no different. What is different is that there is real fear that America is on the brink of something terribly destructive. We have come to question who we are as a nation, and what we stand for.

Our media has been transformed by the advent of the internet. Newspapers and magazines, long the staple of Americans interested in the world around them, are no longer the sole sources of news. Television has taken on an even greater role than in the past. Belief in "fake news" has often surpassed that of "trusted news". Part of us has lost trust in what we are being told by government and by a media that all-too-often is guided by a quest for profit instead of a quest for revealing truth over fiction.

Just like a marriage, the relationship between our citizens, our institutions, and our government has been based on trust. In the past, we trusted what our government told us. We trusted statements and actions of agencies and institutions. We believed the news that we heard through the various media platforms. Trust, that most basic of stable relationships, has been shattered and the causes of that lack of trust go back many years.

A poison that has infected our society is an inflated regard for the importance of money over more important values that should be motivating and directing our efforts. If the polls are correct, we are an ignorant society. Far too many of us have little conception of the world around us.

Education is a means for a better understanding of those values, but most Americans cannot make sense of our planet and its geography. If we are to properly understand our world and our place as a nation within that world, then we need to have a much better sense of world geography and history. The oft-quoted statement that those who don't know of the mistakes of the past are bound to make the same mistakes, seems obvious. Yet knowledge of world and even American history is not a strength of our populous.

If asked, would the reader be able to recount a majority of the virtues? As stated in "Ethics and Virtue" as proposed by Santa Clara University, "Virtues are attitudes, dispositions, or character traits that enable us to be and to act in ways that develop (our) potential. They enable us to pursue the ideals we have adopted. Examples of virtues (include): Honesty, courage, compassion, generosity, fidelity, integrity, fairness, self-control, and prudence."

Our churches have long taught us the virtues, but our polls also tell us that many Americans do not attend church and have not had a religious upbringing. According to Wikipedia, "Virtue is moral excellence. A virtue is a trait or quality that is deemed to be morally good and thus is valued as a foundation of principle and good moral being. In other words, it is a behavior that shows high moral standards: doing what is right and avoiding what is wrong."

The author's father once told him: "I regret that my generation, which lived through the Great Depression, passed down to your generation an over-inflated consideration of the value of money." That is now more relevant than ever.

This book is designed to give perspective on the causes of our divisions and to suggest ideas and alternatives available to us. Part of the solution includes the necessity of reestablishing trust and adherence to higher values with which to guide us.

While appearing dire, our situation can be cured, but it will take an awakening and a dedication on the part of our citizens. We need to redirect the paths we have been traveling. We need to reevaluate what it means to be a great nation. We need to restructure many of the systems that are the fabric of our country. As it is with struggling sports teams, we need to get back to basics.

The process of reenergizing our country and rebuilding that needed trust will take time and it will take a renewed commitment from our citizens.

The author has a strong belief that we will someday look back at today's troubles and divisions that are shattering our country, and be thankful that the threat was not well-directed nor was it well-led. We have suffered a needed awakening to the internal threats posed by demigods.

Our military is a source of pride for our nation and a bulwark against external threats. The author has long believed that a greater threat to our country lies internally and not from external nations and ideologies. Hopefully, our current troubles will act as a wake-up call that allows us to pass those laws needed to protect our country from ever again having to revisit the nightmare we have been facing.

PHOTOS GALLERIES—AMERICAN NATIONAL PARKS:

This book is critical of many things about America. The author has attempted to be constructive in his suggestions about how we can improve. With all the negatives, it is helpful to remember who we still are and who and what we have been.

While we certainly have national faults, there are also many areas where America could be considered outstanding. It would take far more than the pages of this book to properly include what is and has made us a great nation. What the author has included are three documents that should be seen and read to remind ourselves of just what a great country we do have. Two documents: America- An Exceptional Country and Our National Wonders may be found in the Supporting Document Section at the end of this book.

A third document is in six parts and is included within the book chapters. America and its territories have 63 national parks. We invented the National Park system and gave it to the world. From Yellowstone National Park, established on March 1, 1872, to the latest established, New River Gorge, established in 2021, the National Park system is the largest in the world. America is unique and uniquely beautiful. It is also very diverse.

Those qualities of beauty and diversity are included in the six Photo Gallery presentations. All 63 parks are shown. Nowhere on earth is there a country that has nearly as many spectacular places to visit. The reader is invited to scroll through the photo galleries to experience once again the sense of wonder and awe at what is our physical America. Enjoy the experience.

Good luck and good reading.

Table of Contents

Table of Contents

Part 1

Our Collective Being

Chapter One

Structure & Restructure
American Government & Institutions

"Each generation should have the solemn opportunity to update the constitution every nineteen or twenty years, thus allowing it to be handed on, with periodical repairs, from generation to generation, to the end of time." — **Thomas Jefferson, third President of the United States and author of the American Declaration of Independence.**

"The Founding Fathers did not, of course, follow Jefferson's advice." We have only convened one constitutional convention, and that was in 1787. The convention did provide us with our Constitution and provided a means to update, which is the process of amending. The American Constitution can be amended only by votes of two-thirds of the House and Senate and three-fourths of state legislatures.

However, some state legislatures did follow Jefferson's advice and provided for periodic state constitutional revision. Kentucky, Massachusetts, and New Hampshire "embraced periodic convention referenda in the late 18th century, and today 14 state constitutions provide for them. Some 100 such votes have been held over the course of American history, succeeding a total of 25 times in eight different states."

Over the years, many have agreed with the Founding Fathers, that our Constitution is well-structured. In comparison to the structures in other countries, America is very well-constructed. However, we can be better. We can rebuild to be better prepared to meet the challenges of an ever-changing country and world.

Threats to the ability of our citizenry to direct the course of our nation, abound.

Jefferson's idea of a periodic constitutional convention seems unworkable. Changing the basic law of the land every generation would create chaos. But the idea of a single constitutional convention seems prudent and now appears to be a necessity. There are too many current flaws in today's America' that would overwhelm the amendment process to correct. The flaws were not the fault of our Founding Fathers. After all, we have survived as the world's longest running democracy, based on our Constitution, for 234 years as of 2023. The Founding Fathers could not have foreseen what has become the greatest internal threat to our democracy, the need for campaign money which has led to such deep-seeded corruption.

Before we reconvene in a constitutional convention, it would be beneficial if we could reestablish trust in one another before any good could come from another convention. We also do not have anyone of the stature of George Washington who independently oversaw the only federal constitutional convention that we have convened. In today's poisonous environment, we need to reestablish the respect for one another that will be necessary to direct the many debates needed.

However, having said that, the importance of the needed changes are such that the convention should be convened sometime within the next ten years, if possible. The question remains, can we reestablish the needed trust in just ten years?

SPECIAL INTERESTS:

It costs candidates for office in the United States money to run campaigns and lots of it. This means that candidates become beholden to the providers of funds and are unduly influenced by them. Businesses, institutions, and other organizations normally must account to stockholders and boards of directors for monies spent.

While some do allocate funding for just causes, far too many corporations expect a return on their "investment". In return for "investing" in campaigns, businesses and other organizations expect favorable votes or treatment. Thus, the merits of proposed bills take a backseat to special interests. That the many attempts to pass bills to rectify the system have been defeated, or not even allowed to come to a vote, speaks to the depth of corruption in our Congress. Senators and Representatives seem not to want to upset the current system that obviously enriches their bank accounts. Corrective action for this abuse will require a much higher level of interest on the part of the electorate to force a proper vote to restructure the corrupt system of "donations?".

GERRYMANDERING:

Definition of gerrymandering: "To manipulate the boundaries of an electoral constituency so as to favor one party or class." Elected representatives are much more beholden to those who elected them if they are faced with the possibility of defeat in an election. Our Founding Fathers expected free and fair elections that were based more on policies than personalities and parties. An actual vote is meant to allow for the throwing of representatives out of office, if necessary.

Gerrymandering is allowed and practiced in our country. It is possibly the most undemocratic institution in this democratic republic. In the redistricting of states after each federal census, individual states are required to redraw the boundaries of districts to distribute voters more evenly among those districts represented by Congressional representatives. It is also needed to determine the number of representatives allowed for each state based on the relative populations of the states.

When the author was in high school, his congressional district was comprised of the following counties: Ventura, Santa Barbara, San Luis Obispo, and Monterrey, all in California. The district boundaries were the boundaries of the counties. That is fair and does not give preference for any particular political party. Today, districts have convoluted boundaries that defy logic. The districts so constituted are terribly unfair and unduly slanted in favor of one party over the other.

As currently practiced, gerrymandering makes a district "safe" and dependable for voting in favor of one party. When a district is considered safe for a party, the elected representative does not have to worry about the concerns of his or her constituents. All they really must do is pay "lip service" to their constituent concerns. Gerrymandered districts make it almost impossible to turn a representative out of office. It is a nasty, undemocratic, practice and crying for change.

Gerrymandering can be rectified by passing a law establishing criteria for the drawing of district boundaries. Restrictions could include wording similar to the following: "District boundaries may have a maximum of only five sides, two of which have to be straight lines. A side may be defined as a geographical feature such as a river, mountain range, or seacoast. It may also be defined as a major highway, irrigation canal, or a political boundary such as the limits of a city, the boundaries of a county or state."

Whatever the wording, we must change this most undemocratic of institutions. In today's poisonous political climate, it is doubtful if even the most reasonable of suggested changes will win a majority of votes. It is the depth of that corruption that is so disturbing to those Americans who remember a time of collegial workings of our Congress. Representative government demands compromise and today's political parties rarely allow it.

CONGRESSIONAL REPRESENTATION:

Our Congress currently has 435 voting representatives. Additionally, five delegates and one resident commissioner serve as non-voting members of the House representing: the District of Columbia (DC), the Commonwealth of Puerto Rico, the islands of American Samoa, the island of Guam, the U.S. Virgin Islands, and the Commonwealth of Northern Mariana Islands.

American Samoa, Guam, the American Virgin Islands, and the Northern Mariana Islands are American territories that do not have sufficient economies or populations to be considered for statehood. However, Puerto Rico should be allowed immediate statehood and thus be allowed to vote in Congress. The nearby Virgin Islands could be included in that state. Puerto Rico has over three million residents and deserves recognition and the ability to stand equally with the states. We are past the period of claiming territory for an indefinite time. Puerto Rico was the second colony established by Columbus, in 1493, when he claimed the Caribbean for the Spanish Crown.

Our Pacific Island groups and the individual Pacific islands that belong to America should be later-considered for a combined statehood, perhaps along with other Pacific Island groups that might be favorable to uniting with the United States. Individually owned Pacific islands may have more than one island, such as Wake, which consists of two distinct islands. The individual American islands include: Baker, Howland, Jarvis, Johnston Atoll, Kingman Reef, Midway Atoll, Palmyra Atoll, Wake, and Guam. Guam is the only fully developed island with a population approaching 200,000 and a large military presence.

Currently, America supports several island groups with infrastructure maintenance via the Pacific Seabees and we also have defense treaties with several island groups, principally the former members of the American Trust Territories of the Pacific: the Marshall Islands, the Caroline Islands (including Yap), and the Republic of Palau. In addition to providing defense, we provide funding and access to social services.

With the advent of global warming, formerly reluctant island nations may look favorably to union with the United States if the threats caused by rising sea levels are addressed. Any consideration of union with Pacific islands has to include the threat posed by China and its current attempts to counter American influence in the Pacific.

Congress should also consider expanding its non-voting representation to include Native

Americans. For example, an Alaskan Native Delegate could represent those of Eskimo, Aleut, Athabascan, and Tlingit descent. Their combined population is 112,942, far more than populations of current states when they were first admitted to the Union.

Other American native tribes and their populations include the following:

Tribe:	Population (2020):
Cherokee	729,533
Navaho & Pueblo	372,282
Sioux & Blackfeet Sioux	239,110
Choctaw	158,774
Chippewa	149,669
Iroquois Nations	80,822

THE ELECTORAL COLLEGE:

Over the years, since its inception, many have criticized the Electoral College as being undemocratic in that it is essentially a winner-take-all system for each state. The College was the result of compromise in the first Constitutional Convention. When they were discussing the structure of the union, the smaller states feared the power and influence of the larger states. They felt that a simple majority vote of all Americans would result in their individual state influences being overwhelmed by those states with much larger populations.

The College, while seeming anachronistic, has worked as envisioned by the smaller states. Their influence in our elections has far outweighed their size. However, that greater influence means that those living in the larger states lose proportional influence. The effect is that it often disenfranchises voters in larger states who cast ballots that just pad the margin of victory for a particular candidate. It disallows consideration of the margin of victory in each state. Those arguments have merit as five American Presidents have lost the popular vote to their opponent, yet won the presidency.

Election:	President:	Margin:
1824	**John Quincy Adams** lost to Andrew Jackson	-38,221 votes
1876	**Rutherford B. Hayes** lost to Samuel Tilden	-252,666 votes
1888	**Benjamin Harrison** lost to Grover Cleveland	-90,596 votes
2000	**George W. Bush** lost to Al Gore	-537,179 votes
2016	**Donald Trump** lost to Hillary Clinton	-2,868,686 votes

In the 2016 election, Republican Donald Trump beat his Democratic opponent Hillary Clinton, while losing the popular vote by 2,868,686. That victory would have turned into a loss to Clinton if the vote from California would have been fairly counted. Clinton won California by 62.2% of the vote with a plurality of 4,269,978 votes. Those votes were effectively not counted.

The Electoral College has 538 members. Each member is equivalent to one vote in the College. To win the Presidency, a candidate must win 270 Electoral College votes. In 2016, California had

55 of those 538 votes. Those 55 votes were earned by Clinton. The problem is that she would have earned them if she had won by only one vote instead of the 4,269,978 votes that were cast for her. Effectively, 4,269,977 California votes did not count. The presidential election was national and not a state election. Shouldn't all votes, no matter from what state, matter in a national election?

For California, because it is a solid "blue state" (standing for leaning to the Democrat Party), it seems not to matter in any national election. It is not a battleground state. Republican and Democratic candidates seemingly only covet California as a source of revenue to the candidate in the form of donations to the candidate. For both parties, why waste time campaigning in a state that is a lock to vote Democrat?

There is an unspoken danger in ignoring California, or any other populous state, in national elections. Growing up, the author felt more allegiance to California than he did for the federal union. It was a time when the state was still very insular. There was half a continent of very sparsely-populated states between California and the heavily populated Eastern States. He was not alone in feeling isolated and treated as an irrelevancy nationally. On more than one occasion, serious discussion was made on the editorial pages of more than one major California newspaper, including the very influential Los Angeles Times, about the possibility of seceding from the national union. That discussion has been muted for over 40 years, with the inclusion of so many immigrants from other states and other nations.

Texas, however, is a much different story. According to the *Texas Tribune*, the State Republican Executive Committee, the governing body of the Republican Party of Texas, voted on a proposal for Texas to secede from the United States. The Executive Committee vote was whether to place a non-binding proposal on their state ballot. The measure was defeated, but the very fact that it came to a vote is cause for worry. "The ballot language…read, **"If the Federal Government continues to disregard the Constitution and the sovereignty of the State of Texas, the State of Texas should reassert its prior status as an independent nation."**

An additional cause for worry is what the Russian Federation does with any type of dissatisfaction it senses in America. According to the same *Texas Tribune*, a US Senate sponsored report claimed that: "The Russian-based Internet Research Agency used two social media accounts, "Heart of Texas" on Facebook, and "@rebeltexas" on Instagram, to spread falsehoods and exert divisions during the 2016 elections."

The Internet Research Agency, from its offices in St. Petersburg, Russia, hacked into Democrat and Republican e-mails and then spread false information. The Internet Research Agency is an arm of the Russian GRU, which is the Russian military intelligence agency, equivalent to the American CIA.

The Mueller Report indicted several reported Russian spies and 12 Russian nationals working for the so-called Research Agency. In addition, Konstantin Kilimnik, a longtime Paul Manafort associate who worked with Manafort in Ukraine, was indicted by Mueller as a Russian spy. Manafort served for a time as campaign manager for the Trump 2016 presidential campaign. This does not mean that Manafort was working for or supporting the Russians in any capacity. It does mean that he was subject to Russian influence. Could the current poisonous divisions between the Democrats and the Republicans be the result of planned Russian disinformation?

In today's world, any consideration of a state seceding from the United States seems bizarre. California itself is very relevant and has power nationally. Yet, what happened before can happen again. It just seems prudent to eliminate injustices that might be a catalyst in future elections voted by state electorates that may be more involved than at present. The same arguments hold true for states, other than California and Texas, with relatively large populations:

STATE:	POPULATION (2022):
California	39,613,493
Texas	29,730,311
Florida	21,944,577
New York	19,299,981

LISTING of GDP by NATION with STATES INCLUDED (2022):

(1)	China	$ 13.49 trillion
(2)	**United States** (minus California, Texas & New York)	
		$ 12.55 trillion
(3)	Japan	$ 4.97 trillion
(4)	Germany	$ 4.00 trillion
(5)	**California (estimated by Bloomberg to overtake Germany in 2023.**	
		$ 3.56 trillion
(6)	United Kingdom	$ 2.83 trillion
(7)	France	$ 2.78 trillion
(8)	India	$ 2.72 trillion
(9)	**Texas**	**$ 2.35 trillion**
(10)	Italy	$ 2.07 trillion
(11)	**New York**	**$ 2.03 trillion**

Both Texas and California have the infrastructure and power to become very successful nations, if they ever separated from our union. It behooves us to rectify any injustice that might entice future leaders of the major states to attempt separation. California has often been compared to a separate country. However, Texas, with favorable corporate laws and minus state income taxes, is moving rapidly up the listings of population and gross domestic products (GDP). If the current trends continue, Texas will be rivaling California in both population and GDP in a matter of a few decades.

States with that much voting and financial power have to be heard and we need to ensure that their votes count as much as any other state. The fairness doctrine almost demands that the electoral college system be scrapped. The Electoral College System is an anachronism and needs to be eliminated in favor of a simple inclusive national vote. It would be only fair that, in a federal election, votes should be counted on a national and not a state system. The process of amending the Constitution is an arduous and time-consuming one, but it needs to be done to address this injustice.

JUSTICE and INJUSTICE

THE EXTREME (SUPREME) COURT:

The current troubles nationally and the precipitous drop in the prestige and respect for the Supreme Court have caused many to question if our structure needs to be changed. "The Constitution does not stipulate the number of Supreme Court Justices; the number is set instead by Congress. There have been as few as six Justices, but since 1869 there have been nine Justices, including one Chief Justice."

A necessary part of any structural change is that, in our current climate of upheaval, changes cannot be drastic. We need national stability and any discussion of changing the number of Justices is counterproductive. If one political party changes the number of Justices to solve an immediate problem, the other political party can then just undo what was done when it again comes to power. We need to maintain stability where we are able.

THE JUSTICE DEPARTMENT:

The Federal Justice Department has been under executive control since its inception. Under President Trump, it became politicized, which is a grave danger for the independence of justice. The idea of transferring control of the Justice Department from the executive branch to the judicial branch, should be considered.

There are many pros and cons in any consideration of that magnitude. The inner workings of Justice demand to be heard from those deeply involved and with knowledge much deeper than that of the author. It may be unworkable, but the vision of what a politicized Justice Department could do is chilling. It almost happened under former President Trump. That prospect also demands that a discussion be opened on how to better protect Justice from the threat of politicization.

Inspector General's (IGs) are another consideration. The Executive Branch should never be allowed to fire IGs.

THE DANGERS of EXECUTIVE ORDERS:

As currently used, Presidential Executive Orders are a danger to our democracy. They circumvent the constitutional powers of the Legislative Branch without any laws that reduce or control the amount and type of use. So far, it has not resulted in any constitutional crisis, but the threat remains that it could.

The Legislative Branch needs to again consider limitations that allow presidential emergency powers in today's occasional need for a quick executive response, but also limit the use of those powers and also address the types of use.

Handled judiciously, executive orders can be beneficial to quick decisions in a world where quick decisions are sometimes necessary. But they have been and are being abused. There are few checks on their use. Extreme use of executive orders could lead to dictatorial government and a means of bypassing the system of checks and balances incorporated in our Constitution.

SMALL-CLAIMS COURTS:

The author, by virtue of owning and running a medium-sized retail business for 34 years, is very familiar with small-claims courts. The nature of his business required him to often file suit in small-claims courts to claim monies owed. It also caused him to represent his business as a defendant in other cases.

Small-claims courts are designed to save individuals and businesses the, sometimes exorbitant, legal costs of other civil trials. Lawyers are not allowed at small-claims court trials, although they do sometimes attempt to use the privileges allowed them in Superior and Appellate Courts.

Superior Courts are sometimes called Trial Courts. They handle all civil cases, such as family law, probate, juvenile, and other civil cases. They also handle all criminal cases and oversee: small-claims courts, appeals of small-claims cases, appeals of civil cases involving $25,000 or less, and appeals of infractions like traffic and misdemeanor cases. There are two Appellate Courts in California: the Courts of Appeal and the California Supreme Court.

Small-claims cases are held in Superior Courtrooms. An individual or sole proprietor may sue for up to $10,000 in small-claims. Corporations and other entities are limited to a maximum of $5,000. That amount has not changed since the author was in business and, due to inflation, should be increased.

Small-claims courts are due some other changes. Most small claims cases are settled out of court, a method strongly endorsed by the Superior Court judges that hear the cases. Prior to court appearances, plaintiffs are allowed by law to subpoena certain document of a defendant. In practice, that just does not work. Any defendant who has appeared before in a small claims court action knows that there is no teeth in the subpoena requirement.

The author's experience in small-claims involved appearances in one to three court trials within each year for a total of 34 years. Rules allow that: if a defendant does not bring subpoenaed documents to the trial, the plaintiff may go to the judge to request the judge demand the defendant bring the required documents. Judges do not like to sit in on small-claims actions. That is almost always evident. They do not like to deal with "minor" cases. Every time that the author attempted to ask a judge to demand that a defendant produce certain subpoenaed documents that were not produced, his request was not favored. In fact, not once in 34 years of small-claims actions, did any judge ever agree to see the author or hear his plea. He never saw a judge in chambers. Not once. If there is no teeth in a law, or if those entrusted to uphold the law do not comply with the law, then respect for that law is diminished. Subpoenas should have meaning. In small-claims actions, they don't.

Superior Court Judges are due respect and the system demands that respect. However, the courts and system do not show respect for defendants and plaintiffs in small claims actions. Judges often act as though anything involving small-claims is a nuisance. While judges want settlements without a trial, the system does not show a respect for those settlements. There are no rooms where discussions may be held. During the authors' experience, the courts did not even provide chairs or tables. Instead, defendants and plaintiffs had to find an open space, usually in hallways, to sit on the floor. The indignity of wearing a suit, sitting on the floor, having to dodge a public who could then eavesdrop on discussions was difficult and somewhat humiliating. The judges and the so-called court just did not seem to care.

While the small-claims system does have an appellate process, those appeals have to do with appealing a judgment itself. If a judgment allows payments over time and the defendant does not pay as agreed, the plaintiff has no recourse that is cost effective. Bad actors are allowed to continue to be bad actors. That lack of teeth also applies to regular Superior Court judgments. Legal and court costs are such that defendant's lawyers know that, in certain cases with a low dollar judgment, the costs of trying to get a defendant to pay a judgment is often more than the judgment itself. That is not justice.

The author was so incensed at one small claims judgment that he risked being held in contempt, when he told the judge that "this judgment is not fair or right and justice is not being done". He also told the judge that "the court risks the loss of respect for the court system by business". The surprising response from the judge: "I agree with you. There are 1,500 judges in California and we all feed from the same trough," as though that might explain why he could issue a lousy verdict.

SUPERIOR COURTS:

The court system all too often rewards lawyers for frivolous lawsuits. Since judges were lawyers before they became judges, they all come from the same fraternity. Often, judges will take the path of least resistance. Case in point: The author once attended a trial in the Superior   Court in Santa Monica, California. He was representing his rental company in a lawsuit brought by the former company GTE. The case was that a contractor had rented a dump truck and had backed it into a GTE telephone pole and knocked it down. California law states that a renter is responsible for damages incurred during a rental if the renter was the cause of that damage. It is supposed to protect a rental company.

The author's company was subpoenaed along with the contractor. The author showed and the contractor was absent. The expected judgment demanded that the contractor pay GTE for its loss. Since the contractor was absent and the only checkbook present was that of the author, the judge then rewarded the contractor by demanding that the author pay the full cost and demanded a check be written on the spot. Just because a law states one thing does not mean it will be complied with. Judges are free to issue whatever judgments that they feel are right for that day. Is that justice?

Another judge ruled against the author when he was plaintiff in an action that involved a contractor who illegally staged an accident in one location to account for the contractor's destruction of one of the author's water trucks at another location. A school district had rented the water truck for an "on site" job and the contractor hired by the district used the truck on another job miles from the district and managed to destroy the truck by rolling it down a ravine. The judge turned out to be a friend of the defense attorney and they were both members of the same country club. Is that justice?

"DEEP POCKETS":

Another case involved the author's manager at one of his rental yards. The manager wore the company uniform shirt, as required. He decided to buy some groceries before going home and was driving in uniform in his car two hours after business closure. He was then involved in a traffic accident.

The police report of the accident laid the entire blame on the other party. He caused the accident. Also, he was driving on a suspended California driver's license. Additionally, the investigating officer found an open bottle of liquor in the car and suspected that the other driver was under the influence. He ordered the driver to go to the nearest hospital for a breathalyzer test. The driver did not show up at the hospital as ordered.

Unfortunately, the drunk driver had a passenger who was thrown out of the car onto the pavement. He sustained injuries that created a hospital bill of over $200,000. The system wants payment for those costs.

The guilty driver had no insurance, also required by California law. Who is to pay?

The driver also had no money, resulting in the author's manager, who was just an innocent party to the accident and was a victim as his car was severely damaged, getting sued. But the manager was by no means a wealthy man. However, he was wearing a company uniform shirt. The drunk driver's attorney sensed a deep pocket. He sued the author's company.

The suit did not go anywhere, but it did cause the company to spend three years defending itself against "discovery" and cost the company significant legal fees. There was no justice in that court action that allowed discovery. The entire matter was preposterously stupid. However, the time and money lost in defending such stupidity has to come from somewhere. Those costs had to be partially passed to the company customers, the public. The presiding judge rewarded the attorney for the guilty party by allowing him to charge billable hours. Not sure of where the money came to pay those hours, but they came from somewhere? Often the author witnessed judges who seemed to consider that, since a suit had been filed, someone should get paid. And almost always judgments seemed to favor additional billable hours for the attorneys.

The above stories are true in every detail. Sadly, they are very common stories of businesses forced to deal with a structure that too often rewards and enriches attorneys for filing frivolous lawsuits. Another cost that is also forced to be passed on to consumers is the cost of liability insurance premiums caused by such lawsuits. That just increases time that is wasted when it could be used much more productively. It also added to the cost of living for the public. Is that justice?

MISUSE of the SYSTEM:

The author listed the above aggravations to explain what has contributed to the inefficiencies of our justice system. He is not sure what could be done to rectify? Even with its many faults, the justice system does seem to work at times. One of its many faults is that of the time required to comply with certain court requirements. Lawyers are allowed an inordinate amount of time to work their cases. There is almost never any form of punishment for lawyers that fail to meet deadlines required of the courts. It almost seems designed to pad lawyer's pocketbooks by requiring such long time-periods to complete cases.

To lawyers, it is all billable time. With "deep pockets" defendants, they can use the long time-delays in processing a case, especially one that involves appeals, to their advantage. They can drag out a case for years.

General contractors are also guilty of misuse. Some contractors are known for "stiffing" subcontractors. They hire a sub to perform some duties on a jobsite. Then, after completion of the sub's work, the general contractor in charge of the work can find an excuse, any excuse, to not pay for the work done. The author watched this happen to subs at a large shopping center construction site where the general contractor and subcontractors all used many of his heavy construction machines. These situations often result in sad endings. Many subs jump at the chance to work a large project, even one that might require a long period prior to payment for services. Too many of those subs so stiffed must legitimately declare bankruptcy.

President Trump was known for his many construction projects, particularly in New York and New Jersey. When he participated in the Republican Primary election in 2016, he was the defendant in 3,500 court cases where the plaintiffs claimed he found excuse after excuse never to pay his sub and general contractors. They may have been civil issues, but also moral ones.

BANKRUPTCY COURTS:

The author sat on two bankruptcy court committees. He also filed a bankruptcy suit that was merged with many other similar bankruptcy claims in one larger lawsuit. He is somewhat familiar with how the bankruptcy court system operates. He never filed a personal bankruptcy nor did he ever file bankruptcy for one of his companies. All bankruptcy actions involved other companies.

The bankruptcy process is terribly corrupt.

In one court, the author did not even meet with the other members of the committee. Somehow, a decision was made outside of the committee that is empowered to make those decisions. It had to have been between the assigned judge and the attorneys involved. Perhaps that was the case and it was legitimate, but the committee did not ever hear from the court.

In a second bankruptcy action, many meetings were held for a very active committee. Committee research found many hidden assets not claimed on the required bankruptcy court filings by the defendant contractor. The committee found a vacation home not listed and several Mercedes cars of worth. In particular, the committee chairwoman was very conscientious and worked hard to get the large contractor to pay the creditors, including the $60,000 due her company.

The author and several other committee members were required to drive to Fresno from Southern California for each meeting. That distance was no problem if the committee showed progress, which it did. No other committee members or creditors in the action received any money, just the company that employed the very effective committee chair. With the debt paid, her company could no longer support her committee work and she left the committee.

The court rules have an attorney representing the court explain the court and how it works. He is then assigned to the committee and helps the committee in its deliberations. The committee was so effective that it was able to change the contractor's original filing from a Chapter 11 to a Chapter 7 bankruptcy. Chapter 11 would have allowed the contractor to continue running his company without necessarily paying off any of the debt represented by the committee members. Chapter 7 required the contractor to close his business and use his assets to pay off the legitimate claims.

The attorney failed to inform the committee that, once the action changed from a Chapter 11 to a Chapter 7, the committee would be disbanded. He waited until after the action to inform. The committee then had no power to force the contractor to sell off his vacation home or sell his several Mercedes cars that he had hidden from the court. Those assets had been discovered by committee members. However, the court did not forget those assets.

The Chapter 11 committee had identified assets worth well over a million dollars more than the monies owed to all the committee members and all others who had similar claims that the committee represented. Those assets were then taken over by a Trustee of the Court. Since the assets had been well-identified, selling of the assets when necessary and payment of the debts should have been able to have been accomplished very quickly by the Trustee. Not so.

The Trustee and the Court Judge kept the action open, without payment of any kind to the committee members or to any other creditor, for eleven years. During that time the author was in telephone contact with the trustee, and advised the trustee about selling drivable assets at auction. The cars and certain construction equipment was then sold at auction. After that, nothing from the court.

The author then sent two letters to the judge and only received one in reply, a very unsatisfactory reply. It was apparent from the letter and his actions, that the Judge was very familiar with the Trustee. At the end of the eleven years, the case was finally closed. During the eleven years, the court and the trustee were paid for their "efforts". At the end of the 11 years, the assets were gone and not one payment was ever sent to those who were left holding the bag when the contractor reneged on his payments for services and supplies. The judge and trustee pocketed the monies owed to the creditors. That is corrupt justice.

THE COURT is not the COURT:

The reader is asked to bear an extensive explanation of a final bankruptcy court action. It involved Continental Airlines and its employees. It also involved the federal bankruptcy laws. At the time, the bankruptcy laws allowed the notorious actions of a company trying to take control of Continental. Those laws have been changed to disallow the very actions that took place. This narrative is not about the laws. It is about how the bankruptcy court handled the case. Its actions were appalling and the entire court system should be investigated.

Accountability is dealt with in another chapter. Lack of accountability should always be suspected when large monies are involved. Wishfully, it would be quite helpful if some enterprising journalist would do some investigative reporting on two units of government that have never really had any meaningful accounting. Those entities are: The Bankruptcy Courts and the Bureau of Land Management (BLM). "All bankruptcy cases are handled in federal courts under rules outlined in the U.S. Bankruptcy Code."

The BLM is another matter. There is no known instance that the author is aware of the BLM operating in a corrupt manner. However, the BLM is the largest landowner in America. It handles leases of various items such as cattle, logging, and mining, each of which can be very lucrative. With the money involved, and the lack of any known accountability available to the public, it just makes sense that crimes could have been committed. Indeed, all branches of government should have a proper level of public accountability.

According to the Bureau of Land Management, it has over 8,800 employees entrusted to "administer public lands on the basis of multiple use and sustained yield of resources." Their control is vast. In their words: "We manage 245 million acres of public lands and 700 million acres of mineral estate. The level and limitations of Federal control are dictated by the Federal Land Policy and Management Act. With that level of control and with the dollars involved, the temptations must be immense? While not implying that crimes have been committed, it might be beneficial for the media to look into both the Bankruptcy Court and the BLM.

At the time of the bankruptcy action, Continental was flush with money. Francisco Lorenzo, who took over the company in an adversarial action, was planning on creating the largest airline in the Free World. Eventually he did, but his methods forced the government to deny him from participating in any airline ever again. How they did that is a mystery, but they did it nonetheless.

Continental Airlines declared bankruptcy and abrogated all their union contracts. That action went against the gentleman's system that then existed between airlines, the FAA, and the unions. They all acted pretty much together on many issues. All were effective when they worked together and created a system to thwart the skyjacking of airline aircraft.

The FARs (Federal Air Regulations), were created by the FAA for the protection of the traveling public, the airlines, and airline employees. Included in the FARs were provisions that protected the flying public. Airline pilots were restricted from flying too many hours under adverse conditions. The FAA, aware that all union contracts with the airlines had hour and time restrictions to protect the safety of commercial flying, apparently felt that there was no need to enact regulations for issues that had already been addressed in the contracts. Most protecting provisions were in place, but not all.

When Lorenzo abrogated the pilot contract, he eliminated those safety protections. Specifically eliminated were the back-side-of-the-clock provisions, which involved night flying. He also cut pilot pay in half and eliminated the retirement program, thereby pocketing the money that had been reserved in banks for pilot retirements. No such payments to the retirement system were ever made during Lorenzo's time with Continental. Somehow, he did it despite the federal ERISA laws that prohibited such actions.

However, those incidents are not part of this narrative about the irresponsibility and high level of corruption shown by the Bankruptcy Court. What was most disturbing, was that the Court seemed not to care about the illegality of its actions and how it might be perceived. They acted as though they were immune.

After the Saturday afternoon bankruptcy filing, the first scheduled flight for Continental, who continued flying its scheduled flights, was Flight #1 from LAX to Honolulu, Hawaii. The author was one of the three pilots scheduled for that flight. He refused to fly under the conditions imposed by Continental. Subsequent to that action, he received two regular checks from Continental for flight time earned. Additionally, he received three checks for per diem earned. All of those checks bounced, even though the company had lots of money. The author had written a thesis for an MBA program about the Continental Planning Process. He became well aware of company accounts and assets.

He first filed with the federal Department of Labor, requesting payment for the bounced checks. When a class-action suit was filed on behalf of all Continental pilots, the Department merged his case with the class action case. At the time, Continental's headquarters were located in Houston, Texas. The Bankruptcy Court chosen to hear the case was located in Biloxi, Mississippi. When Biloxi was chosen, a bankruptcy judge in Houston asked "judicial privilege" and was then allowed to transfer to Biloxi to judge the case.

Preparations for the trial required pilots to file documents with the Court showing monies owed. Keep in mind that Continental was flush with money and still did not honor the checks that they printed. The then-bankruptcy laws allowed corporations to declare bankruptcy for reasons other than financial condition. The Houston lawyers hired by the Court were the same law firm that had been employed for years by Continental. The return address for the filings, shown on the Court stationery, was the same as that of the Continental legal team. The request for filings had a 30-day time limit, stating that if the documents were not received in those 30 days, that they would then be declared null and void.

After the author's submission, the court repeatedly asked for the same submission of documents, each time repeating a stipulation of the Court that all documents had to be submitted within 30 days of the submission request. The same document request was mailed six times to the author from the Bankruptcy Court, requiring the same documents to be submitted six times. This was over the summer months when many pilots were on vacation and perhaps would not be physically able to continue to send the same documents so many times. Every submission by the author to the Court was triple checked to ensure against errors and to ensure completeness. Never did the Court contact the author at any time in any manner to complain about anything in the documents submitted or to comment about anything. No notice of document acceptance was ever received.

The Houston judge favored Continental on each individual action. It took another ten years and the pro bono civil court action of a compassionate law firm, to rectify the injustice and provide a retirement for the pilot group. The judgment stipulated that Continental set up a retirement annuity, which they did. It also stipulated that Continental provide $90,000 in the form of payments and stocks, and the first $30,000 was paid in stock at the direction of the civil court. However, nobody ever saw the other $60,000 that was to be paid over time.

An interesting occurrence after judgment was rendered: The bankruptcy judge returned to Houston and announced that the Continental case would be his last and that he would be retiring from the bench. However, he was a lucky man. Continental hired him within three weeks of his "retirement" at a salary in excess of $200,000. Isn't it nice that he got his "retirement" when he had denied retirement for a whole company of pilots, even though that retirement was guaranteed and funded by Continental in its abrogated contract.

Please excuse the author's rather caustic remarks. The issue was the performance of the Court. In every conceivable way, the Court acted in a corrupt manner. Congress needs to pass laws and take actions to prevent the Court from handling cases in such a manner. Trust of government is dwindling. To recapture that trust, government in all its forms must behave in a trustworthy manner. The chances of that happening, in today's environment, seem very remote.

"A man may die, nations may rise and fall, but an idea lives on."
— **John F. Kennedy, remarks in Greenville, North Carolina, February 8, 1963**

Chapter Two
Society, Heritage, & Race
Our People & Our Past

"Purebred dogs not only have increased incidences of inherited diseases, but also heightened health issues, such as hip dysplasia in large breeds like the German Shepherd and the Saint Bernard." —**Animal Science professors at the University of California, Davis**

<u>OUR RACES:</u>

Over the years, the issue of race has been at the heart of much of the world's troubles. While a certain level of pride is essential in a productive society, if carried too far it involves feelings of superiority by one race over other races. It happened in Germany under Adolph Hitler when his theory of Aryan Race supremacy catapulted much of the world into a catastrophic world-wide war that killed and maimed so many millions of human beings, displaced even more millions, destroyed much of Europe, and used up precious world resources.

The issue of one race's pride over another has been a problem for America since blacks first unwillingly set foot on Virginia soil in 1619. Those who espouse the superiority of one race over another have it all wrong. Depending on one's religious beliefs, either God or Nature seems to have intended that purebred tendencies among mammals have acted as a detriment to the survival and success of species.

The 10-campus University of California system designated U.C. Davis as its agricultural campus. The above quote about purebred dogs from Davis can also be attributed to humans. Scott Solomon, who teaches biosciences at Rice University, has recently written (2016) a book titled: *Future Humans: Inside the Science of Our Continuing Evolution*. An inclusion, in blue (below), from the book is provided. Please excuse the length of the inclusion, but it is of such importance to any discussion of race and human health & longevity, that it deserves to be read in its entirety:

"Differences in physical traits between human populations accumulated slowly over tens of thousands of years. As people spread across the globe and adapted to local conditions, a combination of natural selection and cultural innovation led to physical distinctions. But these groups did not remain apart. Contact between groups, whether through trade or conflict, led to the exchange of both genes and ideas. Recent insights from the sequencing of hundreds of thousands of human genomes in the past decade have revealed that our species' history has been punctuated by many episodes of migration and genetic exchange. The mixing of human groups is nothing new.

What is new is the rate of mixing currently underway. Globalization means that our species is more mobile than ever before. International migration has reached record heights, as has the number of interracial marriages, leading to a surge of multiracial people. While genetic differences between human populations do not fall neatly along racial lines, race nevertheless provides insight into the extent of population hybridization currently underway. This reshuffling of human populations is affecting the very structure of the human gene pool.

Archaeological evidence suggests that Homo Sapiens came into existence roughly 200,000 years ago in east Africa. By 50,000 years ago, or possibly earlier, people had begun to spread out of Africa, across the Arabian Peninsula and into Eurasia, perhaps driven by a changing climate that necessitated a search for new food sources. They made their way across now flooded land bridges to reach Australia and the Americas, and eventually came to inhabit even the most remote Pacific islands."

Recent archaeological evidence has indicted that Homo Sapiens quite possibly crossed the then-dry Bering Strait as long ago as 50,000 years ago. Currently, the Bering Strait separates Alaska from Russia by 55 miles. With the melting of much of the world's glaciers and ice caps, that distance will continue to widen. During ice ages, the Bering Strait became dry as significant amounts of world seawater were captured in Antarctica and Greenland ice.

To this author, significant racial differences than those of the Africans accompanied emigrants to the new world. Those differences must have been created over a longer period than indicated above for the emergence of humans from Africa to Europe and Asia. The appearance of humans in Asia must have occurred well over 100,000 years ago.

Some movements of human populations mentioned by Solomon have occurred very recently. The voyages of Polynesian discovery included huge, multi-decked, canoes from the Society Islands that discovered Hawaii in the 1300s. Hawaiian explorers then found New Zealand to become one of several migrations to that country, including one from China, that populated that remote island nation.

Even in Africa, some human migrations occurred recently. While South Africa was populated from ancient times by "Pygmy foragers, Khoisan-speaking hunter-gatherers, Nilo-Saharan-speaking herders and Cushitic-speaking pastoralists", Bantu-speaking farmers started to migrate south as late as 1000 A.D. The author has talked to South Africans of English origin who told the author that the Bantus did not occupy some areas of South Africa until after the Boar and British arrivals. Evidence is sketchy, but their claim could not be verified by research.

Continuing with Solomon's discussion: "Evidence of these ancient migrations can be found by examining the DNA of living people as well as DNA recovered from ancient skeletons. In some cases, the genome studies corroborate archaeological and historical records of human movements. The Mongol Empire, the Arab slave trade, the spread of Bantu-speaking peoples across much of Africa and the effects of European colonialism have all left a predictable record within our genomes. In other cases, the genetic data provide surprises and can help archaeologists and historians settle controversies. For example, until recently, it was thought that the America's were settled by a single wave of nomads who traveled across a land bridge spanning the Bering Strait. But recent genome analyses, which include samples from a wide range of indigenous groups, suggest that the Americas might have been colonized by at least four independent waves of settlers.

We are a restless species, and our genomes reveal that even the most intimidating geographical barriers have managed only to somewhat restrict human movements. Today, international migration is increasing at 1 to 2 percent per year, with 244 million people in 2015 living in a country other than that one in which they were born. The biological implications of this massive experiment in interbreeding we are now witnessing will not be known for generations. But applying what we know about genetics and evolution can help us predict our future, including whether humans will be able to continue adapting to the constantly changing conditions on Earth.

Biological adaptation is a result of natural selection, and natural selection requires diversity. Think of natural selection like a sieve separating one generation from the next. Only the genes from those individuals that are well suited to their environment at that time will reproduce, passing their genes through the sieve to the next generation. Changing conditions alter the shape of the sieve's holes and thereby which genes can pass through. The more variation there is in the population, the better the chances that some genes present in a generation will be able to pass through the sieve and be inherited by future generations. Unfortunately for us, humans are not very diverse.

We Homo Sapiens have less genetic diversity than do many species of chimpanzees, gorillas and orangutans—our closest living relatives—despite the fact that each of these are so few in number that they are considered either endangered or critically endangered. Our low diversity is due to the fact that we have only recently become so numerous (whereas the opposite is true for our primate cousins). There are now roughly 7.5 billion living humans, but just 100 years ago there were fewer than 2 billion. Our population has exploded in the recent past, and is continuing to grow, with some 130 million babies born each year. Each baby carries an average 60 new mutations in its genes. With these new gene variants comes the potential for future evolutionary change.

Our ability to continue to adapt to the changing conditions on Earth improves as new genetic variation is introduced to our gene pool through mutations. But the entire human gene pool is made of many smaller gene pools, each corresponding to a particular population. The movement of people around the Earth is mixing these populations, allowing genes to flow back and forth between gene pools, with several important implications for our ongoing evolution.

Let's start with the downsides. Like all species, human groups became adapted to local environments as we spread around the world. Yet the rapid movement of people with distinct characteristics means that people today are more likely to live in an environment for which they are not biologically well-suited.

Consider natural resistance to infectious diseases, which evolved in places where such diseases were common. Such geographical associations are being eroded by global migration. The prevalence of malaria, which continues to cause some 400,000 deaths each year and is especially deadly to children, has resulted in the evolution of physiological protections from infection. Examples include sickle cell disease and thalassaemia—blood conditions that can create health problems of their own but that nevertheless afford protection from the deadly disease and were therefore favored by natural selection in regions where malaria was common. Today, sickle cell and thalassaemia exist in places without malaria as a result both of migration and of the local eradication of malaria.

Likewise, many people live in regions where their skin pigmentation is not ideal for the local sunlight intensity. The color of human skin is determined by the amount of pigment eumelanin, which acts as a natural sunscreen. Having a lot of eumelanin is an advantage for those who live in a place where sunlight is intense and, since our species originated in tropical Africa, the first humans were probably dark-skinned. Lighter skin evolved later in populations that migrated out of the tropics, into regions where sunlight hits the Earth more obliquely.

It seems to the author that the Neanderthals, who existed all over Western Europe, but primarily in the colder, northern regions, were blond with blue eyes. Almost all species of animal that migrated north changed their colors to white. Black bears ventured north and became the polar bears. Arctic foxes and hare have white fur. Siberian Huskies have blue eyes. Arctic wolves are white. Homo Sapiens who live in northern climates often have blond hair and blue eyes. It is characteristic of some Germans and many Scandinavians.

The usual depiction of Neanderthals as hairy, bent over, and with dark skin, evolved due to the first German discovery of the species in the Neander Valley and the skeleton of the Neanderthal was affected by severe arthritis that adversely affected his skeletal makeup, which seemed to have caused several misjudgments.

Not only is eumelanin needed less in such regions, it is actually problematic because our bodies require sunlight to penetrate the skin in order to produce vitamin D. With too much eumelanin, dark-skinned people living at high latitudes risk developing nutritional disorders such as rickets, which cause the skeleton to become deformed. This trade-off--having either too much or too little sunlight penetrating the skin--caused human populations to evolve eumelanin levels that are appropriate for their region. As people move around the world, mismatches between eumelanin and local sunlight intensity result in skin cancer and vitamin D deficiencies, both of which are considered epidemics in some regions.

As populations blend, medium skin tones will become more common. Eumelanin production is determined my numerous genes, so when people with different skin tones have children, these children inherit a combination of gene versions from each parent, resulting in skin tones that are likely to be intermediate between that of their parents.

Such blending is expected for complex traits encoded by multiple genes, such as skin pigmentation or height. But some characteristics, such as having dry earwax or thick hair, are controlled by just a single gene. Blending is not possible for these traits, which a person either has or does not have, based on the genes inherited from the parents. What population-mixing mighty cause, however, is combinations of traits that were previously rare, such as dark skin and blue eyes. Just such a combination can already be found in the Cape Verde islands, whose modern population is descended from Portuguese and West Africans.

In many parts of the world, blending is well underway. In highly diverse urban centers, such as Singapore, inter-ethnic marriages are rising quickly--from just 7.6% of all marriages in 1990 to 21.5% in 2015. In the United States, interracial marriages have doubled since 1980. Not surprisingly, the number of multiracial US children climbed 10-fold over roughly the same time span, up from just 1% of all births in 1970 to 10% in 2013. In Brazil, where European, African, and indigenous populations have been mixing for centuries, some 43% of the population identifies as "pardo", or mixed-race, according to the 2010 Brazil Federal Census.

A distinct advantage of this blending is that beneficial traits present in one population can make their way into another. For instance, should a mutation appear somewhere in Southeast Asia that provides protection against the Zika virus, it wouldn't help those facing the current outbreak in South and Central America. Yet if someone with the mutation moved to South America and established a family there, the mutation could save lives and hence be passed to future generations.

A striking example comes from one of the highest altitude regions on Earth, the Tibetan Plateau. Because the air is thinner at higher altitudes, there is less oxygen available to breathe--40% less in the case of the Tibetan Plateau, much of which exceeds 13,000 feet above sea level.

Low oxygen levels are especially problematic for childbirth, and complications such as pregnancy disorders are more common at higher altitudes. Although people from lower altitudes who spend extended amounts of time at high altitude can partially adjust by making more red blood cells to capture oxygen, this is an imperfect solution as it can lead to a condition known as chronic mountain sickness.

After a tryst between a modern human and a Denisovan, a child was conceived, who left descendants, some of whom became Tibetans."

Denisovans were another branch of human population that separated, along with the Neanderthals, "from modern (Cro Magnon) lineage early in the Middle Pleistocene" era (possibly as long as 600,000 years ago). Roughly "400,000 years ago, the Denisovans and Neanderthals themselves split into separate branches.

The Denisovans ranged from Siberia to Southeast Asia and may have persisted until as recently as 30,000 years ago, based on their genetic legacy in living Southeast Asians." Thus, the disappearance of both the Denisovans and Neanderthals occurred at about the same time. Evidence exists that the Denisovans and Neanderthals also successfully mated.

Tibetans, whose ancestors have lived on the Plateau for at least 30,000 years, are well-adapted to the low-oxygen environment. In a paper published in 2014, the geneticist Anna Di Rienzi, the anthropologist Cynthia Beall, and colleagues showed that Tibetans can trace their ancestry to two previously distinct populations, related to modern Han Chinese, and Sherpa. By examining the genomes of all three living populations, Tibetans, Han Chinese, and Sherpa—the researchers pieced together a sequence of events in which people from the lowlands related to the modern Han Chinese migrated to higher altitudes, where they mixed with those already present, who were relatives of the Sherpa. Beneficial gene versions were thought to already be present in the relatives of the Sherpa, and acquiring those gene versions helped the newcomers to survive and pass on their genes.

But how did the relatives of the Sherpa come to acquire the beneficial versions of their genes in the first place? This too seems to be a result of mixing—not just between two different human populations, but between two different species, that of the modern humans and Denisovans, as mentioned above. Thus, the beneficial gene that has allowed modern humans living at high altitudes to thrive, came from the Denisovans.

Traces of Denisovan DNA can be found in modern people living across much of South and East Asia, Australia, New Guinea, and Oceania. Likewise, genes from Neanderthals, who lived in western Eurasia, can be found in all living human populations, except Africans. Genomic surveys have recently detected evidence of mixing with additional extinct relatives of modern humans,

Neanderthals, and Denisovans, but who thus far (have been) unknown species from the fossil records.

The benefits that come from mixing genes from different populations are well-know to plant and animal breeders. Hybrid corn, for example, outperforms pure varieties when planted in the same fields…Today, according to the US Department of Agriculture, 95% of all corn grown in the US is hybrid corn, which is 20% more productive and uses 25% less land.

Mixing genes is not only beneficial; when mixing doesn't occur, there can be negative consequences. Consider purebred dogs. A 2013 study from the University of California Davis, compared veterinary records of 27,254 purebred and mixed-breed dogs, and identified 10 different genetic disorders, including elbow dysplasia and cataracts, that purebred dogs are more likely to suffer than mixed-breeds. Generations of exclusively same-breed mating has caused an accumulation of recessive alleles (in DNA sequencing), which are likely to be masked by a dominant allele when crossed with a different breed.

Similar effects are found in humans. About 10% of all marriages today occur among close relatives, defined as second cousins or closer. The highest rates are in North Africa and the Middle East, and among immigrants from these regions, where marriage among kin is often encouraged for religious or social reasons. Although genetic counseling is needed to determine the precise risks, in general, the more closely related the parents are, the more likely their children will have birth defects or genetic disorders. The children of first cousins are 2-3% more likely to have certain birth defects, including deafness and heart defects, and 2-4% more likely to have recessive genetic disorders." It seems that God or Nature is trying to tell us that diversity in mate selection is the best method of preserving and strengthening the species.

"While marriages among relatives remain common in certain regions, the worldwide trend is in the opposite direction. When both parents are very distantly related, as happens when their ancestors come from different human populations, the chances of both having a recessive allele for the same gene is extremely low. Consequently, as the world's population becomes increasingly mixed, some genetic disorders will become less and less common.

If the history of life on Earth can teach us anything, it is this: as conditions change, species either adapt or become extinct. In our time of considerable environmental change, humanity should consider its options. No species, even the almighty Homo Sapiens, can stop evolution completely. But we can choose to limit our capacity for ongoing biological adaptation in an effort to remain ever the same by keeping populations isolated. Of course, such decisions are not made by humanity as a whole, but by individuals and governments. Nationalism and xenophobia, on the rise in the United States and Europe, threaten to decrease genetic exchange between populations, stifling our ability to continue evolving and adapting.

Alternatively, we can embrace immigration and globalization in an effort to position ourselves for a brighter future. The underlying causes of the current high rates of human migration are likely to persist, and perhaps to increase, as the global human population continues to grow. Access to natural resources, such as fresh water, have long driven population movements, and these might become even more important drivers of migration as the world's population expands. Likewise, as economic development proceeds, the number of resources used by each person will continue to rise, putting further pressure on scarce resources and further motivating people to move in search of better conditions.

Sea levels are expected to continue rising as a result of global climate change, and this is likely to drive large-scale population movements away from low-lying coastal areas as they become uninhabitable. In short, the reshuffling of populations that results from movements of people around the world will continue to shape the structure of our gene pool—and, by extension, our future evolution—for many generations to come."

The lesson from above is unmistakable. While acceptance of other races is a humane and compassionate thing to do, there are many other reasons to do so. Instead of unreasonable opposition to intermarriage and an equally unreasonable prejudice against other races, our society should embrace all races, if for no other reason than it is beneficial to the health and longevity of our species.

Besides, the choice of one's mate is a private matter and an issue of freedom. There are many forms of freedom and the choice of a spouse is one of them. When the author and many others chose to fight for this country, one of the strongest elements of our society that motivated their willingness to fight was the issue of freedom.

Regarding fighting wars: Our world society will never truly be able to call ourselves civilized until we have finally and irrevocably renounced warfare in deed as well as dictate. One of the many causes of warfare are the supposed differences between the races. It is generally assumed that a total mixing of Earth's races would result in brown-colored children. As a worldwide society, we will eliminate one major cause of warfare if our decedents result in our siring of only brown children. The tolerance required to effectuate such a change will be discussed in chapter 13.

THE PROMISE OF DNA SEQUENCING:

DNA analysis has many exciting and promising uses other than as a crime-solving asset or to answer the background questions of individuals. It may prove to be the single most important tool available for disproving racial "purity" or the existence of some "master race."

Recent research is finding proof that any consideration of a "master race" is truly mythical. The German's who followed Hitler's ideas thought of themselves a superior. The current German national anthem announces "Deutschland Uber Alles" meaning "Germany Over All" in English. The factual matter is that the German "race" is no race at all. They are a combination, not only of racial mixing, but the mixing of entirely different species.

The English themselves are a mixture of several German tribes, several Scandinavian invasions, the Norman invasion, the Roman occupation, and of the ancient Bretons. An article in November of 2022, states that two distinct species of humans were found in common caves in both England and Wales. They lived between 15,000 and 13,500 years ago.

These pre-historic remains are the oldest human DNA found in the United Kingdom. They have even been given a distinct name, the Magdalenians. "They were "remarkably small and ecologically fragile humans." Their remains were distinctly different than other remains of humans found together in the same caves. Evidence suggests that they chased large mammals and crossed into the British Isles when there was a land bridge between what is now France and Britain just after the last ice age.

The presence of "carved human bones and cups made from skulls that were found in the caves are consistent with the idea that Magdalenians might have eaten other humans." According to "Luc Amkreutz, an archaeologist at the National Museum of Antiquities in the Netherlands, the (Magdalenians) are clearly not the same group of modern humans that (are found) everywhere." Thus, even the ancient Bretons appear to be a mixing of two different species of humans, just as the Neanderthals and Denisovans.

We are all a combination of different human species and better off for it.

"Genome-wide ancestry estimates of African Americans show average proportions of 73.2% African, 24.0% European, and 0.8% Native- American ancestry." As sequencing becomes more precise and widespread, that estimate will change. The African-American population has been surprised by the high percentage of white blood in what was perceived by blacks as black and who have totally identified themselves as black. Dr. Henry Luis Gates Jr., the moderator and producer of *Finding Your Roots* has always considered himself black. His finding that he is 50% European has changed his outlook. Many of the blacks on his show, after having found a high incidence of European blood in their ancestry, have also had to reevaluate themselves as Americans. DNA is thus helping redefine what it means to be American and also contributing to bringing us all together.

Black blood among white Americans amounts to almost 4% of the entire white population, an additional surprise to affected whites. Latino populations have significant variables as to black or Indian blood and those variables are caused by location and the histories of those locations in the United States.

The current inexpensive DNA testing provided by organizations such as Ancestry.com show only generalized locations of ancestors. However, as more and more individuals test, the greater the data base and the more precise information becomes available. Those who have sequenced in the past may find updates available that show much more precise information.

From an anthropological standpoint, the results over time could answer some thought-provoking questions and solve mysteries whose answers have proved elusive. It may also create more questions than answers.

Author's Notes: *The author would like to share several observations made over time. He has visited 40 islands in the Pacific and has come away with several considerations. The arguments of Thor Heyerdahl have merit. His observations that the Polynesians and Mexicans have certain linguistic similarities coincide with the author's thought that there are so many cultural similarities, that it is unlikely that it is coincidental.*

In 1974, the author visited the island of Pohnpei in the Pacific Caroline Islands. He was forced to wade in waist-deep seawater to visit the ancient city of Nan Madol. Today it is probably a tourist attraction. Then it was remote and hard to access. Nan Madol is an archaeological site that was a large city comparable to Venice, Italy in its many canals and intricate water features. It included over 100 man-made islands built of basaltic logs. Where did the people who built Nan Madol come from and where did they disappear to? The main fortress is also built of basaltic logs measuring 40 feet high. Several gravesites were found inside the fortress. Will DNA finally answer the questions about the builders?

It has recently been discovered that a Peruvian tribe on the Amazon side of the Andes and located on the edge of the Amazonian mountain jungles is over 50% inhabited by people who are red-headed. DNA analysis found that they are of European (at least 50%) and Indian descent. How, when and why did they get to their current home?

The author is curious as to the origins of the native populations of the Pacific. When the Chinese crossed Taiwan Straight they found ancient tribes on Taiwan and have placed them on reservations. When the Japanese emigrated to their current islands many centuries ago, they found a primitive tribe of Caucasians that they have called the Ainu. They place the Ainu on reservations. Where did they come from?

When the Spanish arrived in the Philippines, they mixed with the people they found on the islands. Those people had themselves arrived many centuries before to find the islands inhabited by black pygmies that they called the Negritos. Half of the Negritos on Northern Luzon as late as the 1960s were civilized and often lived outside of the jungle. The other half were still head-hunters. The Philippine Islands are located due west of the islands of Palau, which are part of Melanesia and thus have black populations. The Solomons and Fiji are also Melanesian. How do the Negro pygmies of the Philippines relate to the giant blacks of Fiji or to the natives of New Guinea? When the Spanish discovered and colonized the islands of the Central Pacific, where did the natives they discovered come from? We may never know, but DNA does give us a very powerful tool to try to find answers.

Just how diverse are the many distinct populations of our world? Will DNA determine the origins of many of the world's tribes, including those located throughout Europe?

OUR HERITAGE, OUR SOCIETY, & OUR PEOPLE:

During World War II, Hitler referred to his enemies, the British Empire and the America Empire, as Anglo-Saxon. Both Germanic tribes emigrated to Britain, Scotland and Ireland from the German states of Anglia and Saxony. But times have changed. Caucasian-Americans came from a variety of nation states, mostly all European. After arrival in the New World, most Caucasians started to refer to themselves as Anglo-Saxon, regardless of their ethnic identity. We considered ourselves an Anglo-Saxon nation. No more.

While many consider that the U.S. is multicultural, that is still not the case. The multiplicity of foreign language radio and television stations across the country have made the cultural assimilation of various new, ethnic Americans more difficult, but after a generation and after learning the language, the children of most immigrants become part of the American culture, however changed by the arrival of those same immigrants.

The subject of immigration will be dealt with in a later chapter, but it is deserving of a short discussion now: The issue of immigration, both legal and illegal, is of paramount importance. Asian and Latin American immigrants are populating all of our states. These people either are or will become Americans and are a significant part of our future. They currently provide the labor without which our economy will collapse.

If our immigration laws are unusable or unworkable, then we must change the laws. We must regain control of our borders. We pride ourselves that we are a nation of laws, yet all too often we only seem to use the laws that benefit certain groups. It is unfair to those who have used the legal means to become citizens if those who arrive at our southern border can legally ignore the many years required of legal immigrants and quickly cross our borders.

Our borders consist of those who arrive by water as well as those by land. While we concentrate on those who arrive at our southern border, potential immigrants from other countries have largely slipped through the media cracks and are largely unknown. However, any visit to Asian restaurants around the country will spot many employees who barely speak English. They obviously did not go through the American educational system. Stories abound about their arrival by sea.

That is speculation. But the facts support that speculation: Using California as an example, it "is home to almost 11 million immigrants—about a quarter of the foreign-born population of the entire United States. In 2019, the most current year of data, 27% of California's population was foreign born, more than double the percentage in the rest of the country. Foreign-born residents represented at least one-third of the population in five California counties: Santa Clara (39%), San Mateo (35%), Los Angeles (34%), San Francisco (34%), and Alameda County (33%). Half of California children have at least one immigrant parent." That is truly an amazing statistic and brings up the important factor of assimilation.

"The vast majority of California's immigrants were born in Latin America (50%) or Asia (39%). California has sizable populations of immigrants from dozens of countries. The leading countries of origin are Mexico (3.9 million), the Philippines (859,000), China (796,000), Vietnam (539,000) and India (513,000). However, among immigrants who arrived between 2010 and 2019, more than half (53%) were born in Asia, while 31% were born in Latin America. Even with recent migration slowdowns, Asia is the leading source of recent immigrants to California, by a factor of over 2 to 1. It seems that the secret immigration from Asia is not so secret anymore.

"More than half (53%) of California immigrants are naturalized US citizens and another 25% have some other legal status, including green cards and visas. According to the Center for Migration Studies, a New York institution, about 22% of immigrants in California are undocumented. From 2010 to 2019, the number of undocumented immigrants in the state declined from 2.9 million to 2.3 million. The prior accepted name for undocumented immigrants was illegal immigrants. The reasons for the renaming remain hazy as they still are illegal in every sense of the word.

The Los Angeles Unified School System is the second largest in the United States. The Los Angeles County population is over 10.4 million, which is larger than most states. According to **https://achieve.lausd.net** the number of languages spoken in the Los Angeles Unified School District is 94, other than English. How can they teach with that number of languages requiring teachers that speak the language, as required by California law? How does the school system provide for so many foreign-speaking citizens and also provide a quality education? The current fact is, they can't. And the process of assimilation of so many into our larger culture is difficult in the extreme. But, all such waves of immigrants in our past have assimilated. It is just a question of how long will assimilation take? With so many students from various countries, our culture is bound to change in unknown ways.

Our nation is changing and nostalgia for how it used to be is counterproductive. We must work together to heal our wounds and accept the fact that others who may not look like us, are also as American as we are. Let's take pride in our diversity as it is a source of strength, not weakness. Those who lament the large number of foreigners crossing our borders, both legally and illegally, will one day wish that we had more.

WASHINGTON, DISTRICT of COLUMBIA LANDMARKS:

The White House, home of the Executive Branch of government.
Photo courtesy of Steemit.

Photo Gallery One

National Parks in the Pacific Southwest

California, Hawaii, American Samoa

Joshua Tree National Park, California

Yosemite National Park, California

Channel Islands National Park, California

Lassen Volcanic National Park, California

American Samoa National Park, Island of Tutuila, Samoa

Redwood National Park, California

Pinnacles National Park, California

Hawaii Volcanos National Park, Island of Hawaii

Haleakala National Park, Island of Maui, Hawaii

Kings Canyon National Park, California

Death Valley National Park, California

Sequoia National Park, California

Chapter Three
Identity Politics
Our Leaders & Followers

"Politics have become far too important to entrust to the politicians." — **President Dwight D. Eisenhower's remarks, Business Council, Hot Springs, Virginia, 10-20-1962**

INDIVIDUAL POLITICAL IDENTITY:

Unfortunately, adherence to political parties these days is almost too alike to fan's adherence to sports teams. Sports fans who elect to follow a certain team, come to identify with that team. The team becomes part of their identity. Selection of what political parties to back are too often based on that identity and not on the ideas and policies of the individual parties. Identities may be based on "religion, ethnic group, social background, or other, for exclusive political alliances, thus moving away from traditional" party politics. Connections thus become much deeper than just based on position in the political spectrum or adherence to particular policies.

It is similar to the sentiment shown by an American Naval Officer during the 19th century. Commodore Stephen Decatur "gained immense admiration and accolades for his naval expeditions and adventures." In particular, he was feted by the British Admiralty. "British Admiral Horatio Nelson remarked that (his) expedition (to rid the pirates from the Barbary Coast) was one of the boldest and daring acts of the age."

In April, 1816, Decatur was welcomed back to the United States as a hero. "He was honored at a banquet, where he raised his glass for a toast and said: "Our country...may she always be in the right; but our country, right or wrong!"

The author cannot agree with his sentiments. In fact, he strongly disagrees. Our country should always, to the best of its abilities, stand for the right, never for the wrong. Adherence to political parties often has the same sentiment as voiced by Decatur: "Our party, right or wrong". Voting for a political party often is more visceral than a selection of sides due to policies or actions. It often becomes a vote for the voter himself or herself. How that is corrected is almost impossible to determine since it seems almost impossible to correct. Our only option to correct needs reestablishment of trust, the exposure of lies, education, and the need for discussion between the various sides of our political spectrum. It may not be rectified in our society until generations pass?

POLITICAL SPECTRUM:

The old definitions used to describe a person's political beliefs no longer apply. The political spectrum has shifted and that shift has been significant. Consider the Republican Party Platform of 2012. The long-worded platform consisted of the following:

(1) Statements against large scale government, government spending, and increases in the national debt

(2) Belief in Jefferson's "wise and frugal government"

(3) Keeping minimum taxation, litigation, and regulation

(4) Stand against tyranny

(5) Adherence to the Rule of Law

(6) Restoration of Constitutional Government

(7) Maximum economic freedom

(8) Belief in a strong military and our free enterprise system

(9) Free market policies with full parity in trade with China

(10) Supported small business

(11) Balanced budgets

(12) Glorified personal housing

(13) Free trade agreements

(14) Supporting national Right to Work laws

(15) Against same-sex marriages

(16) For a Balanced Budget Amendment for the Constitution

(17) Supporting State's Rights and the right to keep and bear arms

(18) Protecting the Electoral College & private property

(19) Against abortions and for energy independence

(20) For nuclear energy, renewable energy, and limitations on the EPA

(21) For restructuring government to reverse the centralizing of power

(22) No more "Too Big to Fail"

(23) Appointment of Constitutional Jurists instead of judicial activists

(24) Turning part of the Postal System over to private enterprise

(25) For legal immigration and against illegal immigration

(26) Repealing Obamacare & tort reform to eliminate frivolous malpractice lawsuits

A full reading of the entire, voluminous platform would result in even more to support, or to condemn. Admittedly, most party platforms in the past have been "window dressing" that bore scant resemblance to actual party actions. However, for conservatives, it all sounds pretty good. It is also in line with prior party platforms.

The Republican Party was formed from the ruins of the Whig Party in February, 1854. For every presidential election from that time until the election of 2016, the party had a platform. It wrote a platform in 2016, but the convention threw it out. In essence, the party was saying that they had no policies to formally support. It thus allowed their party leader, Trump, to decide what policies he supported and thus they became the party positions, regardless of what party members supported, they were and are all expected to follow what he believes.

In 2020, the arduously written 2016 platform that was thrown out, was resurrected word-for-word for the 2020 convention. They had resurrected the "window dressing" for the party rank and file. Party action did follow some of the platform positions, but the elimination of any platform for Trump's period in office meant that, as President and de-facto party leaders, what he did and said served as the platform. The shift to the right under Trump has been mind-boggling.

Many Republicans in the past identified themselves as Goldwater Conservatives. In those days, it was hard to find those who admitted to being conservative. Today, a Goldwater Conservative might be considered a liberal, the spectrum has shifted so drastically to the right.

For Trump, it seems he was searching for a platform that suited his needs. As did Reagan and the elder Bush, Trump once supported free choice for a woman regarding abortion. They all switched their stands, at a time and manner that seemed to indicate that the change was for political and not for moral or truly ideological reasons. Indeed, Trump himself was registered as an Independent and also a Democrat before becoming Republican, all within the 21st century. He seemed to be searching for a stated philosophy to further his personal aims and ambitions and not necessarily due to his convictions. It is questionable if Trump has any personal convictions?

THE MIXED BLESSINGS of MEDIA POLLS:

Unfortunately, politicians switching positions, even on moral issues, is quite common. One would think that moral convictions would be more deeply held than political or philosophical. Yet the siren calls of power and influence have blurred the priorities. Moral issues, such as abortion, should be left to families as it involves the freedom to choose what is best for the individual and family. It is not the business of government to intervene in those decisions.

Ideally, leaders should cast their votes to place the country on a path that the representatives feel is in the best interests of the country, and not the best interests of the individual or party. Yet that is usually not the case. They deal with moral issues that should be left alone. They do it because it plays well with the public. They seemingly do it for votes to ensure longevity in office.

The modern addition of public opinion polls can be considered from both a positive and negative viewpoint. One might think that polls would improve democracy. After all, if voters would consider that their representatives are truly representative, instead of agents, then it might be considered positive. Representatives represent. A better understanding of what the public wants should be considered a benefit to democracy and honest polls provide that understanding. Yet, are the representative's motives to represent or are they acting on considerations of what position might gain them benefit for reelection? A foundation for our system is an assumption that our representatives are better able to make decisions on what is best for our country, the long-term as well as short, than the changing and often selfish beliefs and positions of the public. Are our overall objectives electability or proper governance?

TOTALITARIANISM, FASCISM, DEMOCRACY, and CAPITALISM:

Dictatorships have often been considered as the most efficient forms of government, if the dictator is competent and has the best interests of his public in his actions. Yet, history shows that dictatorships usually are eliminated through an often-bloody revolution. One of the beauties of democracy is that the transfer of power is by evolution and not revolution. One can argue that voting in a democracy should be based on an allowed electorate that is informed on history and issues. That is not true democracy and thus has a built-in danger to the longevity of the democracy. If all people in a democratic republic, regardless of any other consideration other than citizenship, are allowed to vote (one person, one vote), then all voters can feel that they have an equal say in how our country is run and in what direction we are heading. It means evolutionary change.

That assumes that voters feel that their vote counts. The low percentages of those casting ballots in our elections attests to a feeling, at least in part of the electorate, that their votes do not count. Gerrymandering does not foster a feeling, in "safe" districts, that their votes count, for those adhering to the party that is out of district power. Even if the registered party of the voter is the same as that in power, voters have voiced the question of "why should my vote count? It is all pre-determined".

Another factor in need of change, is that our elected leaders should follow the will of the electorate if that will has already been the subject of a referendum. In California, we have a process of the electorate voting on issues that normally would be handled by the legislature. Californians have repeatedly voted for the death penalty. Governmental leaders have reversed that vote of the majority and have supported a policy against the death penalty based on their personal moral philosophy. The death penalty is an intense issue and is not the subject of this discussion. My personal preference or that of others, is not the issue here. The issue is whether our leaders will support the voted will of the people if that will is not the will of the leaders? Readers may ask, "how is that any different than your point that elected representatives should vote on how their vote will act in the best interests of America." The author's answer would be that votes should be state issues and not moral issues. In most cases, the California legislature reneged on their responsibility to discuss and vote on controversial issues, and threw the vote to the referendum process, which often does not allow a proper discussion of the issue. Once that vote has been allowed, then the Governor and legislature should allow an honest vote of the people if that vote might not coincide with their wishes.

The danger to democracy posed by the recent actions of the Republicans nationally in trying to subvert the vote of all the people, is a collective belief of the Republicans, supported by their actions, that they want to continue in power and are willing to destroy the very system that has determined political power for over 200 years. By leaders ignoring the will of the majority, voters often feel that their leaders "don't give a damn what I think, so why should I vote if it doesn't matter?" That apathy can lead to dictatorial forms of government, including fascism.

Fascism can be a very efficient way of governing. Fascist leaders can make instantaneous decisions and decisions made in concert with an overall plan for the economy. Mussolini in Italy initially ran a very efficient government, at least in comparison to prior Italian governments. Hitler was even more efficient in Germany, starting in 1933. The problem with most dictatorial leaders is that they are not benevolent. Unfettered egos can lead a society in very dangerous directions.

A reading of German history from the early 1920s to the ascension of Hitler to power in 1933, is a lesson in how not to allow totalitarian government to be created. As did Mussolini, Hitler allowed the capitalistic corporations to thrive, which was in opposition to what Nazism stood for, which was National Socialism. Hitler's system, although very efficient, was based on a very big lie. Hitler's unfettered power allowed the Germans to eradicate many more than the Jews in their gas chambers.

Official Air Force numbers list over 6,000,000 Jews killed in the concentration camps. They also list over 12,000,000 Russian soldiers murdered, 6,000,000 German citizens slaughtered who opposed the Nazi regime, 3,000,000 Polish citizens gassed, 350,000 Gypsies killed, and an untold number of their "so-called deviants and homosexuals" eliminated. Thankfully, the Jews have kept the knowledge of that enormous atrocity alive. Only the numbers show that it was far larger than even the Jews admit.

For this discussion, other than a form of socialism, the only true counter to totalitarianism is a true democracy. Even with its inefficiencies, it manages to keep leaders in check. On the other hand, totalitarianism in whatever form, including an unconstitutional monarchy, can let loose those forces that can lead to the carnage of the world wars of the 20th century.

Communism was another system that proved unworkable. A reading of the Communist Manifesto shows that a true communistic system would be ideal for humankind. But every country that has been created as Communistic, has resorted to totalitarian control, which is the antithesis of true communism. The Soviet Union adopted communism, but Stalin converted it to his own means and paranoid visions. The problem with the Manifesto is that it seemed to consider the moral and ethical side of humanity was in the large majority. However, history has shown that, although ideal, the Communist Manifesto was unworkable in governing society.

Communism does provide, through its collective farms, a sense of community that is admirable, as do the kibbutz farms of Israel and Israel is not Communistic, but socialistic, and is a democracy that allows a true vote of its citizens.

The beauty of capitalism is that it recognizes that a stronger motivation of those in a capitalistic system is that of a drive to better oneself and one's children. The great motivating factor is greed. Greed produces. A responsible capitalistic system takes some of that revenue provided by greed and distributes it to others less able to provide or less fortunate in other ways. It could be called benevolent capitalism or compassionate capitalism.

A great motivating factor in capitalism itself is that the use of the capital created may be donated for the benefit of society, whether it is American or worldwide. Warren Buffett and Bill and Melinda Gates are representative of that benevolent use. For those who donate for structures, organizations, or other uses, a motivating factor for them is that they can choose where the money goes and not giving that choice to the government. Also, a desire for a legacy, if their names are affixed to the structures, is also a great motivation.

That benevolent benefit of capitalism has to come from the capitalists themselves. In that, their actions are based on altruism and not regulation. The challenge posed by Buffett, and for others in addition to himself, to give back substantial portions of their wealth to society in whatever form desired, has been positively met with a significant number who have come forward and donated or pledged to donate.

It is for the common good and, if it becomes a revered norm of society, it will lead to a much better America.

"Democracy cannot succeed unless those who express their choice are prepared to choose wisely."
— **Franklin D. Roosevelt, President of the United States (1933-1945)**

"Education is a human right with immense power to transform. On its foundation rest the cornerstones of freedom, democracy." — **Kofi Annan, Ghanaian diplomat who served as the 7th Secretary-General of the United Nations**

Chapter Four
Religion and Tolerance
Church and State

"You will permit me to observe that the path of true piety is so plain as to require but little pollical direction." — **George Washington, First American President**
speaking on the need for separation of Church and State.

The quote from George Washington above denoted a philosophy of religious tolerance. According to the Christian Science Monitor, "he was an Anglican, or Episcopalian, in practice. In spirit, however, he was ecumenical, contributing to various churches and corresponding with such diverse groups as Roman Catholics, Quakers, and Jews, each of whom noted his toleration."

Washington, who chaired both the national convention to establish the Articles of Incorporation as well as chairing the Constitutional Convention, was among those who created the First Amendment's Establishment Clause, which prohibits the government from making any law "respecting an establishment of religion." The clause, adopted on December 15, 1791, forbids the government from "establishing an official religion, but also prohibits government actions that unduly favor one religion over another." It had a dual purpose. It protects the affairs of state from undue interference from any religion, but conversely protects religion from governmental interference.

The Federal Constitution goes on to say, "The Senators and Representatives before mentioned, and the Members of the several State Legislatures, and all executive and judicial Officers, both of the United States and of the several States, shall be bound by Oath or Affirmation, to support this Constitution; but no religious Test shall ever be required as a Qualification to any Office or public Trust under the United States."

Clearly, the founders of the United States wanted to explicitly codify the need for a separation between religion and the affairs of state. Thus, early on in the history of our country, the separation of Church and State became the law of the land.

Washington was not the only founder who favored the separation. Benjamin Franklin also supported separation: "The number, the industry, and the morality of the Priesthood, and the devotion of the people have been manifestly increased by the total separation of the Church from the State." Thomas Jefferson, the author of the Declaration of Independence and the third president of the nascent republic also declared: "I contemplate with sovereign reverence that act of the whole American people which declared that their legislature should make no law respecting the establishment of religion or prohibiting the free exercise thereof, thus building a wall of separation between Church and State." Some religious scholars might say that Jefferson was protecting religion from government interference, which he was. But his statement and subsequent actions also clarified the duality of his statement. It protected each from the other.

John Adams, the second president of the United States affirmed that: "The Government of the United States of America is not, in any sense, founded on the Christian religion." Thus, each of the first three presidents of the United States agreed that religion has no place in politics.

It has become abundantly clear that the lawful separation has been frequently breeched by those who would preach politics from church pulpits. Thus, Evangelicals are violating our Constitution when they try to convince their parishioners to espouse a certain political belief or act in a certain political manner.

Republicans have always espoused that the Constitution is inviolate. They repeatedly argue that in the selection of justices for the Supreme Court and other, lower courts, the justices should base their decisions on the original Constitutional meanings. According to Pew Research Center, "Republicans, by more than two-to-one (69% to 29%), say that justices should base their rulings on the Constitution's original meaning rather than on what it means in current times."

If that is indeed the case, then Republicans are guilty of hypocrisy on a grand scale. One cannot pick and choose between what provisions of the Constitution to espouse and which to condemn. It is either the law of the land or it is not. If Republicans fully support constitutional protections of gun rights, as they continually espouse their support for the Second Amendment, then they must also support the provisions of the First Amendment that tells them that they cannot impose religion, in whatever form, into our politics. Yet the Republicans continually do so.

Author's Note: *The author is not a Democrat. He was born into a family of Republicans going back to their creation in 1854. He was a Republican all his life and only became an Independent in 2021 because the Republican Party, in his estimation, had abandoned the tenants that it had held dear for so long. He left the party because it was not acting in the best interest of the American public or in the best interests of democracy and the rule of law.*

A woman's right to decide the fate of her own body is embodied in constitutional protections of those rights. It is a freedom issue and one for which many of us fought to defend. Abortion, as it is voiced by Republicans, is in violation of some fundamental moral and religious code. They say it is morally unjust and against the laws of God. They have thus imposed an aspect of their religious beliefs on society as a whole. Tolerance, as espoused by Washington and the Bible, is not what they are practicing. Abortion is a family matter and not in the realm of government action. Government, as directed by the Constitution, must stay out of religion and the abortion controversy is all about religion. Conversely, religion must stay out of government.

Catholics and Evangelists both preach government action to support their religious beliefs as it involves abortion. Republicans, who have long coveted limited government and have often cried against government involving itself in the personal affairs of its citizens, have now persuaded government to close down abortion and planned parenthood clinics and have even proposed criminal actions and even executions for both participating doctors, involved families, and even violated children whose lives have been shattered. Republicans cry out against their opposition saying that the Democrats are soft on crime. Yet the author knows of no greater cause of crime than being forced to raise an unwanted child, who then lashes out at a society that did not give him or her the love and respect that we all deserve.

The Republicans are guilty of a rejection of much of what they previously stood for as a political party. They now seem to preach an intolerance of others and the opinions of others. It is a most undemocratic stance. A definition of tolerance is: "The ability or willingness to tolerate something, in particular the existence of opinion or behavior that one does not necessarily agree with."

THE BIBLE and TOLERANCE:

From the Bible: "Do not use your freedom as an opportunity for the flesh, but through love serve one another. For the whole of law is fulfilled in one word: 'You shall love your neighbor as yourself.'" Galatians 5:10-6:18. "I...urge you to walk in a manner worthy of the calling to which you have been called, with all humility and gentleness, with patience, bearing with one another in love, eager to maintain the unity of the Spirit in the bond of peace." Ephesians 4:1-3. "We ask you brothers, to respect those who labor among you and....to esteem them very highly in love." Thessalonians 3:18.

"Let us not love in word or talk, but in deed and in truth.": John 3:16-5:18. "Whoever closes his ear to the cry of the poor will himself call out and not be answered." Proverbs 21:13. "So whatever you wish that others would do to you, do also to them, for this is the Law of the Prophets." Mathew 7:12. "And have mercy on those who doubt." Jude 1:22. "We were all baptized into one body—Jews or Greeks, slaves or free—and all were made to drink of one Spirit." 1 Corinthians 12:12-27. "Love your enemies and pray for those who persecute you." Mathew 5:44-45. "Be kind to one another, tenderhearted, forgiving one another." Ephesians 4:30-32.

"Have nothing to do with foolish, ignorant controversies; you know that they breed quarrels. And the Lords' servant must not be quarrelsome, but kind to everyone, able to teach, patiently, enduring evil, correcting his opponents with gentleness." 2 Timothy 2:22-26. "Gracious words are like a honeycomb, sweetness to the soul." Proverbs 16:24. "Always being prepared to make a defense to anyone who asks you for a reason for the hope that is in you; yet do it with gentleness and respect." 1 Peter 3:15. "All of you, have unity of mind, sympathy, brotherly love, a tender heart, and a humble mind. Do not repay evil for evil, or reviling for reviling, but on the contrary, bless, for to this you were called." 1 Peter 3:8-11. "Judge not that you be not judged." Mathew 7:1. "Let him who is without sin among you be the first to throw a stone." John 8:7.

"Let not the one who eats despise the one who abstains, and let not the one who abstains pass judgment on the one who eats." "Who are you to pass judgment on the servant of another?" Romans 14:1-4. "With all humility and gentleness, with patience, bearing with one another in love." Ephesians 4:2.

The reader gets the idea. Much of the Bible is devoted to the need for tolerance. Others may be able to quote sections of the Bible that promote intolerance, but I would be very careful if I were to extol the virtues of intolerance. The Bible promotes the idea of a just God, and shows a strong belief that justice, tolerance, and mercy should guide human actions on Earth.

Religions, other than Christianity, also believe in tolerance. It is just some misguided adherents to some religions who practice an intolerance that is not a part of the ethical and moral values extolled by their religion. All too often in world history, religion has been used for political purposes.

THE HEREAFTER:

Throughout history, societies have wondered about the hereafter. Almost every society has evolved a creation theory. For most of human history, the religious structure that was built around creation theory, has usually, excepting sacrificial religion, been a force for the good.

Of course, many can also tell of crises in the world created by religion. Certainly, the British created several religious crises by its methods of designating political boundaries and its seeming policy of divide and conquer, or in many cases, divide and control. To this day, the Palestinian crisis and that of the entire Middle East can be partially laid at the feet of the British who controlled the area for many years. British religious powder kegs exploded in Northern Ireland and in Fiji, to name a few others.

In the case of Fiji, it had to do with imported East Indian workers to work the sugar cane fields, and the draconian British law that only allowed 8% of land ownership to devolve to the Indians, who are approximately 50% of the Fijian population.

Many of those religious controversies resulted in violence. But the main causes were the artificial political boundaries imposed. In defense of later British actions, they often were meant to be benevolent. However, our own American experience with British boundaries is an example of earlier divide and control policies of the British Empire.

Why do you suppose that America started out with 13 states? Why did England, and later Britain, first establish so many colonies? Part of the reason was that the English Crown elected to offer foreign soil in the New World to private, commercial enterprises in return for development of those independent colonies. It was a smart policy which ensured private organizations and individuals bore the costs of exploration and development, as long as the development was in the best interests of the Crown. Spain, on the other hand, had to dip into its treasury many times to fund voyages of exploration and discovery.

Having said that, it still seems likely that a strong policy of the Crown was to create enough different entities as to almost ensure that they would stay separate and thus not a threat to the Crown and England. Almost assuredly, the English masters of the Admiralty and the Crown had to be astonished that the British colonies of the New World, other than the Maritimes and the rest of Canada, were able to come together and field a well-trained army of militia soldiers.

In spite of the religious nature of many of the world's crisis points, religion itself has served an admirable service to mankind. While offering many different "histories" of the creation, it has given hope to mankind that his time on Earth may not be his only time. It has thus created a foundation for life based on a moral code. It has eliminated fear from many of the world's people, for each of the world's religions have a moral code to guide human actions.

The Christian moral code resembles the codes of other religions. Briefly, it includes: respect, honesty, compassion, hard work, kindness, gratitude, sharing, cooperation, responsibility and generosity. No matter what one's religious beliefs, adherence to the above code will provide a solid basis for a good and successful life.

Part of the world's current problems lie in the fact that many of those who profess to follow the standards of their religion, often act in opposition to those standards. Thus, religious extremism in the United States is as dangerous as that of some of the Islamic states. Islam, as practiced in some Middle Eastern countries, is of an all-or-nothing variety. The messianic religious devotion and the disallowance of the tenants of other religions to the point of sacrificing their lives in a supposed service to Allah, is a great cause of the problems of the world and of the United States and other Western powers, in particular. The Koran does not espouse suicide as a means to kill others. The Bible and the Quran both teach tolerance. The practices of far too many religious conservatives from all major religions can only be described as intolerant.

Part of the extremism in the Middle East can be attributed to an intolerance in the West. History is filled with far too many examples of Western leaders showing intolerance of those leaders in the Middle East. If we are to progress toward a more just world society, our Western leaders must show a greater respect of the religious and social beliefs of others who don't practice Christianity. The key is showing respect.

RELATIONS with ISRAEL:

Part of that respect should be in the form of fair actions. If we continue to blindly follow and support the Israeli Governments' actions, we do ourselves and the world an injustice. While the creation of Israel was a blessing, the rights of the Palestinians have all too often been ignored. Their rights to the land of Palestine, exceed those of the Israelis. But a homeland for the Jews was a must after the injustices and atrocities against the Jews during World War II. The giving up of anciently-held Palestinian lands has created a responsibility on the part of Israelis to treat the Palestinians with respect and allow them equality within Israel. That has not happened. . For the future peace of the world, Israel must show a respect and tolerance for the Palestinians and act with fairness toward them and their aspirations. You don't correct a wrong with another wrong.

The concept of monotheism reached Palestine from Greece as it slowly worked its way around the Eastern Mediterranean. Islam, Christianity, and Judaism, all Middle Eastern religions, adopted monotheism. A strong case can be made that all three religions have the same God. Unfortunately, if you tell an Evangelical Christian that his or hers is the same God as the Muslims, you are not likely to receive a kind reply.

To bring us all together, either in this country or in others, we need to show that we have much more in common than we have differences. We need to concentrate on those commonalities. Over the centuries of its existence, the United States has served as a sentinel for tolerance and the blending of diversity. We can stand for the same thing again, but it needs a recommitment from us all.

INFINITY and the UNIVERSE, a CASE for RELIGION:

Diversity of opinion has been a hallmark of the United States. That includes the varying concepts of religion. Most have certain convictions that are closely-held. Often those convictions are the same as the church to which a person may belong. The United States protects those individual concepts. It is a precious freedom.

The author sometime prays, but has often wondered to what he is praying? Those who might condemn religious beliefs often say that there is no proof. How do we establish proof? Religious-minded people state that we need to have faith. Faith in what?

A case for the possibility of a supreme being can be made in that nothing is impossible. Our very existence is proof. Consider infinity. Scientists talk about our universe and about the Big Bang Theory of our expanding universe. How can that be? How can we judge a specific universe when we live in an infinite universe? To many, our universe is what we can see through our amazing orbiting telescopes. Yet, that is governed by our senses. It seems that an expanding universe may be just an individual pulsation, as how can an infinite universe expand? Expand into what? Infinity means that the universe is already there, wherever there may be?

The concept of infinity makes anything possible. If something has happened once, it can happen an infinite number of times. We search for life on other planets, yet infinity demands that the universe is filled with life in varying forms. The Earth itself is an example of the huge multiplicity of life forms. Infinity tells us that life in human form is spread throughout the universe and in infinite numbers. Will we ever meet any of these other lifeforms? It is doubtful. God or nature has provided an infinite distance between lifeforms and to travel between seems impossible, yet infinity tells us that it is possible, yet improbable. Until humans discover a transformative method of travel, we are bound to our little corner of the universe. That there is no convincing evidence that we have been visited by beings from other worlds, might mean that the intention of God is that we try to maintain our existence without outside help? What is the intention of God? Science seems to show that there is some sort of universal design? What is that design and what forces are yet to be discovered?

Human minds are tied to a finite world. Science is tied to establishing proofs for theories and propositions. We strive to find the truths of our universe and establish laws that govern it. Yet our minds cannot really understand how something can be infinite. It is impossible according to our thoughts and how we humans think. Yet the converse is impossible. We cannot have a world without end, yet we also cannot have a world with end. If it ends, what is outside? Is there nothing outside? Isn't space itself an endless nothing?

The same is true with time. When did it start? If it started, what happened before it started? It is impossible to our limited thought that time could be infinite itself, but it is also impossible to be finite. Time and space are concepts that cannot be totally understood by any mind, including that of Einstein.

If a finite universe is impossible, and an infinite universe is impossible, and a finite consideration of time is impossible, yet an infinite time is also impossible, cannot any religious belief be possible? It is a question that cannot ever be answered, but it is food-for-thought for those who might question those beliefs held by others. It is another example of our need for tolerance of other concepts and other beliefs.

"We are Americans because we practice democracy and believe in republican government, not because we practice revealed religion and believe in Bible-based government." — **John Stuart Mill**

Photo Gallery Two
National Parks in the Pacific Northwest
Alaska, Washington, Oregon

Denali National Park, Alaska

Kenai Fjords National Park, Alaska

Crater Lake National Park, Oregon

Pinnacles National Park, California

Olympic National Park, Washington

North Cascades National Park, Washington

Lake Clark National Park, Alaska

Gates to the Arctic National Park, Alaska

Glacier Bay National Park, Alaska

Kobuk Valley National Park, Alaska

Wrangell – St. Elias National Park, Alaska

Katmai National Park, Alaska

Chapter Five
Business, the Economy, and Labor
Increasing Productivity

"That which is not inspected, deteriorates."— **General of the Army and President of the United States Dwight David Eisenhower at a News Conference 5-12-1954**

With consideration that ours is a strong economy and our dollar is even more so, the strength of our economy, and the increased value of our dollar, is dependent on the overall efficiency of the economy. That means that, overall, each worker continues to increase his unit measure of production. That productivity increase is usually dependent on things entirely outside the workers control, such as automation or better and more efficient production and processing. Automation allows an industry to produce the same or more and do it with less employees, thereby increasing the unit productivity of those employees remaining at a company after automation is complete.

Automation of industries can be a very good thing. But there is a concurrent responsibility on the part of the industry that is automating, to either provide a descent retirement for the affected, laid-off, employees or to provide cross-training to allow employment elsewhere.

AMERICAN AGRICULTURE in the WORLD ECONOMY:

Possibly our greatest need for automation is that of agriculture, especially that of the harvesting of agricultural products. That is no easy thing. The author's father was General Manager of the Citrus Industry Research Association, a short-lived but productive effort to mechanize the citrus industry that was sponsored by the University of California, Sunkist Growers, and several fruit processing companies. Its task was to encourage the creation of equipment to modernize the handling of citrus fruit from the orchards to the grocery markets. It was also to evaluate the equipment. A final requirement was to work with packing houses and other fruit handling agencies to test out the equipment. It is easier, much easier, to automate the picking and processing of citrus, or any other fruit or nut tree, than it is to automate the harvesting of what are called "truck crops".

Truck crops include various types of berries or vegetables that grow on bushes or plants close to the ground. Harvesting of truck crops can require back-breaking labor and cries out for some type of automation. Yet, to-date we have not found an answer. But, if there is a strong enough will to find answers, there is always a way.

"Food drives the world." Apart from clean water, access to adequate food is the primary concern and motivation for most people on earth. That makes agriculture one of the largest and most significant of the world's industries. Agricultural productivity is important not only for a country's balance of trade, but the security and health of its population."

As of 2019, the United States is the top exporter of agricultural products in the world.

(1) United States $ 118,300,000,000.
(2) Netherlands $ 79,000,000,000.
(3) Germany $ 70,800,000,000.
(4) France $ 68,000,000,000.
(5) Brazil $ 55,400,000,000.

That does not mean we are the top producer. That honor belongs to China. The U.S. is 49% higher in the value of its agricultural exports than the second leading producer, which is the Netherlands specializing in the production of flowers for export.

With a population of over 335,000,000, the United States produces significant amounts of food for internal consumption. The chart below shows the United States and other leading producers in the world for agricultural commodities. Of surprise and great significance is China's production. It is not a major exporter of food due to it having to feed 1.4 billion Chinese, yet it is the leading producer for more products than all the rest of the countries listed below put together.

LEADING AGRICULTURAL PRODUCERS (Data supplied by Wikipedia):

The following shows the ten agricultural commodities where the United States is the leading world producer (10): Corn, sorghum, blueberries, milk, chicken, beef, turkeys, almonds, pistachios, and cheese.

The following lists American production of 35 other products and our world production ranking in parentheses:

UNITED STATES: Cotton (3), lettuce (2), lentils (5), onions (3), green peas (4), cauliflower and broccoli (3), potatoes (5), spinach (2), soybeans (2), carrots and turnips (3), pumpkin and squash (5), safflower (3), sugar beets (4), tomatoes (4), pears (2), grapes (4), oranges (4), apples (2), raspberries (4), strawberries (2), cherries (2), beer (2), wine (4), pork (2), hazelnuts (3), walnuts (2), tobacco (5), honey (5), eggs (3), sawn wood (2), paper & paper products (2), wood pulp (2).

The following lists the commodities where China is the leading world producer:

CHINA (35): Paper products, wood, wool, silk, tobacco, honey, eggs, caviar, garlic, chili peppers, walnuts, peanuts, chestnuts, duck, geese, goats, rabbits, sheep, pork, beer, tea, watermelon, kiwi fruit, strawberries, plums, apples, peaches, grapes, pears, tomatoes, sweet potatoes, cucumbers, pumpkins, spinach, potatoes, eggplant, cauliflower and broccoli, lettuce, cabbage, green beans, green peas, wheat, cotton, rice.

RUSSIA (7): Barley, buckwheat, sunflower seeds, sugar beets, gooseberries, raspberries, currants

INDIA (16): Wood fuel, jute, ginger, cashew nuts, buffalo, lemons, limes, mangoes, guavas, bananas, okra, chickpeas, onions, dry beans, millet.

BRAZIL (6): Sisal, Brazil nuts, coffee, oranges, sugar cane, soybeans

The United States is considered a developed country, although we are still expanding the development of urban areas and planting crops in areas previously used only for grazing cattle. In that, we should still be considered a developing country. The only other one on the list of top producers that might be considered still developing is Brazil, which is continually eliminating Amazon jungle to make way for farms.

The export chart on the previous page has the surprising Netherlands in second place. That is due to the high value of its products, which include flowers and live plants, which "Netherlands supplies nearly half of the global total."

Despite the fact that some farming regions in the United States are losing farm land to development, the value of our produce keeps increasing. Those parts of the country that require irrigation are employing the Israeli-developed drip irrigation system that allows the use of rolling topography previously only used for cattle, sheep, or goats. Another method that the U.S. is employing to increase production on the same or less acreage, is the use of genetically modified strains.

The importance of the above is that of exports, for that adds to the strength of any economy through a favorable balance-of-payments. The balance of payments is simply the revenue produced from any type of export, such as agriculture or industrial products and services, minus the cost of importing the same. A net gain is a positive balance. Regarding value of the products, the fact that the United States is above every other country is significant. The large margin is even more significant.

According to the U.S. Department of Agriculture, since 1948 the available land for agricultural production in the United States dropped 30% through 2017. During that time, the value of total agricultural output increased 290%. Even considering inflation, that is efficiency.

Farming used to be a totally labor-intensive industry. It is no longer. During that evaluation period from 1948 to 2017, needed agriculture-related labor dropped 75%. That also indicates efficient production and the trend, especially with increased mechanization, is likely to continue upward for the foreseeable future.

POLITICAL CONSIDERATIONS:

American political parties have varied perceptions regarding our economy. The Republicans feel the less government interference the better. Democrats feel big government is necessary to help our economy. Both outlooks have merit. Like any industry, the various industries within the overall agricultural industry are in a constant state of evolution as new equipment, new processes, and new discoveries come into use. Government has been instrumental in development in that the funding for research more often comes from government than industry associations. The private and public partnership has been hugely successful in establishing the United States as the foremost agricultural exporting nation in the world. Yet government is also guilty of overregulating. The proper level of regulation of business has to be constantly reevaluated to ensure that the interests of the public are protected while the level of industrial production is not harmed and that regulation does not harm business efficiencies.

The level of business taxation is critical. Business donations to political campaigns often result in business taxes going down. That is an unfortunate byproduct of our system of lobbying. When lobbying influences changes in business taxation, it is always meant for big business. If small business benefits, it only means that it was happenstance. What is good for big business is not always good for small business and small business is a huge driver of our economy. It is always a fine line of decision between providing adequate revenue for government and overproviding.

We can't afford to tax to a level that is detrimental to business, but also business needs to pay its fair share of taxes to keep other forms of taxation at reasonable levels. It is a fine line that always needs to be evaluated. Of course, any business owner would say that any tax is detrimental. Legislators should keep in mind a lesson that the author's father learned at the USC Gould School of Law: "The power to tax is the power to destroy."

When California Governor Pete Wilson first went to Sacramento, he was greatly surprised that there were no lobbyists for small business. Yet at the time, small business in California was responsible for 90% of the economy. It still is. Big business lobbying is for big business and the interests of big business are often at odds with the interests of small business. In fact, big business sometimes sponsors laws that enable big business to steal business unfairly from small business. It behooves legislators at all levels of our government to consider the situation, the consequences, and the needs of small business, while they evaluate bills sponsored by large business interests.

The Republican fear of government interference in business and heavy taxation has merit. But so does the Democrat belief in the benefit of government. Growing up on a citrus farm, the author saw the good provided by government support of agriculture. Without government research and advice, our agriculture economy would have never progressed as it has. Yet he has also seen, in his 34 years of running a retail business, that government can make business suffer greatly through over-regulation and an attitude that business is predatory. What government employees often do not understand, is that business creates revenue that provides the business tax funding that, in turn, provides for governmental budgets and the payrolls of government employees. The author's business paid multiple taxes and fees to entities representing all levels of government, city, county, state, and federal. Additionally, business, through payrolls, provides the revenue for individual income taxes and also provides funding for disabilities and unemployment. Because business, both big and small, provides so much revenue for all forms of government in the form of taxes, assessments, and fees, it is concerned that its money not be used in a frivolous manner.

A PERSONAL EXPERIENCE:

The following is related since it was personal and not third person. It is not meant in any way other than to give testimony to an experience that was mirrored tens of thousands of times for small and large businesses throughout California. It is told because it is representative:

In California, the state agencies seem to consider that business is made up of rich owners who have little respect for society. The author assures readers, most small business owners are not made out of money and often have trouble making payroll. Most small business owners consider themselves members of local communities and they respect society as they respect their neighbors. Small business owners are your next-door neighbors. Neighbors who decided to see if they could meet that challenge of working for themselves. The author finally closed his business in 2010 due to the rapacious California governmental attitude toward business and its increasing draw on sources of business revenue during the steep decline in business during the 2007-2010 severe recession.

During the recession, his business lost 60% of its revenue. That is extraordinary and a level the author had never previously seen. Unlike a construction business that did not pay its employees when work was slim, his equipment rental business had to remain open and his employees all had to be paid. Many retail businesses acted in the same manner. They had to remain open even though business had dropped through the floor. His business, as were so many during that period, was perilously close to having to close.

Yet the government in all its forms, (city, county, and state, especially state) did not attempt in any way to help those businesses in peril of failure. Instead, they were constantly thinking up additional methods to tax business so that their governmental revenue was maintained. They often changed the name of taxes and began to call them fees. The change was a successful method to circumvent laws controlling taxation. Taxes are controlled by the state legislature. Fees are largely not.

The amount and type of fees charged were controlled by the individual departments and not controlled by the state legislature and thus government was free to increase fees without effective oversight. The state, in its many forms and agencies, treated business without respect and that attitude has caused many corporations to move to other, more friendly, states. If the author could have moved his businesses to another, more friendly state, he would have done so in a heartbeat, in spite of his being a third generation Californian with a feeling of loyalty to the state.

That is the negative and a negative that needs to be addressed in California. Unfortunately, political control in California is under the total control of the Democrats and their empathy for business is often lacking. Two-party government helps control the excesses of single-party government and California has had single-party control for a long time.

Small business needs the understanding of Democrats as well as Republicans. There are a lot of positives available to government and it has options available for it to change or redirect our economy in the event of further business downturns.

EXCITING FUTURE ECONOMIC OPTIONS:

Henry Ford had a great idea. He thought that by paying his factory workers more than the going hourly labor rate, his employees would then have enough money to purchase his cars. It worked. The idea of the creation of more buying-power helped create a middle class that purchased enough products to help make American business thrive.

Business leaders reversed the Ford thought process when they opted to send their factories to other countries to take advantage of cheaper labor. Their ideas might have favored their businesses, but they greatly hurt the United States. Unemployment rose. Establishing American industries overseas or across the border into Mexico, certainly helped the host countries. Their unemployment went down. Employees that work provide government with tax revenue. Employees without work, use tax revenue in the form of unemployment payments. Our economy and workers suffered.

Many major corporations bypassed large unemployment areas of the "rustbelt" and created call centers overseas. The corporations paid less payroll and Americans received less good and reliable customer service. While seemingly well-trained and knowledgeable, the accents of call center employees, in places like the Philippines, Malaysia, and India, as well as their lack of understanding of the differences in our American language, including the nuances and idioms of our language, often created communication difficulties.

Meanwhile, the Rust Belt states (Indiana, Illinois, Michigan, Missouri, New York, Ohio, Pennsylvania, West Virginia, and Wisconsin) had potential call-center employees, whose native language was American English, on unemployment. Employed workers provide revenue for our economy. Unemployed workers are a draw on our economy. Allowing call centers to be relocated overseas was a terrible idea and certainly unpatriotic for large business management.

An additional consideration regarded manufacturing: The need for manufacturing here at home is ever-present. It is in our national interest to have any military-related manufacturing located within our borders as well as additional internal mining to provide our manufacturing with required scarce metals. Factories that could be transformed to manufacture military aircraft, vehicles, and machinery were relocated overseas, outside of American control. Some of that manufacturing was relocated to China.

We have relied on China to manufacture those items, and China allowed American manufacturing and business to relocate within its borders in return for extracting business knowledge that it could then use when it created its own like-industries. Amazon utilized Chinese manufacturing in a big way. It was good for Amazon. It was good for American purchasers. But it was not good for America since China is probably our biggest geopolitical threat and there is a good chance we will be involved in war with China within the next several decades. We rely on China to provide those necessary rare metals. Let's bring those factories and call centers home where we then can offer employment and the security of having those war-related enterprises back within our own borders. .

While some industries are usually always in decline in any major economy such as ours, there are many exciting new directions and new industries that are worth consideration and industrial and governmental investment: Health-related industries like biotechnology and gene therapy; environmental industries such as wind energy, nuclear energy, clean ups of our lands and oceans; transportation innovations such as the bullet train being built in California's Central Valley and the concept of transportation via pneumatic tubes; space explorations that might take man to Mars; manufacturing robots to automate manufacturing; creating "smart cars" that are controlled and integrated into an overall transportation network that will eliminate accidents; other forms of Artificial Intelligence (AI) that will transform our lives and radically change so many aspects of our economy. Talk about increases in productivity and the efficiency of automated labor, AI will constitute a revolution in our lives, just as television, computers, and the internet have changed us.

Some may question my inclusion of nuclear energy under environmental improvements. Currently coal-fired and natural-gas fired electrical generation plants create several types of pollution. Nuclear generation provides very efficient power and very little adverse bi-products. Research may eventually find beneficial uses for those nuclear bi-products, such as radioactive waste.

The location of nuclear power generation stations is of concern. Nuclear needs water for proper cooling and that has made ocean-side locations a favorite. Our Pacific Coast is vulnerable to severe earthquakes and that makes location critical, especially in California. The 1994 Northridge Quake was caused by a subterranean earthquake fault that was previously unknown. There is no known way to determine subterranean faults meaning we cannot, with assurance, build a nuclear plant in California without risk.

However, each year finds the development of further safety features that make nuclear generation a very safe option. Locating nuclear plants in desert areas of our West could then power our national grid. Those desert areas are not subject to earthquakes, tsunamis, tornadoes, or severe storms.

"TOO BIG TO FAIL":

There are five areas, other than the obvious, that should be of concern to business and our government as it relates to our economy and to the well-being of the United States: The first relates to the size of businesses.

"Too big to fail" is an idea promoted by leaders of large businesses. Their aim was to encourage the provision of taxpayer revenue to support large businesses in danger of failure. Their efforts were successful. But at what cost?

There is a psychological aspect to the potential failure of business. Fear of failure promotes caution and usually prevents investment in questionable enterprises or methods of operation. If a business is considered "too big to fail", those business leaders do not have that fear. It is a different mind-set, which is similar to that of many governmental employees. They always have the "cushion" of taxpayer revenue to bail them out if they get into trouble. Fear of failure is a great motivator.

No business should be too big to fail. It is an uneconomic fallacy. The chance of failure promotes an accountability. Failure usually involves human mistakes and those who made the mistakes should be accountable. If there is a need for a certain service or product, failure of one large company will be followed by its replacement with another, like company. Trained employees of the failed company can then find employment with the new company. It is the failed management that made the mistakes that is thus faced with an accounting for their actions or lack of action.

MERGERS & ACQUISITIONS:

Mergers are often not a good idea for the well-being of an economy. Our government has a very good anti-trust division that evaluates mergers. There are certainly situations where mergers of like businesses are needed for survival. The competition in an industry might make size the difference between success or a slow demise. The economies of scale are at work in those situations.

However, mergers, especially between unlike companies, usually are only in the best interest of management and the stockholders, and not in the best interest of the employees, the consumers, or the economy. And mergers of unlike companies do not promote efficiencies. They make the acquiring company more vulnerable to long-term failure.

Mergers are often explained to the public that it promotes more efficiency in production and thus a product will be sold at a lower cost to the public. Not so. Mergers are never meant to be in the public interest. Mergers are always meant to be in the interest of management.

Mergers can destroy huge companies that have been in business for many generations. Case in point: Sears Roebuck and Company at one time was responsible for over 1% of the entire American GNP (Gross National Product). Instead of continued concentration on their well-established lines of business, they got greedy and overreached. They merged with or acquired businesses that were not in Sears type of business. The slow death of Sears stores across the county was a sad thing to witness.

Gillette is an example of a company acquiring another business for defensive purposes: It bought Wilkinson, manufacturer of the Wilkinson Sword Blade. Anyone who shaved with Wilkinson found out that, with one blade, they could shave for a month. It constituted a threat to Gillette and they paid top dollar for Wilkinson. Users of the Sword Blade watched as Gillette continued to use the Wilkinson name and slowly reduced the effectiveness of the blades. When Wilkinson blades finally became as lousy as Gillette, Gillette merged the two and eliminated the threat. Users then paid the same price for a days' shaving as they had previously paid for a month's shave. Did the America economy benefit by this transaction? Did American consumers benefit?

As a former commercial airline captain, the author has seen many airline mergers that did not make sense. Sometimes it involved a mismatch of equipment. Other times it involved dissimilar corporate cultures. Often it resulted in lower morale and lower employee pay. They never resulted in lower ticket prices for the public. The only exception to that would be Southwest. Southwest often lowers ticket prices, but that is based on wise corporate decision making and staying with a common type of aircraft and thus realizing huge benefits in parts, equipment, and training. Southwest did not have to merge with anyone.

Theoretically, mergers and acquisitions are supposed to be of benefit to the public. At least that is what many management teams would like us to believe. In truth, they almost always resulted in employee layoffs. They almost always resulted in less employee pay. They almost always resulted in greater management benefits and pay. The benefits to the public were hard to discern.

"RUBBER STAMP" BOARDS of DIRECTORS:

This is a difficult aspect to think of ways to improve, but it does constitute a problem. Management usually installs directors who are either friends or confidants of management. Boards are supposed to oversee management, but that is rarely achieved in practice. Accountability also suffers. Mismanagement should have adverse consequences for management. All too often, managers of public held companies are given pay and benefit raises after overseeing terrible years where corporations lost money and the stockholder value diminished. During mergers, officers of a money-losing enterprise are often given "golden parachutes" by their Boards that include exorbitant amounts of retirement money, which in no way was related to performance. It is the stockholders who lose in these transactions due to the loss of revenue which affects the bottom line. Customers also lose, simply due to the fact of the extravagantly higher corporate management compensation, which equates to higher product costs to show profit.

THE ADVERSE EFFECTS on BUSINESS DUE TO COVID:

COVID did far more damage to business and our society than those obvious health-related sicknesses and counter-measures, both short and long-term. Humans need social interaction for better health. The COVID need for extended isolation, especially in older people, has had a disjointed affect on us. There has been a form of disconnect in our culture. While families still get together, they don't do it as often. The long-term isolation has seemingly become permanent in certain parts of our society. The organizations where we used to socially interconnect, are often unavailable for us and the connection is too often of the Zoom variety.

The Politics of Divisiveness has further accentuated this tendency. We are isolated not only physically, but mentally and emotionally. This needs to change. We need to devise methods to reconnect our people.

Business has been disrupted, not only in supply train issues, but in employees working from home. While some employees are conscientious, others take advantage of the "lack of the bosses' vision" to fabricate work time resulting in a decrease in productivity in some industries. Business needs to physically reconnect its employees and repopulate its offices.

DANGEROUS DISPARITY in INCOMES:

The average or median pay for Chief Executive Officers in the United States is $802,870. The average salary for a factory worker in the United States is $16.48 per hour, which equates to an annual salary of $32,960. The ratio of executive pay to the average worker pay is 24.36 times. Compared to Japan, the median CEO salary in Japan is 65,760,758 yen or $445,368 U.S. dollars. The average factory worker in Japan is paid 2,795,458 yen or $18,932 U.S. dollars, which equates to a CEO to worker ratio of 23.52.

Those figures are almost identical: 24.36 compared to 23.52. However, salaries are not the complete story. To avoid income taxes, American CEOs have been creative. Types of executive compensation include: "base salary, incentive pay, with short term focus, usually in the form of a bonus, enhanced benefits package that usually includes a Supplemental Executive Retirement Plan (SERP), extra benefits and perquisites, such as cars and club memberships, deferred compensation earnings, severance/ buyout/ retirement compensation plans, pay with long-term focus, usually in some combination of stock awards, option awards, and non-equity incentive plan compensation."

According to Wikipedia, "Within the last 30 years, executive compensation or pay has risen dramatically beyond what can be explained by changes in firm size, performance, and industry classification. This has received a wide range of criticism. The top CEOs compensation increased by 940.3% from 1978 to 2018 in the U.S. In 2018, the average CEOs compensation from the top 350 US firms was $17.2 million. The typical worker's annual compensation grew just 11.9% within the same period. The pay and benefit inequality are the highest in the world.

It has been criticized not only as excessive, but also for rewarding failure-- including massive drops in stock prices. It has contributed to much of the national growth in income inequality. Observers differ as to how much of a rise, and the nature of this compensation is a natural result of competition for scarce business talent benefiting stockholder value, and how much is the work of manipulation and self-dealing by management unrelated to supply, demand or reward for performance."

A PERSONAL EXPERIENCE:

The author was an active member of the Air Line Pilots Association when he flew for Continental

Airlines. That was the name of the pilot's union, which did act as more of an association.

The pilot group was proud that they were the lowest-paid in the industry. There was a very strong pride within the entire company, which included other union groups such as the mechanics and flight attendants. Being the lowest paid meant that the pilots were the most efficient. That was neat. The pilots worked hard and came in first, according to the FAA, in the on-time competition among the airlines and they did it for two straight years.

The author then, along with a Pan American pilot, who was an officer in the Pan Am Flight Engineer's Union, researched the executive pay for both Pan Am and Continental. Although Continental was in the second tier of airlines according to size, grouped with Braniff, Western, and National Airlines, they found that its executive pay exceeded that of all the major airlines including Pan Am, United, Delta, American, Northwest, and Eastern. It was then that Continental pilots began to question the wisdom of our salary structure. The Continental executives earned the highest salaries because the pilot group earned the lowest. The feeling of common sacrifice of all employees for the common good began to dissipate. The pride that had always been the hallmark of Continental started to wane.

Such a heavy disparity between executives and workers is dangerous. America for much of its history had a sense that we were all working together to create a great country. Executives in those days seemed to work hand-in-hand with all workers. There seemed to be a mutual respect. That has also dissipated.

The author's partner in his rental firm was a trained executive who received business degrees from Purdue and USC. His career background was with corporate America and he was in line for the Presidency of a major conglomerate when he partnered with the author. He represented the attitudes of the business elite. He also never learned that his partner was employee oriented. On several occasions, he voiced a great disdain for the "working or employee class." If his attitude represented the attitude of an entire management class, then we, as a country, are in trouble.

Attitudes may clash and one group may disrespect the other, but compensation differential can be dangerous. The ability of an employee to provide for his family is paramount. If the "working class" perceives a significant enough differential in their pay compared to the "executive class" then resentment can build. If those excessive executive salaries are often not based on performance, then the resentment can build even faster.

The Russian experience with the uprising against Czar Alexander and the assassinations of him and his family are an example of "lower class" resentment boiling over. The French Revolution is another. The "working class" rose up and slaughtered the "elite class". Not suggesting that it will happen here. But efforts need to be made to ensure that worker resentment is not allowed to grow to uncontrollable excesses and that all employees are valued and treated with the respect we all deserve.

"Money will cease to be master and become the servant of humanity. Democracy will rise superior to the money power." — **Abraham Lincoln, President of the United States (1851-1865)**

Chapter Six
Immigration, Cultures, and Subcultures
Ever-Changing Cultural Dynamic

"The strength of America is that it is not multicultural, but that it is able to accept and absorb other cultures to constantly redefine its own, ever-changing culture. Immigration is a process of the infusion and integration of other peoples, their energies, their talents, their cultures and their ideas into our populous and, in the process, reenergize America." — **The Author**

THE FIRST IMMIGRANTS:

Immigration and this country are linked as perhaps no other country on earth. All our ancestries, if we go back far enough, came to these shores from elsewhere. The first known immigrants trekked down from the north and spread throughout the Americas. They were the ancestors of all the North American Indian tribes, including those that created the great empires of the Toltecs, Aztecs and Mayans. The ancestors of the Mayan and Incas moved down the slender land bridge connecting one America to another and populated South America.

The reasons that humans migrate from one area to another are many and varied. Most have to do with pure survival. Climates change over time and droughts occur that may last for generations. Game depend on water, as do humans, and the ancients hunted for survival. If the game they hunted moved, the ancients had to follow. Devastating floods, or storms, or earthquakes have displaced many tribes. Signs purportedly from the ancient Gods might have created fear? Perhaps lunar or solar eclipses spooked tribal leaders? Human history seems to always be filled with stories of battles or wars between different peoples. Stronger tribal encroachment on weaker tribes' territory have forced many tribes to relocate.

That was apparent to the Anglo-Saxons after their arrival in the English Colonies in the New World. In fact, English encroachment on tribal territories forced tribes to push west in a domino effect. One tribe pushed another which, in turn, pushed another. Finally, the westernmost Great Lakes tribes left their permanent settlements and became nomadic plains Indians. The Sioux were the strongest of those pushed tribes.

History is also filled with tales of adventure. Curiosity is a very human trait and propelled many of the great exploratory voyages of history, including those of Magellan and Lewis and Clark. We now explore the undersea world as well as our universe. Whatever the reasons, our Siberian ancestors spread as far as the very tip of South America- Southern Patagonia. Humans are also one of the most adaptable species on earth. Patagonian tribes were found to exist comfortably-naked in the frigid weather near Cape Horn.

Those ancient ancestors of our first American immigrants crossed a land-bridge from Siberia to Alaska at a time when one of the intermittent ice ages locked up enough water in ice that the dropping sea levels exposed an ocean floor that extended from Siberia to Alaska. Current archaeological evidence points to that crossing occurring some 50,000 years ago. That figure is bound to change as more discoveries are made and more carbon testing is accomplished.

As of January, 2023, new archaeological evidence suggests that humans were wearing animal furs as far back as 300,000 years ago and that they thus could have survived that long in frigid Siberia. New DNA evidence also shows that those who crossed to Alaska returned to Siberia at least four times and created a common culture connected by the land bridge.

Current map showing the Bering Strait that separates Alaska from Siberian Russia. The strait also separates the Bering Sea from the Arctic Ocean. www.ibtimes.com

FIRST EUROPEAN IMMIGRANTS—THE SPANISH & MEXICANS:

The actual first Europeans to permanently settle what became the United States arrived at St. Augustine, Florida in 1565. Settlers in what Spain called Alta California later became American citizens when Mexico ceded it to the United States in 1848 in the Treaty of Guadalupe Hidalgo. While Alta California could be considered the spoils of war, due to the American victory in the Mexican-American War, the U.S. did pay Mexico $15 million for the lands ceded. Mexico had controlled Alta California for 27 years after it gained its independence from Spain.

In 1836, 15 years after Alta California became part of New Spain that was ceded to Mexico, Californio politician, Juan Bautista Alvarado, declared the independence of Alta California from Mexico and stated that it was to be "a free, sovereign, and independent state." His gamble was successful in that be became Governor of California for Mexico and served from 1837 to 1842.

"Californio is a term used to designate a Hispanic Californian, especially those descended from

Man standing on Cape Prince of Wales, Alaska, the westernmost point in North America. He is gazing across the Bering Strait at the mountains of Cape Dezhnev, Chukchi Peninsula, Siberia, Russia, a distance of 51 miles. Naming of Cape Prince of Wales was by Captain James Cook of the British Royal Navy in 1778. www.drivinvibin.com

Spanish and Mexican settlers." The term was used for those who were Californians prior to it actually declaring independence and becoming a Republic. The Californios were a "Spanish-speaking community that has resided in Alta California since 1683 and is made up of varying Spanish, Mexican, Mestizo, Mulato, and (those with) indigenous Californian origins." The Californios "had little use for Mexico and engaged in sporadic revolts during the 1830s and 1840s".

The independent Californios had a culture that "emphasized individual worth, which was based on honor, respect, and machismo". That independence has been a hallmark of Californians almost from the beginning. Anglo-Saxon immigrants from the East arrived by boat, wagon, and train. The vast and unpopulated deserts, mountains and plains that separated them from the eastern populations created a streak of independence in them as well as the Californios.

California successfully declared its independence from Mexico in 1846. Initially, they declared a Republic, which was short-lived. In 1846, during the initial stages of the Mexican-American War, the American Army invaded California. It had marched all the way from Fort Leavenworth, Kansas. The invasion angered Californios who had treated the Anglo-Saxon immigrants to California with respect.

Though vastly outnumbered by the Army, the Californios resisted. They fought hard against superior and better-trained military units. Their resistance culminated in the Battle of San Pasqual, fought between the Californios under the command of Captain Andres Pico, and the American "Army of the West" commanded by General Stephen Kearny. San Pasqual was fought on December 6, 1846, near the present-day city of Escondido. Armed with long, spear-like lances, the Californios charged the better-equipped, but surprised Americans and they killed or wounded over 35% of the soldiers. "The Californios (may have) won the battle, but they lost the war."

Reinforced, General Kearny marched his troops to Los Angeles and again fought Andres Pico only this time he won the battle and occupied Los Angeles on January 10, 1847. Pico not only surrendered Los Angeles, but all of Alta California to the American forces. Commander of the army unit that captured Los Angeles was Lt. Colonel John C. Fremont. With Pico, he "signed the Articles of Capitulation (called the Treaty of Cahuenga) on January 13, 1847.

The treaty that ended the Mexican American War was "signed on February 2, 1848…By its terms, Mexico ceded 55% of its territory, including the present-day states of California, Nevada, Utah, New Mexico, most of Arizona and Colorado, and parts of Oklahoma, Kansas and Wyoming." Collectively, those states were then part of Alta, or Upper California, as opposed to Baja, or Lower California.

"In 1846, approximately 11,500 of California's 14,000 non-indigenous residents (82%) were of Spanish or Mexican descent. By 1850, two years after the discovery of gold in the northern part of the territory, Spanish-speaking Californians were only 15% of the non-Indian population; by 1870, only 4%. However, change came more slowly in the southern region of California. The few Americans who had settled in Southern California prior to its transfer to the United States to some extent had attempted to integrate themselves into the local culture. Frequently, they married into prominent Californio families, learned at least rudimentary Spanish, and converted to the Roman Catholic religion. Some considered themselves Californios. Until the 1870s, Mexican Californians remained a sizable portion of the residents and voters in Southern California. Eventually, however, the press of the growing population of non-Hispanics and economic changes destroyed an old way of life."

Author's Note: *When the author was growing up in a ranching community in Southern California, one of the girls in his high school had descended directly from one of the original Californios of Spanish extraction.*

An excellent discussion of the largely unknown resistance to annexation of California by the Californios may be found in a college thesis. It is titled "Californio Resistance to the U.S. Invasion (of California) of 1846". It was written in 2009 for California State University by Patricia Campos Scheiner. It may be found online under www.scholarworks.calstate.edu/downloads/gf06g3652

During the same period, the author witnessed a huge invasion of his native state by immigrants from the eastern states. Just as the Californios saw their culture overpowered by that of the Anglo-Saxons, he saw his own California culture buried by the overwhelming numbers of newcomers to California in what has been called, "the greatest migration in human history".

Immigrations, in whatever form, cause cultures to change. It is inevitable and new people create necessary change. Mahatma Gandhi said that cultures that are not allowed to change will die. Stagnation is never a good thing.

THE FRENCH, ENGLISH & DUTCH:

In 1604, the first permanent French immigrants, whose descendants eventually became American citizens, established the French colony of Port Royal in what became Nova Scotia. That area later became known as Acadia. Acadians were eventually driven out of Acadia by the English and settled in the Louisiana Territory, or as known to them as "La Louisiane". The Acadians intermarried with the local Indians in Louisiana and their offspring became known as "Cajuns", which "was a corruption of the word Acadian".

The Cajuns joined a French population that were citizens of a part of New France west of the Mississippi River. That area was claimed by France in 1682 and slowly developed into a sparsely-populated colony of France. In 1803, Napoleon sold the Louisiana Territory to the United States and its French citizens thus became American.

The first permanent English to settle America were part of a flotilla of ships that arrived to establish Jamestown in 1607. Jamestown became part of the Virginia Colony, which eventually became the State of Virginia. The exploding populations of the English, and later the other European-Americans, eventually inundated that of the many Indian cultures. While many Indians became part of the Anglo culture, many remained on the tribal reservations, which became home to many Indian subcultures existing side-by-side with the dominant Anglo culture.

The first Dutch to settle in America were mostly Walloons and their slave-bound servants. They arrived in the newly-created Dutch colony of New Holland in 1624. They arrived "by the shipload, landing at Governor's Island and initially dispensing to Fort Orange", which later became Schenectady, New York.

In 1664, New Holland was militarily taken by naval forces ordered by King James of England. That started the Dutch-Anglo War that was concluded in 1667 with all Dutch properties and claims ceded to the English. That also included the remnants of New Sweden, which also included a sizable Finnish population. Large German immigrant populations soon followed, arriving in the Provinces of New York and Pennsylvania. Thus began the massive process of amalgamation of the many different languages and cultures that then constituted America.

SUBCULTURES:

Subcultures are defined as "a cultural group within a larger culture, often having beliefs or interests at variance with those of the larger culture." The black population of America could be defined as a subculture, although it is slowly integrating into the dominant, largely-white, American culture. The black population, for several reasons too complex to even begin to be discussed here, were segregated by color from the time that they were forcibly brought to this country. The English who enslaved blacks in America, came from a different culture in England where segregation was largely by class instead of by color of skin.

Indian tribes existing on reservations are also a subculture. America is trying to better the economic conditions on the reservations by allowing gambling casinos. The effort has been largely very successful. Casinos are part of a larger plan to try to atone for past injustices practiced on the tribes. It is also an attempt to integrate more tribal members into the dominant American culture.

Normally the existence of a subculture within a larger culture is not a good thing for the dominant culture. The persistence of the differences between the dominant culture and a subculture often leads to a festering of grievances by the subculture against the dominant. Every immigrant wave into the United States has created ghettos where those of common language and culture tend to congregate and live. Ghettos then become the home of subcultures until the process of integration into the larger community allowed the ghettos to fade away. The recent trend of the dominant culture to gravitate to private schools is making integration more difficult. Public schools have always been a means for populations concentrated in ghettos to intermarry with other immigrant groups and thus integrate with the dominant culture.

One example of a good subculture is that of the American military. Soldiers, sailors and airmen are concentrated in military facilities across the world. For good reason, they are not allowed to integrate to any degree within surrounding communities. Even in American communities, the military stays largely to itself. By tradition, custom and motivation, military personnel feel that they represent the larger culture; the larger community.

An aspect of military life is the continual movement of personnel between facilities. The author feels that this was promoted as policy to ensure that military personnel would feel more loyal to the military than to the American community. The process creates a feeling of community within the military.

Through the process of reassignment, usually every three years, military personnel are not allowed to become part of surrounding communities and, instead, have further ingrained feelings of loyalty to the military because each assignment is to a familiar military community, but in a different physical location. Often, familiar faces are encountered at the different locations, further cementing the feeling of family and community within the military structure that stays within the confines of the facility. For the purposes of the United States, this is for the overall good and benefits morale and thus allows better military protection of the American community. The danger in this process is if military personnel begin to feel a distancing of the military from the community that it is pledged to protect.

Part of the pay of a military man is psychic pay. Psychic pay is not revenue, but it has immense value to military people. It is the honor received for a willingness to put one's life on the line for the American community with which he or she lives. The military deserves to be honored and should be honored, if for no other reason than it shows a huge return on investment. American industry, in the past, had taken a page from the military in its reassignment practice. To forge loyalty in its employees, corporations often transferred employees from one location to another. Their employees do not spend enough time living in communities to form a lasting bond within those civilian communities. The bonding and loyalty were then transferred to their corporations. At least that seemed to be the plan, and it worked for many decades.

That has been overshadowed of late by counter forces that have largely changed the dynamic. The primary force that has created disillusionment among employees is the deterioration of the treatment of employees by their management. This estrangement constitutes a real danger to our culture and our nation. It is human nature to want to feel appreciated. Corporate practice regarding employees too often is opposite of their stated policies or spoken word. As often stated, "actions speak louder than words". That holds very true for employee groups.

American employees are now known for their lack of loyalty to the companies that employ them. That does not mean that they do not do commendable labor. It does mean that they are likely to look elsewhere for work.

Productivity increases with employee groups that have been with the same company for long duration. Training takes time and takes away from productivity. When employees transfer to other companies, it sometimes takes time to train them. It involves companies having to spend payroll on training which not only involves those being trained, but also those who train.

Japan is famous for the loyalty of employees to their companies. That is because of the strong Japanese sense of honor. It is considered dishonorable for Japanese management to mistreat its employees. That sense of employee loyalty could be considered very cost effective.

Just as there are good and bad businesses, there are good and bad employee unions. When corporate employees feel a lack of appreciation or that they are not paid properly for their efforts, they often turn to unions. Often unions then become locked into contracts that lead to inefficient operations and that is counter to the good of our economy.

We are talking about corporate culture, which is part of the overall American dominant culture. While employee productivity increases with automation, so does it increase with corporate policies and practices that encourage loyalty.

Author's Note: *The author felt that the Airline Pilots Association, to which he belonged for 16 years, was a good union. He was also a business owner for 34 years, 26 of them as President and CEO. He has thus seen the labor situation from both sides and has gained an appreciation for the attitudes and positions of both union members and executives. They both have important stories to tell.*

A PROBLEM WITH TELEVISION:

While some might create a long list of problems with television, this discussion centers on why our current television options have created a problem for our culture. This is not about the violence on TV, or the blatant sexuality, or the offensive words used, or the learned disregard for human life. It is about the proliferation of channels available to the public.

In defense of that statement, the author witnessed an example of why foreign cultures are harder to integrate into our society than they were in times past. When he owned his rental business, he was approached by the Japanese head of American operations for a Japanese manufacturing company. The company was planning to introduce his line of construction equipment to the American market.

The author evaluated the equipment and was pleased with their products. The Japanese had decided to first introduce their equipment in Southern California by selecting a rental company north of Los Angeles and another south. Rental is a good introduction of new products as contractors rent and use.

An agreement was reached and the author's company started to rent and market the Japanese products. The new Director of American Operations met with the author after about six months of sales and rentals. In answer to the author's inquiry about how the Director's wife was enjoying her new America home, the Director confided that he had hoped that living in America, his wife would learn a new culture and a new language.

He said that it was not happening. They lived in the section of Los Angeles called "Little Tokyo" which has a population over 40,000. He related that she shopped in stores that spoke Japanese. The couples they met were all Japanese and spoke Japanese in their homes. Los Angeles television have a variety of foreign language channels with one that exclusively spoke Japanese. She had no impetus to learn English and no interaction with Americans. Her life was no different than what they shared in the real Tokyo.

LOS ANGELES FOREIGN LANGUAGE TELEVISION STATIONS:

Kanal Yek TV (Persian language); KXLA (Japanese); KSCI (Korean); Sky Link TV (Chinese); NAT TV (Thai); KIIO-LD (Armenian); KSCI (Multi-ethnic); KNLA-CD (Multi-ethnic); Mundo Fox (Spanish); KFTR-DT (Spanish); KBEH (Spanish); Estrella TV (Spanish); Telemundo (Spanish); Azteca (Spanish); Deutsches Fernsehen (German); BFM TV (French); 24 TV (Ukrainian); TVN & MTV (both Polish); Geo TV (Pakistani/Urdu); AVS (Hindi); Kenal 5 (Swedish).

The list continues. The point being that foreigners arriving in America haven't the incentives to become part of the national fabric. They can enjoy the benefits of the world's strongest economy without having to become part of the culture. The incentive of learning English is partially gone as well.

Additionally, the proliferation of channels also means that English-speaking Americans are not getting the same news. Differences of opinions are good and many voices can also be good, but information can also be a factor in nation building and individual bonding. We are now visiting uncharted waters in seeing how this proliferation of communication is either hurting or helping us be a stronger nation and culture.

THE ATTITUDES of the WHITE POPULATION:

The native-born white population of the United States is in decline and the trend is accelerating. This is troubling to many whites who have grown up in often all-white communities and have treasured what they consider to be stability. They often feel that their world has become unstable with the presence of a non-white immigrant population that has a higher birthrate. Many feel that their America is slipping away. After all, their white ancestors worked hard, raised large families, and built the farms and factories that helped build America.

They see "affirmative action" affecting their businesses and jobs perhaps because they could not get the raise they counted on because it was given to a less-qualified person who was a person of color. They might see contracts for which they were well-able to fulfill go to others just because they may be led by a different gender or are owned by a black or Hispanic. They might still believe, and rightly so, in fairness that should be a hallmark in all that we do. The author happens to agree. You don't correct a wrong with another wrong.

You do not deny a person a deserved advancement because of his color, nor do you deny to another American company the right to fairly bid on a contract because of the color of the owner's white skin. The color of one's skin, be it white, black, brown, tan, yellow, or magenta, should never matter. But that should also fairly apply if the owner of a company is a white male and if the employee who lost his or her job unfairly is also white. Whites did not buy into the just cause of blacks and browns to be treated fairly and equitably by our society only to see themselves treated with bias against them on the same basis that blacks and browns were treated. Both are equally unfair and "affirmative action" is an affront to those who believe in the equality of races, sexes, religions, and just people.

Also, a cause of resentment among whites is caused by a system that creates an unfair bias against whites. For example: the fair way for students to be accepted by universities is that the universities never allow the color of a person's skin to be a factor in selection. Yet the University of California has allowed selection of blacks to be based on a quota system. Thus, blacks are allowed admission based on the color of their skin. This is another form of affirmative action and is resented by a portion of the white community. What is considered doubly unfair, is that at the top of the selection process, admission is treated fairly. The top applicants for admission are admitted with no consideration of their gender, country of origin, race, ethnicity or skin color. That is the way it should be done. The top applicants to the California system are Asians. They were granted admission because they earned it properly. Blacks and browns do not score as well on the SATs and are thus admitted by a quota system. The University has now decided not to consider the SATs in their selection process. It causes one to wonder what they now use for criteria?

What angers many whites in California is that the white portion of the student body in the University system is only 20%, yet the white population is 37% of the overall California population. Additionally, the white population is responsible for a reported over 80% of the revenue that supports the University system. In other words, whites pay 80% for 20% enrollment. Rightly or wrongly, whites in California often feel that the system is stacked against them in favor of minorities. Since Hispanics now outnumber Anglos in California, the whites are also now a minority. A minority that might have been partially created by an exodus of whites to other states, with Texas at the top of the list.

The above "situation" is provided to show how some white populations may be inclined to follow a leader who has criminal and totalitarian tendencies and who is a great threat to American democracy. What forces may drive intelligent people to follow an unintelligent path?

The author presents the above as a possible means of whites feeling resentful. Reparations are another cause of resentment. The ancestors of most of us served in the Civil War on the Union side. Why should the white families who supported and fought for the freedom of slaves, be required to pay reparations to those who did not serve as slaves themselves and seemingly want to profit at the expense of white taxpayers? Reparations are a slippery slope and will open a "Pandora's Box" by encouraging others to travel the same route.

The reader may not agree with what the author has presented, but many do agree and the disillusionment of that portion of the white community has to be considered. The possible reasons for that disillusionment must be dealt with by our society for our society to survive and thrive. We all: African-Americans, European-Americans, Hispanic-Americans, Native-Americans, Pacific Island-Americans, and Asian-Americans must consider how to deal with the reasons for the white alienation, just as we should evaluate alienation of other Americans. Hyphenated Americans should also consider that most white Americans do not consider themselves European-Americans. They do not align with foreign nations and consider themselves "just Americans."

Yet the declining birthrate among the whites is not the fault of the immigrants. According to the CDC, in 2020, the number of white births in the United States was 1,843,432, while deaths were 2,491,026. Part, but not all of that disparity might have been caused by COVID, which hit the mostly white over 60 population quite hard. At the same time, Asian non-Hispanic births were 219,068 and deaths were only 99,574. Black births were 529,811 and deaths were 451,792, while Hispanic births were 866,713 and deaths were 305,708. Clearly, factors are at work that have caused the white population to plummet. The huge white families that caused the frontier to move so rapidly to the west and that populated so many states, are no more. In fact, many white couples have elected not to have any children at all or, at the most, two children. Two-children families are almost a rule for families in white America, yet that is an unsustainable number. Anglo-Saxons have to accept the fact that their declining percentage of the population is caused by themselves and not others.

IMMIGRATION:

The iconic Golden Gate Bridge which spans the entrance to San Francisco Bay. The bay, as well as Santa Monica Bay, has seen a high number of West Coast immigrants arrive from Asia. Asian

immigration has surpassed Hispanic immigration to the United States. Thanks to DK Findout for providing the photo.

"Today, more than 47 million people living in the U.S. were born in another country, accounting for about one-fifth of the world's 244 million international migrants, and 14.4% of the total American population.

American industry, especially agriculture, depends on Hispanic labor to survive. One only has to go in fast-food restaurants or visit warehouses to know that fact. While Anglo-Saxon farmers cut down the forests and did the back-breaking labor to create our amazing agricultural industry, they no longer want to do the necessary work to sustain it.

The author's father was President of his grower-owned local Sunkist co-operative, which operated an orange packing house. At the time, it was the largest in the world. He sponsored a drive in Texas to hire white workers to come to California to work the orange orchards by picking fruit. The effort was not against Hispanics or anyone else. At the time, nearly all the Sunkist employees were Hispanic. The effort was simply to find labor of any color. At the time, whites in the farming districts would not work to harvest crops. Most felt that the labor was too hard, the working conditions not to their liking, and the pay not enough. They seemed to feel that such manual labor, even though it was performed by their ancestors, was below their dignity.

When the packing house went to Texas, the labor needed to harvest their oranges came from the Braceros who were contract laborers from Mexico and were housed in a camp next to the author's fathers' ranch. They were on 18-month contracts and were a blessing. The great Bracero guest-worker program is no longer. It has been replaced by Hispanic laborers, both legal and illegal. They are willing to perform the back-breaking labor, while whites are not.

When the local packing house had hired enough Texans to fill a bus, they brought it to California. To a man, each white laborer walked off that bus and just walked away. They wanted the free ride to California but not the hard work to earn it. Unfortunately, that is the situation across America. Hispanics are not taking white jobs. Whites just don't want them.

Say what you will about the broken borders and the fact that our immigration laws and practices are in disarray, but without the Hispanic labor provided by our southern border, our American economy would totally collapse.

America desperately needs immigration. It need not come from Hispanic countries, but the needed labor has to come from some group of countries. It appears that our continued disarray at our southern border is the product of design. We could fix the problems in a relatively short time if we had the collective will to do so. At the root of many unsolved problems lies money, and lots of it.

Agriculture has undergone a revolutionary change. Largely gone in most areas are the smaller family farms and ranches. In their place are the large corporation ranches and farms that have huge economies of scale. They are necessarily mechanized, but the prior-mentioned inability to mechanize the harvesting of certain crops has continued the need for huge numbers of laborers. Instead of the contracted guest laborers from Mexico, many of the agricultural companies have replaced guest laborers with fear.

Resumption of labor provided by Bracero-types from Mexico seems like a no brainer. Then why haven't we done it? By allowing disruption at our southern border, illegals are then allowed to cross in ever-increasing numbers. By "allowing" illegals to cross and then find work, it allows fear of deportation among the illegals, which equates to low pay.

Deportation fear also exists among Asians that come to America. While our national focus is on the Hispanics, part of a greater problem lies hidden. Most Americans would be stunned to find out that more Asians cross than Hispanics. Only Asian usually come by boat, a much harder access to identify. In 2018, 37% of all immigrants were Asian while 31% were Hispanic. In that same year, 149,000 of the immigrants were Chinese, while 129,000 were from India. Mexico provided 120,000 and the Philippines, 46,000.

There is a desperate need for our government to finally correct the immigration laws. But it seems the motivation is not there to accomplish it. Current rules still allow it to be out of control. Neither political party is able to fix it and it appears that the agricultural lobby is so strong that it may be a while before it is accomplished.

For the reader to better understand our American immigration, some facts might help.

Black immigration has led to 4,618,555 foreign-born blacks living in the US in 2019. They come from: Jamaica (17%), Haiti (16%), Nigeria (8%), Ghana (6%), Ethiopia (6%), with the remaining 47% coming from 146 countries.

Hispanic immigration accounted for 44% of the 46.7 million foreign-born in the US. Of those, 10.5 million are unauthorized, 20.7 million are naturalized US citizens, 12.3 million are lawful permanent residents, and 2.2 million are lawful temporary residents.

Foreign-born populations in 2018 by country of origin and not by race or ethnicity were: Europe & Canadian (13%), Asians (28%), Mexicans (25%), Other Latin Americans (25%). In 2018, US-born women had over 3,000,000 births, while immigrant women had 760,000 births.

One fact might prove surprising to Americans and that is the education levels of immigrants. Many Americans think of Hispanics when immigration issues are discussed. But many different countries are homes to many of our immigrants.

Following is the percentage of immigrants, in 2018, who have an advanced degree:

American-born citizens	33%
Foreign born in US	32%
Country of Origin:	
East and Southeast Asia	40%
Central Asia	57%
South Asia	71%
Oceania	37%
Europe	44%
Canada and North America	50%
Caribbean	22%
Central America	11%
South America	34%
Mexico	7%
Middle East & N. Africa	50%
Sub-Sahara Africa	40%

The figures show that Central America and Mexico, at 11% and 7% provided mainly manual labor. With the exception of those two sources, and those emigrating from the Caribbean, every country and area sending immigrants to the United States had a higher education level than the average American who was native-born. If judged solely on education, immigration is greatly improving America with the infusion of foreigners, especially from Asia.

In closing, the author would like to add two personal experiences regarding education and immigration. The university system in the United States is second to none. American universities educate many foreign born. The result is that many of those who come for education stay and become very productive members of our society. In California, many doctors and nurses are foreign born and have filled our hospitals with highly qualified people. UCLA produces large numbers at its huge health care educational area that is fully one-third of an already huge campus.

UCLA, University of California- Los Angeles is public. The other major university in the Los Angeles area is USC, University of Southern California, which is private. Of interest is that one-quarter of the USC undergraduate student body, comes from mainland China. This is, not only a lucrative enterprise for USC as those are full-pay students, it is also a wonderful way for potential adversarial nations to learn about America and Americans. And perhaps also to learn about American football.

The second observance of the author regards the process that those who arrive legally go through to emigrate to the United States. That legal process takes years. Is it fair to those who play by the rules to have them see illegals be given preferential treatment by giving them citizenship after they broke the law by sneaking across the border? It is a legitimate question to ask of ourselves. Are we a just nation? Are we a fair nation? Are we a Rule of Law nation like we endlessly profess?

The author has friends who emigrated to this country as adults from Northwestern Europe. When they watch our country give preferential treatment to those who arrive at our southern border unannounced, without having gone through the same process that took them years to accomplish, aren't they justified to have anger at this country for not using our own laws? It makes one wonder who is influencing the debate? Are foreign nations that would do us harm manipulating social media to cause confusion and allow Americans to lose faith in our systems? Are agricultural interests doing the same to satisfy their own selfish motives?

Currently Hispanics are dying in the deserts of Arizona. Their attempts to unlawfully enter the United States have created unacceptable dangers for the illegals. We are working to improve conditions, but those conditions will remain until we have finally reached a bi-lateral understanding and fairly reorganize our immigration system.

If our immigration laws are not working, let's change the laws to fairly accommodate our need. We need workers, so let's get our workers through immigration or guest worker programs, but do it so that all who want to come are treated the same and all are also treated fairly and humanely. Let's again become a Rule of Law nation.

"Deliberation and debate is the way you stir the soul of our democracy." — **Jesse Jackson**

"Democracy, which is a charming form of government, full of variety and disorder, and dispensing a sort of equality to equals and un-equals alike." — **Plato**

Part 2

Community & Collective Needs

Chapter Seven

Regional and National Transportation

Safe, Swift, and Effective

"If you asked people what they wanted, they would have said 'faster horses.'" — **Henry Ford, founder of the Ford Motor Company and inventor of the moving assembly line for industrial production. He also invented the five-day, 40-hour workweek, which is now standard.**

HISTORY of the DEVELOPMENT of TRANSPORTATION:

The development of faster and more efficient methods of transportation has always proceeded leaps of development for world commerce. Faster and better transportation has been fundamental.

The first major advancement in the transport of humans and the produce of humans occurred around 4,000 BC when horses, camels and donkeys were first domesticated. Before that, walking was the best and only method. Horses, camels, and donkeys provided transport for people, enabling them a much more efficient means of hunting game by allowing them to follow the game and to launch spears to down their prey.

Domesticated animals allowed humans to visit neighboring villages more-easily, which were then being built for mutual protection; for a better means of trading; for the creation of small industries; for the common use of developed water; for ease of maintaining farms and orchards, and as an option to the then-practice of a nomadic lifestyle.

Humans quickly learned that domesticated donkeys could carry significant weights and that camels could do the same in scorching climates with little water to go around. Horses were built for speed while donkeys became the animal of choice for carrying produce from their pastures and between villages to quicken trade and rudimentary commerce.

Five hundred years later, the most important invention of all, created wheels. Instead of carrying products on their backs, donkeys and horses could then pull carts equipped with fixed wheels that were loaded with much more than the animals could carry. At the same time, river boats were invented and quickly utilized for travel and transport.

In 2,000 BC, the first chariots were built. They were used primarily for human transport and were also a primary weapon of war, at least until the wartime uses of horses became widespread around 1,000 BC. Chariots were then relegated for travel.

The Romans paved their first roads in 312 BC. This immensely increased the utility of the roadways and their comfortable use. Prior to paving, roads were subject to the slowing effects of rain and the potholes created by the standing water. Paving also greatly reduced the wear and tear on the wheels of their carts, wagons, and chariots.

The world had to wait another 1,350 years for the next major advancement. The Chinese invented the compass, which eliminated the guesswork often created by ill-defined roads or questionable "Y"s in the roads, or crossroads. Wagon travelers, as well as riders of horse, were then able to avoid getting lost in roadless areas devoid of any type of signage.

In 1662, a thoughtful European hitched multiple horses in front of a long wagon mounted with multiple seats. Thus, the first horse-drawn public bus was invented. In 1783, the first hot-air balloon was launched and eighteen years later the first steam 'road locomotive' was run. Another thirteen years passed before the steam locomotive was placed on rails. Two years after that, the earliest bicycle was made.

The first year of the "century of transportation", 1900, saw the German Ferdinand von Zeppelin launch a controllable airship that had its own propulsion. The first craft was supported by internal gas cells built inside a covered frame. It was 420 feet long and cigar-shaped. Beneath the gas structure were "two external cars, each of which contained a 16-horsepower engine geared to two propellers. A sliding weight secured to the keel afforded vertical control by raising or lowering the nose, while rudders were provided for horizontal control." It attained a speed approaching 20 miles per hour.

Two later-built craft attained world recognition: the Graf Zeppelin was built in 1928, while the giant Hindenburg made its maiden voyage in 1936. Graf Zeppelin was decommissioned in 1937 after having made 590 flights, including 144 ocean crossings. In 1929, it covered 21,500 miles in a world flight that was completed in 21 days.

The Hindenburg "was 804 feet long and powered by four 1,100 horsepower diesel engines, giving it a maximum speed of 84 miles per hour," while carrying 100 passengers. In 1937, the Hindenburg caught fire while landing at Lakehurst, New Jersey after having made an ocean crossing. Thirty-six passengers lost their lives. The tragedy marked the end of use of the dirigibles for commercial use.

The "Transportation Century" saw a hugely accelerating pace of advances in transportation. In 1904, the Wright Brothers flew their first motor-driven aircraft. In 1908, Henry Ford manufactured his first automobile. In 1942, the Germans launched their V-2 rocket. While a weapon of war, the V-2 was the predecessor of the peacetime American rockets that enabled their conquest of space. Werner von Braun was the leader of the German V-2 effort and came to the United States after the end of World War II to direct the American rocket efforts.

Two years after World War II, America flew its first supersonic flight in an aircraft. America lost out to the Soviet Union, when they launched the first man-made orbiting satellite, Sputnik 1. America launched its own satellite shortly thereafter and it literally "rocketed" into space with a huge program that saw Americans land on the moon in 1969 and, in 1981, fly their first Space Shuttle.

While several space agencies, Japanese, Russian, European, and American are creating faster and more creative means of space travel, American private contractors, such as Lockheed Martin, Northrop Grumman, and Raytheon Technologies, in partnership with DARPA (Defense Advanced Research Project Agency) are leading the way in the development of hypersonic vehicles that fly within the earth's atmosphere.

Hypersonic speeds are classified, but hypersonic vehicles fly faster than a mile a second and endure "scorching 2,000-degree F temperatures". The author piloted supersonic aircraft and once reached a speed of 1.91 Mach at an altitude of 55,000 feet. It was a flight testing the accuracy of "energy maneuverability" charts and using wing-tip external fuel tanks. The vortex of the tanks somehow enabled the flight to accelerate during the entire climb from 25,000 feet and the aircraft was still accelerating at the 55,000-foot level when he elected to terminate the climb. The flight was unauthorized and exceeded the manufacturers limits of 1.6 Mach on the wing-tip fuel tanks, but he was curious as to how the manufacturers data shown on the energy charts equated with actual flying in an operational aircraft. He has always maintained his interest in high-performance flying.

Curiosity has often been the catalyst for discoveries. When he was unable to duplicate the superlative climb characteristics of the tanks when he tried to climb without wing-tip tanks, he speculated that it might be an interesting aeronautical find. While stationed in South Vietnam, he asked a squadron mate, who was scheduled to transfer to the Test Pilot School at Edwards Air Force Base in Southern California, if he would test it out and Kurt Haderlie replied that he would try. Unfortunately, Kurt was killed on a test flight shortly after his transfer.

As an aside, the author's maternal grandfather was a chemist and an entrepreneur. He started Los Angeles Chemical Company. One of his businesses was the mining of alluvial silt, which is used in the drilling of oil wells. For his mining, he leased the entire Muroc (Rogers) Dry Lake, which is in the Southern California Mojave Desert. In 1933, the United States decided that it needed an Army Material Command base for the Air Corps near the Pacific. The Army Air Corp, through eminent domain, then took over Muroc from the author's grandfather and built what became Muroc Army Air Force (AFF) Base.

After the end of WWII, the AFF created the 2759th Experimental Wing which first evaluated the German Me-262, the world's first jet fighter. From that, the AAF created the F-80 Shooting Star, which saw service in the Korean War along with the F-86 Sabre.

In 1947, Muroc was transferred to the newly created US Air Force and was renamed Muroc Air Force Base. In December 1949, Muroc was again renamed after Captain Glen Edwards, a USAAF veteran and test pilot for the Experimental Wing who had been killed. The Experimental Wing was deactivated and replaced by the Air Force Flight Test Center on June 25, 1951. The USAF Test Pilot School was later created and housed at Edwards to evaluate and prepare test pilots for the Flight Test Center.

The AAF selected Muroc for flight test partially because of the expected crashes during flight test. Muroc was in the high desert and was at a distance from any population center. The expected crashes were due to the mortality rate for Edwards test pilots being 50%. After World War II, the Pentagon created the United States Air Force out of the Army Air Corp and Edwards then housed the U.S. Air Force Test Pilot School.

Since the 1980s, rumors have abounded in the aviation community about the existence of a hypersonic aircraft called the "Aurora". Many doubted its existence. It was real.

The author had a discussion with one of the Aurora test-pilots who had retired to heading up a manufacturing company in the Newbury Park section of Thousand Oaks, California. The test-pilot told of a weekly test, flown on Thursdays, of the Aurora flown overwater approaching Southern California at over 4,000 miles per hour. The tests off the SoCal coast were abandoned due to the

Wikipedia: Artist's conception of the Aurora.

usual sonic booms.

Rumors still abound about the hypersonics. It has been proven that the "Transportation Century" ended while seeing hypersonic aircraft speeds in excess of 5,000 miles per hour. It is amazing to contemplate that the century began with 20 mph speeds in a dirigible and ended with flying "bullets" traveling 5,000 mph.

The author participated in the Vietnam War. Even in the 1960s, operational fighter-bombers were extremely fast. On an attack mission against Southern Laos, he escorted an aircraft from his flight who had an engine shot out. They landed at an American air base named Ubon in the jungles of Northeastern Thailand. The pilot of the damaged aircraft had failed to properly pull and bank after a strafe run using the planes' Gatling cannon. He pulled but failed to bank, causing him to catch up to the bullets he had shot and they, in turn, shot out one of his two engines. F-4 pilots flew at speeds faster than the bullets they fired and that was back in 1966. Transportation speeds are advancing so rapidly that it is hard to keep up.

The author has also seen written material attesting to unmanned, hypersonic testing speeds in excess of 13,000 miles per hour. These tests were also under the control of DARPA. Advances in military aircraft often are later transferred to civilian aircraft production. What will this century provide in the way of commercial, passenger-carrying, aircraft?

PUBLIC TRANSPORTATION:
"For every $1 billion we invest in public transportation, we create 30,000 jobs, save thousands of dollars a year for each commuter, and dramatically cut greenhouse gas emissions."
— **Bernie Sanders, Vermont Senator, and former candidate for president of the United States.**

A recent drive by car from the northern end of the City of Ventura in Southern California, to the northern city limits of San Diego, covered 210 miles. With-the-exception of freeway travel through the massive Marine Camp Pendleton, the entire trip saw commercial or residential development on either one side or both sides of the roadway. Never a break.

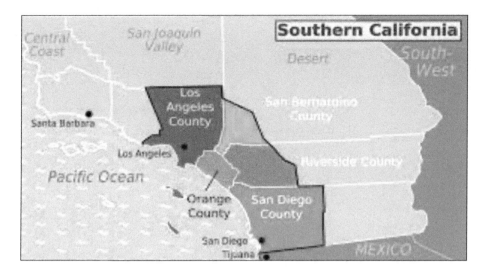

Map courtesy of www.en.wikivoyage.org

The map shown above delineates three full counties: Los Angeles, Orange, and San Diego, and the populated portions of Riverside and San Bernardino counties, shown in green and light purple. The land to the east in both counties is barren desert with scant population.

The area shown covers all the drive mentioned on the previous page, with the exception of Ventura County, which lies just to the west of Los Angeles County. The total population of the colored map portion was 21,289,563 in 2022. If Ventura County is added, the total comes to 22,137,510. That is an enormous number concentrated in such a limited area. The breakdown by county is shown below:

Los Angeles County	10,053,089
San Diego County	3,339,298
Orange County	3,222,341
Riverside County	2,463,893
San Bernardino County	2,210,942
Ventura County	847,947

Unfortunately, concentrated populations of this magnitude are very common in China. They are even getting to be common in the United States. California has two of them that are massive, including the San Francisco Bay area, which houses over 8 million. If the world does not stop its insane population increase, then huge problems will develop regarding sufficient food and water for the growing numbers. Also, transportation will have to be handled on a regional basis.

The hard-to-read map (next page) is of the Los Angeles Metrolink rail system. It extends lines to Ventura, Orange, San Bernardino, and Riverside counties. It reaches Oceanside in San Diego County as well. In places, it shares rails with Amtrak. This is truly a regional approach.

San Francisco has its own regional system named BART or Bay Area Rapid Transit. The equally

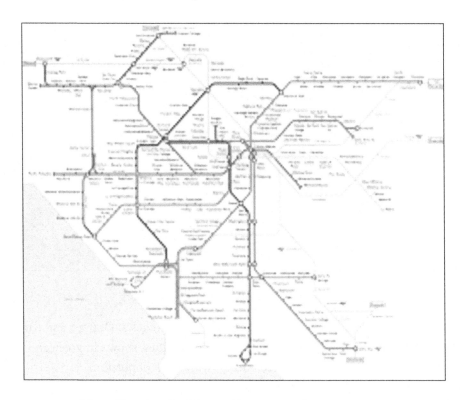

Map of Los Angeles Metrorail, courtesy of pinterest.com

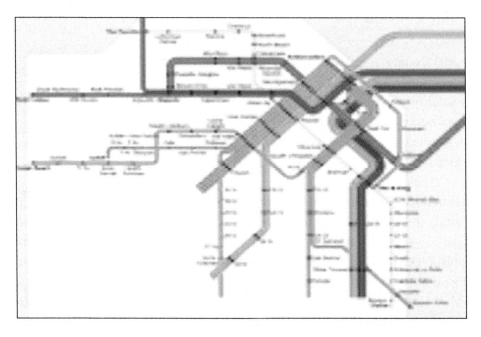

Map of Los Angeles Metrorail, courtesy of pinterest.com

hard-to-read, but colorful, map of the BART system, on the previous page, extends from San Francisco County to Marin County to the north, to San Mateo County to the south, and to Alameda and Contra Costa Counties across the bay to the east.

The California regional systems are a must and should be emulated by other population centers in the United States. In fact, many areas are fast-building similar systems to keep up with demand. The greater the number of L.A. Metrolink and Amtrak stations available, and the greater frequency of travel, the greater the anticipated use by the average Southern California commuting resident'

"Any businessman will tell you that transportation is fundamental to success."
— **John Hickenlooper, Senator, and former Governor of Colorado.**

As Senator Hickenlooper noted, transportation is fundamental. Both regional systems in California are expanding rapidly. BART is sponsoring a four-station expansion to take "riders deep underground to downtown San Jose, Santa Clara and the rest of Silicon Valley, at an estimated cost of $9.8 billion, when it tentatively opens at the end of this decade."

Texas is another state with a rapidly expanding population and rapidly expanding industries. Its population is approaching 30 million as California's is approaching 40 million. Texas has three mega population centers that are rapidly expanding: Houston, Dallas-Fort Worth, and Austin-San Antonio, which someday will join growth. If Texas were a sovereign nation, its economy "would be the 9th largest in the world, ahead of Australia, Mexico, Spain, and Russia". It needs those transportation networks to build ahead of growth.

Regional transportation is already benefiting California. According to Bloomberg, as reported on 10-24-2022: In 2023, California will surpass Germany to become the 4th largest economy in the world. It will then be surpassed by only the United States (without California), China, and Japan.

HIGH SPEED RAIL:

Currently, France has over 2,800 kilometers of high-speed rail lines, "which allow speeds up to 200 mph." China has the world's largest high-speed railway network at 40,000 kilometers or 24,855 miles. Its system is capable of accommodating high-speed trains running at 217 mph. France also is one of the world leaders in nuclear power. They currently have 56 operable reactors supplying clean power to their citizens.

The only high-speed rail system in the United States is being constructed in California. The initial section is in the Central Valley and 119 miles are under construction. Construction has been paid for by the State, but anticipated Federal revenue is expected in the amount of $8 billion.

The system is owned by the California High-Speed Rail Authority and its first operating segment is due to be opened in 2029. The map (next page) shows the various segments (11) in different colors. The completion year of the entire system is unknown because of funding that is not locked down. While France is a relatively small country in comparison, China is physically larger than the U.S. With consideration of their 25,000 miles of high-speed rail, we have a lot of catching up to do.

It is hoped that the California experience will entice other states to emulate and perhaps the federal

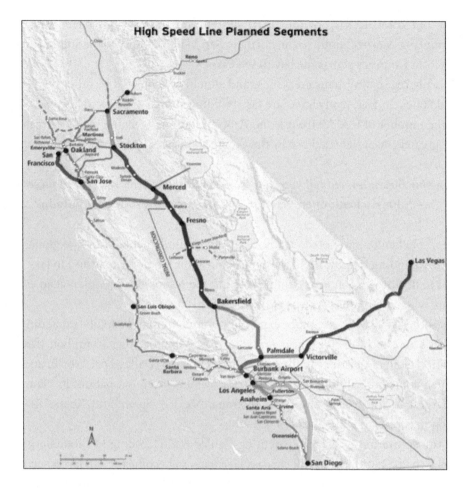

Map courtesy of www.hsrail.org

government will get involved, other than their possible funding. It would be a great improvement if the California north-south routing could be extended up to Vancouver in British Columbia and that east-west lines would start to connect the coasts.

HYPERLOOP TECHNOLOGY:

While several futuristic theories for transportation systems have been proposed, the author feels that hyperloop technology offers the best chance of ultimate success. The following is extracted from *"Evolution of Pneumatic Tube Transportation"* which may be found online at www.tomorrowsworldtoday.com.

HISTORY:

"In 1845, the London and Croydon Railway built an experimental cargo station in which the area between the rails and train created a vacuum, causing the train to be propelled forward by atmospheric pressure. The railroad abandoned the experiment after two years of difficulty.

Picking up where the Croydon Railway left off, the Crystal Palace atmospheric railway was used in London in 1864. The system featured a fan that was 22 feet in diameter to propel the train; the fan's blade would reverse to suck the carriage back along the track for return journeys. This railway was used for just two months before it was shut down and was never expanded.

Over a century later in 1967, Alfred Beach built a pneumatic subway train in New York. The subway propelled the cars along long tubes by using compressed air. The perfection of electric multiple-unit traction and vehicles occurred shortly after this experiment, so an expanded pneumatic system was not deemed worthwhile, and Beach's subway shut down.

Also in the 1960s, the US government considered running a vactrain between Philadelphia and New York City. A vactrain combines pneumatic tubes with maglev technology, meaning that a magnetically levitated train moves through a vacuum seal tube. The project was later deemed too expensive and was scrapped. Similarly, a Gravity-Vacuum Transit system was proposed for California in 1967, but it was never built.

Other, similar projects were continually designed or proposed throughout the end of the 20th century, with the same sad results. In France, a prototype (that was) like a levitation train, but with cushions of air instead of magnetic resistance for propulsion, was created. However, a lack of funding, the steep cost of infrastructure, and the lead scientist's death, caused the project to end in 1975. Additionally, in the 1990s a team of researchers at the Massachusetts Institute of Technology began developing a vacuum tube that would transport passengers from New York to Boston in just 45 minutes. The test loop was built, but the project did not continue.

By now, the reader might be convinced that this technology may not be in our future.

FUTURE POTENTIAL—THE HYPERLOOP:

"However, the possibility of pneumatic tube transportation has increased dramatically in the 21st century. It is estimated that the global pneumatic tube systems market will reach $2.8 billion by 2026, showing its staying power in the future.

The US government recognizes this, and as a result, the US Department of Transportation unveiled a guidance document to establish regulations for hyperloop technology in July of 2021. A hyperloop is the newest technology for pneumatic tube transportation, and it uses magnetic levitation and vacuum pumps to propel passengers. This announcement marks the first government agency in the world to establish regulations for the hyperloop, and makes the technology eligible for federal railway funding, increasing its likelihood of commercialization.

There are currently two companies that are frontrunners for the first commercially available hyperloop: Virgin Hyperloop and Hyperloop Transportation Technologies. Virgin Hyperloop has tested its system on its testing track called the DevLoop located in the desert outside Las Vegas.

In July 2017, Virgin Hyperloop announced that it successfully completed its first full-system hyperloop test in a vacuum environment. A month later, they revealed that their Hyperloop One reached 192 mph and covered the entire 500m DevLoop distance. In November 2021, Virgin completed its first passenger test.

Currently, Virgin is looking for a new, longer test track, so they can better test commercial options. It is also working with local government agencies in Texas to determine hyperloop's feasibility,

HyperloopTTs test track in Toulouse, France. Photo courtesy of HyperloopTT.

HyperloopTTs levitated train inside the hyperloop tube. Courtesy of <u>www.newcivilengineer.com</u>

including a system that would connect Dallas with Fort Worth, a 32-mile trip.

Next, Hyperloop Transportation Technologies (HyperloopTT) has advanced their Hyperloop. The startup began building its own 50-mile test track in Quay Valley, California in 2016. The startup was built off Elon Musk's published proposal for the Hyperloop in 2013 where Musk detailed how Hyperloop Alpha would be made up of enclosed capsules or pods moving through a system of tubes on skis that levitated on a cushion of air. Musk did not patent it for himself, but instead registered the design using the open-source project model."

The "open-source model is a decentralized software development model that encourages open collaboration. A main principle of open-source software development is peer production, with products such as source code, blueprints, and documentation freely available to the public."

It remains to be seen if the hyperloop proves commercially viable. The estimated 600 miles-per-hour speed is eye-opening. One encouraging fact is the interest and investment of Elon Musk. The South African turned American has proven to be a master engineer, a credible executive, and to be a master investor. Unfortunately, and perhaps a sign of his concentration on his other enterprises, such as Twitter, SpaceX and Tesla, the hyperloop test tube in Lawndale, California is being dismantled in November and December, 2022 due to non-operation.

It is clear, that the technology is on the precipice of either another massive failure, or an answer for our future. Airline travel means having to access a commercial airport that has sufficiently long runways. Adverse weather can ground flights. A hyperloop system avoids weather delays and the flexible establishment of hyperloop stations could be placed anywhere in cities since the system is similar to subways in that travel will usually be underground within congested cities and then can be elevated when conditions permit.

Another positive aspect of hyperloop development is that 80 federal agencies are working on hyperloop. With the federal government so heavily involved, prospects brighten.

It is an exciting prospect and, combined with other rail systems in a comprehensive national system, could provide wonderful and inexpensive transportation for our grandchildren.

"Those who wish to reap the blessing of liberty must undergo the fatigues of supporting it."
— **Thomas Paine**

"Democracy arose from men's thinking that if they are equal in any respect,
they are equal absolutely." — **Aristotle**

"The ballot is stronger than the bullet." — **Abraham Lincoln**

Chapter Eight

Campaign Costs
& Political Reform

Representatives and Responsibilities

"Money slithers through every part of our political system, corrupting democracy and taking power away from the people. Big companies and billionaires spend millions to push Congress to adopt or block legislation. If they fail, they turn to lobbying federal agencies that are issuing regulations. And if they fail yet again, they run to judges in the courts to block those regulations from taking effect. With money comes time, access, and the corruption of our representative democracy." — **Elizabeth Warren, Senator from Massachusetts**

Political corruption in the United States is so deeply entrenched in the American system that meaningful campaign finance reform is almost impossible to achieve.

Readers are recommended to read a 1989 article in the Hofstra Law Review titled *"On Campaign Finance Reform: The Root of All Evil is Deeply Rooted"* written by Daniel Hays Lowenstein.

Voters need to put identity politics aside as both political parties are guilty of allowing "big money" to rule our government. Countless bills have been proposed for reform and countless bills have failed a Congressional vote or have been placed in limbo status, to die a slow death.

Congressmen and congresswomen are often victims of this evil as is the rest of America. Good Senators and Congresspeople must play by the rules of our current system if they expect to be reelected. It costs money to purchase any form of advertising. It costs money to hire consultants. It costs money to field a staff to get-out-the-vote. It costs money to pay for travel expenses in meeting the voters. Everywhere a candidate turns, he or she needs money to continue.

The Founding Fathers could not have envisioned the cost in time, as well as money, to mount an election campaign. For representatives who must run for election every two years, campaigns take up so much time and money that it is a wonder that any needed policy is formulated. Something must change because each election cycle creates requirements for more money and time.

About the only weapon available to the voting public in America to effectuate needed change is fear. Lobbying itself is a needed part of legislating. It is essential for our elected representatives to take the time necessary to evaluate all aspects of pending legislation. Lobbyists can and do show different viewpoints to be considered. It is when lobbyists go too far and try to influence legislation using "benefits" for the congressmen or women, that lobbying gets its deservedly awful reputation with the public.

The fear factor should come into play to thwart any legislator who receives benefits from lobbyists or others and who then votes on issues of importance to the lobbyist or their special interests. There needs to be severe enough penalties for transgressing and "teeth' in their implementation. Legislators found guilty of being influenced in this manner should be charged and jailed for a sufficient length of time to make the cost of punishment exceed the cost of the crime, and allowing money to influence policy or voting is a crime and should be treated as a crime. Fear of public humiliation is important but it is not enough. The needed fear should include the strong possibility of imprisonment.

Unfortunately, corruption is so deeply entrenched that the court system is guilty as well. Before fear can be used as a weapon against unprincipled representatives, we need to reform our judicial system. Chapter One dealt with needed changes to that system. Chapter Sixteen, titled "Crime, Punishment, Swift Justice, and Judicial Reform" takes it a step or two further.

EVALUATING PENDING LEGISLATION:

The author has included personal experiences within many of these chapters. Reciting the experiences of others can be very important, but the describing of personal experiences can help establish the truth. An example of the need for time to properly evaluate pending legislation is one of those personal experiences of the author.

A PERSONAL EXPERIENCE:

In 1967, the author was assigned duty to fly for NATO in Europe by the United States Air Force. He grew up with guns on the ranch of his parents and was a hunter, who also liked to target practice. He had been on the Air Force Academy Pistol Team. He knew how to safely operate pistols, rifles, and shotguns. He owned two guns that he had acquired from the National Rifle Association (NRA).

Being a bachelor, he had no home in the United States. He was essentially married to the Air Force and his home was wherever the Air Force sent him. The military ships personal belongings of personnel to wherever military men are stationed. In this case, it was RAF Woodbridge in Suffolk County, England. He had his guns along with him in the English Quonset hut that he called home.

Then came the Bobby Kennedy assassination. It was doubly tragic and the nation was again thrown into mourning for a second Kennedy shot and killed. For Congress, it was a rush to judgment. They seemingly felt that they had to do something and do it quickly The anti-gun lobby had been pressing Congress to outlaw the importation of guns for a long time. With the assassination, they saw their chance and a bill outlawing guns to be brought into this country was hurriedly passed.

The reader can sense where this is going. The formulators of the bill did not take into consideration those military men or other governmental employees located overseas. They did not allow an exception. At the end of the author's tour of duty in England, he was forced to smuggle his guns back into the U.S. Think of that. Someone entrusted with the defense of the country is relegated to having to commit a crime to continue possession of what was his to begin with. Admittedly, that was a special case. But special cases abound and are part of most legislation. The good part of lobbying is that special cases can be aired and discussed. In this case, Congress acted too hastily.

The result of the banning of gun imports was that the author hid a Springfield rifle within his personal effects. The shippers placed all personal effects in a large wooden box. Somewhere, they X-rayed the box and the rifle was removed. According to the marine insurance agent that handled the author's property enroute from Europe to New Jersey, the marine unions had negotiated among themselves for pilfering rights. The gun was not removed by government agents.

The NRA 45 pistol was left with a friend in England. He hid it within a box of tape recordings of music, so marked it, and then sent it. It remained the only item successfully smuggled.

That is an argument in favor of lobbying, but lobbying with good intent. Most lobbying is with the sole intent of securing legislation and court action that favors a special interest and is not in the best interests of the public.

WASHINGTON, D.C. LANDMARKS:

United States Capitol Building, Photo courtesy of dissolve.com

United States Supreme Court building in Washington D.C.

CAMPAIGN FINANCE REFORM—CONGRESSIONAL INACTION:

Senator John McCain worked all his legislative life trying to pass campaign-finance reform legislation. In 2001, he submitted a companion bill (S.27) to the originally introduced H.R. 380. The Senate version passed on 4-2-2001, but was stalled in the House. H.R. 2356 was introduced in its place and it was passed by the House on 2-14-2002, and by the Senate on 3-20-2002. The approved bill did not have his name on it, but his submitted prior bill was credited to "McCain-Feingold."

HR2356 was the last legislation to regulate campaign financing. It "was designed to reduce the "role of 'soft money' in campaign financing, by prohibiting national political party committees from raising or spending any funds not subject to federal limits, even for state and local races or issue discussion." It was also designed to prohibit "ads that name a federal candidate within 30 days of a primary or caucus or 60 days of a general election. It prohibited any such ad paid for by a corporation (including non-profits) or ad paid for by an unincorporated entity using any corporate or union general treasury funds."

Key provisions of HR23256 were overturned by the Supreme Court, or as some now call it, the Extreme Court. In the case of Federal Election Commission (FEC) v. Citizen's United, the Court held that the issued ads could not be banned from the months preceding a primary or general election. The Court did, however, uphold the other key provision of the bill.

HR2356 Congressional inaction and the Supreme Court's contrary attitude regarding the necessity for controlling the corrupting influences of money, reflecting that they are complicit in the corruption itself. Otherwise, they would recognize the danger posed to our democracy if money is allowed to dictate. Their oath of allegiance to our Constitution has become a hollow statement without meaning.

OPEN SECRETS:

Highly respected Senators Frank Church and Hugh Scott partnered in 1983 to launch the *Center for Responsive Politics*. Church was a Democrat and Scott, a Republican. Clearly, it was a bipartisan effort to clean up soft money in campaign finance. In 2021, the *Center* merged with the *National Institute on Money in Politics*, an equally respected organization working for the reduction of the power of money in elections.

The new organization is called *Open Secrets* which, according to Wikipedia, "is a nonprofit organization based in Washington DC that tracks data on campaign finance and lobbying." The *Open Secrets* website states that "*Open Secrets* is the nation's premier research and governmental transparency group tracking money in politics and its effect on elections and policy."

According to *Open Secrets*, "since January 3, 2021, congressional lawmakers have introduced more than 50 bills related to campaign finance reform or the role of money-in-politics. Most were never voted out of committee, but several (10) made their way into larger, more comprehensive legislative packages."

Eight of the 10 were introduced by Democrats and two by Republicans. None of the ten are expected to become law. It is not that Congress does not have opportunities to vote on the money issue, it is just that they collectively refuse to vote them into law.

From 2002 to 2021, no legislation was passed. Since January 2021, over 50 opportunities have been presented to committees and Congress without any positive action. How many were presented from 2002 to 2021?

Congress has no will to put restrictions on money. Could it mean that the money they are allowing might find its way into accounts other than those of the various campaign committees?

"Our political life is becoming so expensive, so mechanized and so dominated by professional politicians and public relations men that the idealist who dreams of independent statesmanship is rudely awakened by the necessities of election and accomplishment. And thus, in the days ahead, only the very courageous will be able to make the hard and unpopular decisions necessary for our survival." — **John F. Kennedy, Profiles in Courage, Harper Brothers, 1956**

Photo Gallery Three

National Parks in the American Southwest

Arizona, Nevada, New Mexico, Texas

Grand Canyon National Park, Arizona

Petrified Forest National Park, Arizona

Saguaro National Park, Arizona

Great Basin National Park, Nevada

Carlsbad Caverns National Park, New Mexico

White Sands National Park, New Mexico

Lassen Volcanic National Park, California

Guadalupe National Park, Texas

Chapter Nine
California Taxation, Fees, and Agency Malpractice
Saving the "Golden Goose"

"The power to tax is the power to destroy." — **USC Gould School of Law Professor**

Bloomberg is predicting that California will surpass Germany to become the 4th most powerful economy of the world sometime in 2023, then only surpassed by the economies of the United States, China, and Japan. The state must be doing something right. Right?

The fact is that they could be doing even better if they had more business-friendly agency staffs and fought harder to keep major businesses in California. Since 1850, California's population increased each year. According to the state Department of Finance, "between 2021 and 2022, California's population declined 0.3%", its first decline since statehood. Many factors contributed, not the least is the staggering cost of living, including specially formulated gasoline and sky-high home prices. But most left California because of its high state income taxation, the insanely high overall cost of living, and the terrible business climate. Many employees followed their companies out-of-state. Of those states benefiting from the exodus, Texas has been the biggest beneficiary.

The attitude of disdain for business by state agency staff created a cause of fury among business owners and managers. It is as though they do not understand where the money comes from that pays their salaries and benefits. If some agency employees became aware of the fact that they owe their salaries to the taxed profits of business, they may start paying heed to supporting the "golden goose." The fact is that business employees and the corporations themselves earn the money that is then provided, through a myriad number of taxes and fees, to government to accomplish its missions and to pay the salaries of state employees. Without business, government would be non-existent. Without government, business would thrive.

The author spent 34 years leading a multi-facility company which had to deal with multiple state agencies. Agency staff pay little respect to owners of businesses. The feeling of those on the receiving end is that the staffers seem to regard all businesses and business owners as "made-out-of-money" and in the business of trying to cheat the public. It is galling, but most agency employees act as if they are doing business a favor, when it is the other way around. For some medium and almost all small businesses, the money is rarely there and only during good years. Often it is a struggle to cover payroll and most small business owners pay their employees before they pay themselves. For years, the author went without liability insurance, because he could not afford the severe costs involved.

The responsibilities of business owners are: to provide the best product possible for the public; to provide a return on investment to the stockholders; and to provide a good and safe working environment with adequate pay and benefits for their employees. Contrary to the attitude of the agencies, most business owners care for their employees and take pride in what they provide for their customers.

The author took pride in the fact he had provided health care insurance coverage for his employees throughout the 34 years of running his business. He stuck to that promise to his employees and his business went without liability insurance coverage in those years when there was not enough money to provide for both insurances. He was one accident away from business ruin and bankruptcy. Those sacrifices are commonplace among small business owners who want to provide for their employees, many who have families.

The reason that California has such a vibrant economy is not because of government. California businesses thrive because of the ingenuity of leadership and employees and they do it despite the inefficient regulatory practices of state government. Regulation is a necessary part of the needed protection of the public, but over-regulation is an onerous burden to business that often takes the form of needless paperwork and having to deal with inspectors who often demand and state inaccuracies. State agency employees usually are committed to job protection and thus by creating unnecessary paperwork they add additional work to be done. In many cases this may not be true, but it certainly appears to be for those business owners saddled with the ridiculous responsibilities imposed by the agencies that practice malpractice.

It is a difficult situation and one for which the author has no answer. How do state agency employees entrusted to regulate industries act when their necessary oversights are completed? Free time for those can be deadly for owners of small businesses. All too often those employees seem to dream up ways to create further demand of time and money from businesses. Large businesses have departments to handle state agencies and they usually have very competent legal staff to intimidate the agencies from going after them. Notice to the agencies: Small business does not have those capabilities. Of course, the agencies know this and that is why they often attack the companies that will have least resistance to their often- incomprehensible demands.

AGENCY ABUSE:

Sometimes agency inspectors glory in the power they can exert and make demands that are just an exercise in control and not necessarily in the best interest of the public. The author learned to demand written proof of violations of regulations and often that proof was not forthcoming. A case in point: The Fire Department has inspection authority and can make unannounced inspections. At the time the author was in business, the going rate that a business had to pay for an unannounced Fire Department inspection was $75 per hour. Often those hours consisted of the author explaining items and issues to a new inspector. He had to pay for those lessons.

County environmental health also had authority to make unannounced inspections at any time. There was no limitation to the number of inspections that could be made, which was the same for the Fire Department. Environmental health charged $120 per hour and that was a long time ago. Just as the business community heard that the police, when needing to increase revenue, went out in numbers to write traffic tickets, agencies who were paid per inspection would make multiple inspections that obviously increased their revenue. Businesses began to suspect that some inspections certainly helped pay agency employee salaries.

Some of the results of inspections were infuriating. Case in point: A Fire Department inspector was clearly new on the job and wanting to impress. She wanted to see inside the author's small engines repair building. She noted that the electrical plugs were all the standard 12 inches off the floor. She demanded that they be raised to 18 inches.

At a cost of over $2,000, the plugs were all raised. The next inspector demanded that they be lowered back to the previous 12 inches. When demanded, the second inspector produced the written proof that 12 inches was the rule. The first inspector had demanded without knowing her own regulations. The lesson learned was to always ask for proof when being required to change something. The mistake on the inspectors' part did not save the $4,000 cost to first raise the electrical plugs from 12 inches to 18 and then to lower them back to 12. There were several like instances of regulatory abuse, but the story of the plugs illustrates one of many problems with agents improperly demanding regulatory compliance.

This does not mean that most inspectors are not professional or that most regulations are not needed. It does mean that overzealous agency employees can make life miserable at times for business owners and that precious time and money is lost in needless work.

Another of the author's observations was that business owners or managers and agency employees and managers have very different mindsets. While businesses are always concerned with business revenue, employee morale, profit centers, bottom lines, customer satisfaction, and payroll, agency staff always have tax revenue to fall back on while business has no such safety net. Agency concerns usually are regarding policy, public observances and complaints, and the attitudes and desires of superiors. Both reactions to identical news is often quite different. It might be beneficial if agency staff would spend time with business managers and owners to find out what their concerns are and business owners and managers could do the same for state employees.

TAXATION—A NATIONAL PERSPECTIVE:

According to the Congressional Budget Office (CBO), discretionary spending in the American budget has suffered a 50-year drop from 9.6% of gross domestic product (GDP) in 1973 to an anticipated 5.3% by 2023. Those figures indicate that discretionary spending has steadily gone down over time, replaced with non-discretionary spending, which erodes the legislative power of Congress. That erosion is caused by the national debt. The CBO also states that the federal government will spend $400 billion on interest payments on the national debt this fiscal year. "That is equivalent to just over 8 percent of all federal revenue collection." The debt itself keeps climbing and now stands at $31,257,000,000,000. (10-31-2022) That is 31 trillion dollars. Everett Dirksen was misattributed for a quote that will be paraphrased here: "A trillion here and a trillion there, pretty soon you're talking big money." For the normal person, a trillion is difficult to even conceive.

The federal government likes to claim that much of the debt is internal, which does account for $6.82 trillion. It owes more to itself than any other entity. However, that usually takes the form of using Social Security revenue for the General Fund. The money taken from the Social Security account must be returned at some time because those funds are allocated.

The public portion of the debt is over $24.29 trillion. Of that, "foreign and international investors hold over $7.6 trillion." China is a large investor. The remaining portion of the public debt, $16.7 trillion, is owed to U.S. banks and investors, brokers and dealers, personal trusts and estates, businesses, the Federal Reserve, state and local governments, mutual and pension funds, insurance companies, and holders of savings bonds.

The problem with our national debt is that, while we sometimes need to increase debt to pay for required expenses (such as the recent heavy payments to Ukraine for assistance and to pay for the military supplies and equipment we have provided for them to fight the Russian invaders), we need to pay down the debt when we have a good economy. Unfortunately, that rarely happens.

California has created a Budget Stabilization Account, which is often called the "Rainy-Day Fund." The Governor's Budget Summary for 2022-2023 projected a surplus of $45.7 billion, which includes $20.6 billion for discretionary spending. The budget reflected $34.6 billion for budgetary reserves, which include $20.9 billion for the Rainy-Day Fund. "The Rainy-Day Fund is now at its constitutional maximum (10% of General Fund revenues), which requires $2.4 billion to be dedicated for infrastructure investments." The state debt stands at $143.73 billion. That projected budgetary surplus evaporated and is now a deficit.

It would be advantageous if our federal government achieved a surplus that would allow it to construct a similar rainy-day fund, which could then be spent during economic downturns when federal revenue decreases.

FEES ARE TAXES:

California often charges fees instead of taxes. That is because fees are not subject to the same constitutional restrictions as taxes. Fees are also often described as surcharges or assessments. While changes to taxes must process through the elected legislature, fees are subject to change at the whim of unelected agency employees. When possible, the agencies ensure that they are funded by fees. Following are some fees charged by the State of California:

- California Tire Fee
- Childhood Lead Poisoning Prevention Fee
- Covered Electronic Waste Recycling Fee
- Emergency Telephone Users Surcharge
- Energy Resources Surcharge
- Fire Prevention Fee
- Hazardous Waste Disposal Fee
- Hazardous Waste Environmental Fee
- Hazardous Waste Facility Fee
- Hazardous Waste Generation and Handling Fee
- Integrated Waste Management Fee
- Lead-Acid Battery Fee

- Lumber Products Assessment
- Marine Invasive Species Fee
- Natural Gas Surcharge
- Occupational Lead Poisoning Fee
- Oil Spill Prevention and Administration Fee
- Oil Spill Response Fee
- Underground Storage Tank Maintenance Fee
- Water Rights Fee

The above is merely a partial listing. Citizens may see other charges (fees) that are enumerated on their property tax billings. The above are mostly business-related fees. Not listed are Department of Motor Vehicles fees that cover just about anything conceivable. The reason that the author closed his business doors in 2010, during the height of the Great Recession, was the reaction of state governmental agencies who started to impose additional fees and to manipulate existing fees to pad their lost revenue.

Business owners naively assumed that government would not be so stupid as to do anything to cause business owners to fail. Yet the state agencies reacted to the business downturn by doing anything and everything to regain lost revenue. There was good reason that they lost revenue. Businesses did not have any profit to tax. During downturns, businesses must lay off employees. Agencies often do not.

The author's business lost 60% of its revenue and was barely hanging on when state agencies, on an almost weekly basis, kept sending notices of additional fees or increases in existing fees, or manipulations of existing fees that brought the state more revenue and cost businesses that desperately needed money just to exist.

One of the curses of the tax-and-fee system currently in use is the overlapping of costs to businesses from multiple agencies doing the same thing. Business must deal with city, county, state, and federal inspectors, fees, taxes and paperwork. Always lots of paperwork. Often the four governments were charging fees and taxes for the same things. The biggest violators of common sense were those entrusted to environmental concerns. All too often, representatives of those environmental concerns treated business as though we were committing a crime when all we were trying to do was comply with laws, regulations and ordinances that became more and more restrictive. The duplications of efforts often drove business owners crazy. Other states work together with businesses to solve problems. Not California, and that is one of the reasons why so many businesses are leaving or have left California.

UNFAIR GOVERNMENTAL PRACTICES—An Example:
During the recession of 1990 to 1995, the author installed four, vertical 1,000-gallon propane storage tanks. He did a heavy business selling propane to many different customers, including those who barbecue and drive recreation vehicles. At the time, Cal OSHA was not in existence. The installation was done with extra-heavy re-bar in a hi-tensile concrete base and as much concrete

below ground as above. The concrete-filled bollards protected the tanks and the height of the concrete would cause even the largest tire to bounce back, instead of bouncing over. Much of the installation was in excess of that required by regulation and ALL of it was following all laws and regulations then in existence.

Construction and tank installation was overseen and conducted by the wholesale propane supplier who insured all laws had been properly addressed. Then Cal OSHA was resurrected. The facility was inspected by Cal OSHA and the tanks were deemed in violation. It did not matter that Cal OSHA had not been in business as the time of the installation. The tanks were 33 inches apart and the **new Cal OSHA regulations** said that they had to be 36 inches. The business was then required to take two of the four tanks down at a considerable expense.

That is just one of many such examples of government over-regulation and behaving in an outright brutal manner. There were significant time and monetary costs associated with the installation and they were largely lost because an agency successfully threw its weight around and was able to demand. They successfully demanded that we remove the tanks even though the reason for removal was created after the installation. Above all, it was grossly unfair. How is a business supposed to operate if it complies yet still loses?

CALIFORNIA SMALL BUSINESSES SUBJECT to DOUBLE TAXATION:

The author feels that Investopedia offers the best explanation of the oppressive California business taxes that he has elected to quote them verbatim:

"Business taxes in California are some of the most oppressive of any state. High taxes, combined with the onerous business regulations for which California is also known, have led many businesses in the 21st century to flee the state for places they perceive as more friendly operating grounds, such as Texas or Florida.

Recently a California business owner encapsulated this phenomenon with a state map he circulated on social media; on top of the map he printed, 'The best avenues for business owners in California,' and then highlighted all the interstates and highways leading out of the state.

California imposes higher than average state income taxes on business and personal income. However, that is not the worst part. California is one of the few states that imposes both taxes, business and personal, on small business owners who set up their businesses as pass-through entities, such as S corporations or LLCs.

Businesses formed using these designations avoid double federal income taxation because the income they earn passes through to the business owners where it is then taxed. The federal government considers it double taxation to tax both the business owners on the pass-through income and the business income itself…While most states follow the federal philosophy, California stands out as one that hits business from both sides." In effect, it taxes the business income and then taxes the same income on a personal pass-through.

"California imposes three types of income taxes on businesses: a corporate tax, a franchise tax, and an alternative minimum tax. Nearly all businesses in the state are subject at least to one of these taxes and sometimes more than one.

The corporate tax rate is a flat 8.84%, which is higher than average. Corporations are not subject to the franchise tax, but they are subject to the alternative minimum tax (AMT) at 6.65%, which limits the effectiveness of business writing off expenses against income. The franchise tax applies to S corporations, LLCs, limited partnerships, and limited liability partnerships (LLPs)

Additionally, the state taxes shareholders on any personal income they derive from the corporation. If that income is paid in the form of dividends, California is a particularly brutal state. The state's top marginal tax rate on dividends, at 13.3%, is one of the highest in the United States.

The minimum franchise tax is $800, which also applies to S corporations, even if the S or C corporations claim zero or negative net income. The franchise tax is also paid by business owners of corporations. If S income is passed down to owners, they pay a 1.5% fee in addition to the regular state income tax on the business income.

LLCs pay a graduated franchise tax fee that begins on gross incomes of $250,000 with a flat fee of $900 and it goes up from there in tiered increments. For LLCs with less than $250,000 gross, they pay the flat $800 fee. The net income from an LLC passes through to the owners, who must then pay a personal income tax at marginal rates up to 12.3%. Partnerships and sole proprietorships must pay the $800 franchise tax and business owners must also pay personal income tax on any income that passes through from the partnership."

The California Franchise Tax means a company can lose enough money to approach bankruptcy, but still be forced to pay the $800. Readers are aware that these taxes are in addition to federal income taxes on the same monies.

21st CENTURY ESCAPES:

The Hoover Institution is named after President Herbert Hoover and is housed on the Stanford University Campus. Its Director, Condoleezza Rice, is concerned with the business climate in California. Hoover claims to be the nation's preeminent research center dedicated to generating policy ideas that promote economic growth and prosperity. Their concern is stated in their publication, California on Your Mind under several article including: California Business Exits Soared in 2021, and There is No End in Sight.

"In 2021, California business headquarters left the state at twice their rate in both 2020 and 2019, and at three times their rate in 2018. In the last three years, California lost eleven Fortune 1000 companies, whose exits negatively affect California's economy today. But California is also risking its economic future as much smaller but rapidly growing unique businesses are leaving and taking their innovative ideas with them.

Texas is reaping the rewards of California's terrible business climate. The following Concordia University list of those industries that left California for Texas from 2019 to 2021, doesn't even include Tesla, who left in 2021 for Austin. Of course, it does not hurt that Texas is one of four states that have no state income tax:

Aeromax – Manufacturer of parts and assemblies for military aircraft moved to Fort Worth
Astura – Medical-biomedical company moved to Irving, Texas

CBRE – Fortune 500 company into real estate brokerage. Moved to Dallas

Charles Schwab – Financial services company; moved to Dallas

Filetrail – Record management software company; moved to Austin

Green Dot – Financial products and banking services; moved to Austin

Hewlett Packard Enterprise – Information tech company; moved to Houston

Incora – Supplies aerospace, defense, space, automotive and pharmaceuticals; moved to Fort Worth, TX

KVP International – Veterinary supplies, moved to Grand Prairie, Texas

Oracle – Database software and cloud applications, moved to Austin

Pabst Brewing Company – Country's largest privately owned beer brewer. Moved to San Antonio

Saleen Performance Parts – Automotive parts; moved to Round Rock, Texas

Signeasy – Electronic document signing; moved to Dallas

Smartaction – Artificial Intelligence; moved to Fort Worth, Texas

Smartdraw Software – Computer software; moved to Woodlands, Texas

Sonim Technologies – Cell phone manufacturer; moved to Austin

Wedgewood – Diversified real estate; moved to Fort Worth

These companies that left were only the ones who left for Texas and only during a three-year period. It does not include those who left for other states and those were many, with several large Fortune 500 companies.

"Why are companies leaving? Economics…California state and local economic policies have raised business costs to levels that are so high businesses are choosing to leave behind the many economic benefits of being in California and moving to states with better (business) climates featuring much less regulation, much lower taxes, and lower living costs.

The Hoover headcount of businesses leaving "is almost certainly far too low, since most business relocations are not reported by the media, and relatively few relocations require filing state compliance reports that would trigger documentation of the exit. According to professionals in the business relocation industry" the Hoover headcount "may be too low by a factor of five."

The tabulation did not "take into account California businesses that are retaining headquarters in California but are making large facility investments in other states, such and **Apple** and **Wells Fargo**, who are building large campuses in Texas, and **Disney**, who is doing the same in Florida.

California business exits are occurring across virtually all industries, including manufacturing, aerospace, financial services, real estate, chemicals, and health care. Perhaps the most disturbing is the large number of high-technology businesses that are leaving.

California policy makers have seemingly always thought tech would stay, no matter what." It is this blasé attitude that makes the author think that the state will not reach the level predicted by Bloomberg. "But even tech firms are leaving the Golden State at an accelerating rate. California is also losing small, rapidly growing tech businesses at an increasing rate. Losing smaller businesses has remarkably negative implications for California's economic future, because long-run economic growth requires new, transformative ideas that ultimately displace old ideas, and transformative ideas almost invariably are born in young companies.

That competitive world of business is one of 'out with the old and in with the new' and this process, which economists call 'creative destruction' seems to accelerate every year. **Maxar Technologies** is one of those new businesses that could become transformational. Maxar, which left California for Colorado, is a rapidly growing organization specializing in radar and satellite technologies, providing 90% of the geospacial intelligence used by the US government for protecting our troops and other national security purposes.

Another key departure is **Envirotech Vehicles**, which creates zero-emission trucks, heavy equipment, ad buses, and which left California for Arkansas. Demand for these vehicles will explode in the near future. As the U.S. rapidly moves toward replacing fossil-fuel-powered vehicles with electric vehicles. Yet another California exit is **AquaMetals**, which left for Nevada. AquaMetals has developed a new, unique way of recycling strategic and rare metals, including lithium, which is used in smartphone batteries. They have created metal capture processes that are much more environmentally friendly than existing processes. The demand for lithium and other rare earth metals is expected to skyrocket in the coming years.

California…is at or near the bottom in rankings of business climate and economic policies. The American Legislative Exchange Council, a nonpartisan research organization that produces economic policy evaluations of every state annually, ranks California 48th behind only New Jersey and New York.

The Tax Foundation, a nonpartisan think tank focusing on state and national tax policies, ranks California 49th in its Business Tax Climate Index…Annual surveys of business CEOs and small business owners invariably rank California 50th in terms of the quality of state business climates." The growing business negatives are starting to topple the positives that moved the Golden State population from 10 million at the end of World War II, to 30 million by 1990 and close to 40 million today.

"While California has many natural advantages, its state and local economic policies have created a business climate that is no longer competitive with that of many other states. Policies have driven business and housing cost so high that companies and people are leaving the state for more affordable, less regulated, and less taxed locations. This process will continue until the state's political leaders make very different policy choices that create a different future for California. One that honors its remarkable past."

"Democracy extends the sphere of individual freedom, socialism restricts it."
— **Alexis de Tocqueville**

Chapter Ten
Needed Organizational & Institutional Reform
Crisis in Confidence, The Federal Reserve & Moral Responsibility

"We are only as strong as we are united, as weak as we are divided."
— **J.K. Rowling, author of the seven-volume Harry Potter book series**

American society has been dealt many body-blows when trusted organizations, institutions, and governments turn out to be so flawed that our national trust has eroded in significant ways and degrees.

<u>**CONFIDENCE in INSTITUTIONS:**</u>

American confidence in institutions is at an all-time low and that holds significant danger for the United States going forward. When most of us were children, we looked up to individuals who we respected and whom we wanted to emulate. They were role models for our conduct. We looked up to them for guidance and as an example of how we were expected to act or how we wanted to pattern ourselves after to win acceptance from others.

As adults, if we admired anything, it was usually our institutions. Institutions are the bedrock of any society. For America, our political forefathers or actual forefathers laid the foundation. Our fathers and mothers, with help from others, figuratively built the house in which we live. Institutions are the very fabric of our country and is what keeps us together. That needed togetherness is why we desperately need laudable national goals that we all can look up to. Goals not only show direction, but they are unifying. Damaged institutions also damage the respect we have for our country and the fabric of our country begins to fray. Unfortunately, the lack of respect and confidence is not a new thing. The accelerating rate of decline in confidence is somewhat of a new thing.

A recent Gallup Poll registered the confidence levels Americans have in our various institutions. Those poll results are printed below:

GALLUP POLL: CHANGE in CONFIDENCE in MAJOR U.S. INSTITUTIONS: Single year change in "a great deal of confidence" or "quite a lot of confidence."

INSTITUTION:	YEAR:2021	YEAR:2022	CHANGE IN % POINTS:
Organized Religions	37%	31%	-6
Organized Labor	28%	28%	0
The Military	69%	64%	-5

INSTITUTION:	YEAR:2021	YEAR:2022	CHANGE IN % POINTS:
The Supreme Court	36%	25%	-11
The Presidency	38%	23%	-15
Congress	12%	7%	-5
Public Schools	32%	28%	-4
The Police	51%	45%	-6
Criminal Justice System	20%	14%	-6
Newspapers	21%	16%	-5
Television News	16%	11%	-5
Internet News	19% (2014)	16% (2017)	-3 (in three years)
The medical system	44%	38%	-6
Business: Small	70%	68%	-2
Business: Large Technology	29%	26%	-3
Business: Big	18%	14%	-4
Banks	33%	27%	-6
Science	64%	No updated data	
Health Maintenance (HMOs)	19% (2013)	No prior data	

The numbers are sobering. They should be read with the understanding that the polls registered a drop in confidence in only one year. That is huge. What will be the results in five years, or in ten?

The range of responses in their survey were several, but in the chart Gallup chose to only include those who had, either a great deal of confidence in an institution or quite a lot of confidence.

The three branches of our government took big hits:

The US Presidency took the biggest hit, dropping 15 points, from a 38% approval rate down to 23%. However that is a measure of the drop in percentage, it is not the percentage rate of drop in the past year. That amounts to a drop of 39% of those who had high levels of confidence in 2021.

The Supreme Court took the second largest hit: It went down from a 36% approval rate to 25% or 11 points. That is a 31% drop.

Congress took the smallest drop, from 16% to 11%. But that represents a drop in American confidence of a whopping 42% in only one year.

Our federal government suffered single-year losses of 39%, 31% and 42%. That is not only startling, it is dangerous. The American low regard for our corrupt Congress is so widespread that only 7% of us think a great deal of them or at least quite a lot. That means that 93% of us think: some, little, or none-at-all in the way of respect. Many feel a loathing and disgust. Do Congressmen and Congresswomen think that their rhetoric is masking their actions? The American public is much smarter and discerning than that. They realize what a sorry lot we have leading us and, worse than that, what a broken system that Congress represents.

The Presidency is another example. Two individuals can account for most, if not all, of the lack of confidence, and those are Donald Trump and Joe Biden. Trump is not only unethical, but also unlawful. Just as Nixon famously misstated, "I am not a crook." Trump has shown he is a crook and on a much larger scale than Nixon.

Biden's low rating is partially due to the tainting of opinion of the office itself that was created by Trump. But that is not the only reason the public has lost confidence. It was the hope of many that Biden would start off his administration by placing his highest priority on healing the wounds of our nation. He did not. Instead, he seemed to be playing the same game of politics and not realizing what a dire situation in which our country now finds itself. Instead of healing our wounds, Biden caved to the Progressive side of the Democrat Party and the result was almost unlimited spending. That does not mollify Republicans. It enrages them because that is not seen as showing fiscal responsibility.

Many of those Progressives seemingly take glee concerning the plight that is the Republican Party. Again, many of those Progressives seem to pay more heed to the discomforts of their enemies than the situation of our country and what it might mean to our democratic institutions.

The Democrat practice of spending more money than we receive and thereby increasing the National Debt, is anathema to Republicans. However, they are guilty of it themselves and the data proves it. Republicans only think that their leaders in Congress and the Presidency are much more fiscally responsible than the Democrats. The lure of providing taxpayer money to fund projects that are dear to the hearts of donors is too tempting for members of both parties to resist.

What Republicans think is equally important to how they act. How they think is overwhelmingly influencing the direction of our country. We have seen that in their continual beliefs that, in some instances, black is white and white is black. The author does not blame them. He does strongly blame their leaders in and out of government. He strongly blames portions of the media, like Fox News, who hype the continual lies about our institutions. Fox harbors the greatest guilt. Republican rank and file are guilty only of listening to a few sources of information and they are guilty of trusting in what their conservative leaders have been telling them. One of the author's greatest fears is what will happen when Trump Republicans finally wake up to the grand deception that has been perpetrated on them? An even greater fear is what will happen if they fail to wake up?

Author's Note: *I write the above after having been a lifelong Republican and the latest in a family that have been Republicans since they were created from the Whigs in February 1854. I have always considered myself a conservative, but thinks conservatism, as now practiced under Republicans since 2016, is radicalism. I respect Republicans for their obvious love for country and support for our military. They honor our flag. But so do the Democrats and therein lies my hope for a return to bipartisanship.*

But first, Republicans need to find out the truth about their erstwhile leader, Trump. It was obvious in 2016 that Trump had never ever read our Constitution. His obvious respect for despot dictators is not only curious, but soberingly dangerous. His "floating" of his desire to be named "President for Life" is just another example of his ignorance of our democratic system.

Trump espouses his conservatism, yet in the 21st century, he has been both a registered Independent and a registered Democrat, in addition to now being a registered Republican. Additionally, he used to espouse that he was pro-choice, but changed to a pro-life stance when it became necessary to further his selfish aims. While he is not alone in changing his position, the matter of abortion is a moral issue and how can one have a set of morals that sway with the winds of political storms?

The distressing aspect of the Gallup figures is that they are so low. The satisfactory levels are printed in green, while the dangerous levels are in red. The red is scary, indicating that the confidence level of Americans in its institutions is horrible. The green indicates the respect for our military and for small business, both rate the highest and both are deserving of that confidence.

Another cause of distress is that most categories have dropped so precipitously in only one year. For some institutions, the confidence levels can't get much worse. The chilling part is what will happen to our society if our confidence reaches even closer to zero?

The above chart is also missing a few categories. It does not include the confidence level for firefighters, a level that should be high. Firefighting is one of the few institutions in which the support and respect of our community is highest and it is missing. Consideration of state or local government is also missing, with local being county and city government. It also might be interesting to see how the public regards service clubs who are nonprofit and are philanthropic in nature, such as Rotary, Elks, Kiwanis, Lions, etc. A final evaluation missing from the chart is that of the Federal Reserve. The Federal Reserve, or commonly called the Fed, has so much power that it can legitimately be called the 4th branch of our national government. The Fed is somewhat mysterious to many as it is a shadowy part of government that keeps a low profile. Yet it controls the monetary part and has such a strong influence in our economy. A full explanation of the Federal Reserve is included later in this chapter.

The author spent 10 years in the military. He also spent 34 years owning and running a small business. The military is still filled with men and women of integrity who have spurned higher-paying employment for the privilege of serving our country. They are worthy of our praise.

Regarding small business: When Pete Wilson won the California governorship and arrived in Sacramento, he marveled at the fact that he could find no lobbyist representation of small business. He was right, there is no effective lobby. Yet at the time of Wilson's arrival, small business accounted for fully 90% of the California economy. Small business is also worthy of the praise shown in the poll.

The author took three trips to Sacramento during his time in small business, as a representative of business organizations in Ventura County, California. Each time he sat in on sessions of the then-Senate Insurance and Finance Committee. As is often said: "If you want to eat sausage, don't see how sausage is made." At the time, Willie Brown was kingmaker in the California Senate. He made his presence known every time the author sat in on Insurance and Finance. When the author presented a bill before the same committee, he was inundated with questions and opinions from the many insurance company lobbyists who were present.

While the insurance lobbyists were very much in attendance and their influence seemed significant, it was very apparent that Brown ran the committee and apparently dictated the decisions of the committee. Insurance is now in a separate Insurance Committee and finance is now under the Governance & Finance Committee. The author highly recommends that readers attend committee sessions at their state capitols. They are themselves a lesson in civics. An electorate better informed on how our government operates will usually make better decisions on who operates our government.

While small business does not have the heft of larger corporations regarding corporate money set aside for philanthropic or community investment, it does provide the funding for local youth sports teams and other local high school programs and events. It forms the backbone of local investment while large corporations fill the financial void for larger statewide and national philanthropy.

Small business can also have a heart. When a young boy was killed while riding his bicycle, the author's business and many other nearby businesses chipped in to provide a proper funeral for the boy's impoverished family. The same small group of businesses contributed the funding to provide the local police department with bicycles. It was an attempt to get the police out of their cars and into the businesses so that they could become familiar with business managers and owners, enabling them to then operate together in common cause such as reduction in local area crime. Police understand crime is reduced when there are more "eyes on the street."

A HEARTWARMING EXPERIENCE:

Perhaps the most heartwarming event in the author's business experience occurred when his business was repeatedly burglarized. Three different times his employees arrived at work to find a pile of chicken bones just beyond the entry gate. It was always on a Wednesday. The bones were what was left of the warm chickens that were thrown over the fence by the burglars to keep the two guard dogs occupied. After the third theft, the author fired his dogs.

The first theft took more than a quarter million dollars in equipment. They even stole one of his trucks to haul the equipment away. It was later found down in the district around the twin ports of Los Angeles and Long Beach, which account for close to 50% of American imports. As explained by the Los Angeles police, the stolen merchandise would be driven to the ports and stored in nearby warehouses before being loaded in ships bound for China. It was a form of export. The Port District police did manage to find a few of his stolen items in a warehouse and returned them to him.

The second theft occurred on the following Tuesday night and again discovered on Wednesday. The same pile of chicken bones. It was figured that the thieves were just returning to claim other equipment that they had noticed on their first visit and did not have room for in the stolen moving van.

The heartwarming outcome was the reaction of his county rental competitors. Two other equipment rental companies filled trucks with their own equipment and sent them over for the author to rent until he obtained replacements. They did not charge anything and said to keep the equipment "as long as needed." It was another example of the American concern for others that transcended the competitive motivation.

The author ordered replacements. Six weeks after the second theft, he arrived to find the then-common chicken bones. It was another Wednesday. This time the persistent thieves loaded equipment that included none older than three weeks. They were smart and waited for delivery of the new replacement equipment.

It turned out that the theft was the first among rental companies in California. It was not the last. Other industries were also hit. It became apparent that it was a very sophisticated and large theft ring and it probably operated out of Los Angeles. Tuesday nights were the gang's nights for theft in Ventura County.

The California Rental Association, at the time the largest such organization in the United States since the concept of rental got its start in Los Angeles County, was connected with the local Thousand Oaks, California Police Department. It was a learning experience for both institutions. All California rental companies were alerted as to the methodology of the thieves. The City formed a Crime Prevention Task Force and included the author plus the county sheriff and local police plus being chaired by the Mayor.

The white vans that were used by the theft ring were shown on several security cameras. Armed with that knowledge, the Thousand Oaks police found a white van parked alongside a local freeway, resulting in multiple arrests. It turned out that the theft ring was filled with former military and their operations were marked by military precision. Their torching equipment was better than that of the author. The ring operated out of Los Angeles and were responsible for thefts in nine western states.

The result included prison time for 23 members of the ring and the rehiring of the author's two Dobermans.

THE FEDERAL RESERVE:

Another notable absence from the Gallup confidence figures is that of what is known as the "Fed." The Fed is really the Federal Reserve. Most Americans know about the Fed as it is often in the news when it changes the federal funds rate. The federal funds rate "is the primary tool that the Fed uses to conduct monetary policy. It is the rate that banks pay for overnight borrowing in the federal funds market. Changes in the federal funds rate influence other interest rates that in turn influence borrowing cost for households and businesses as well as broader financial conditions." While monetary policy and control are in the hands of the Fed, fiscal policy is handled by the Executive and Legislative branches of government.

It is important for all Americans to realize what the Federal Reserve System is and how it is structured and operates. It is, effectively, one of four separate branches of our Federal Government. However, it was set up in 1913 instead of in our Constitution. It should be considered one of the four branches by virtue of its power. While the Legislative Branch, in the form of Congress, is empowered by the Constitution to make laws; and the Executive Branch is empowered by the Constitution to enforce the laws and run the government; and while the Judicial Branch, in the form of the Supreme Court, is empowered by the Constitution to interpret the laws; the Federal Reserve controls American monetary policy as opposed to the Executive's power to control fiscal policy. Monetary policy has greater "teeth" than fiscal in stabilizing our national economy.

The definition of monetary policy, according to the *Economic Times*, is: "Monetary policy is the macroeconomic policy laid down by the Central Bank. It involves management of the money supply and interest rate and is the demand side of economic policy used by the government of a country to achieve macroeconomic objectives like inflation, consumption, growth, and liquidity."

There are several myths regarding the Fed. Debunking the myths: The Fed owns gold and/or prints money. Not true. The Fed is audited and audited often. True. The private sector owns the

Federal Reserve Bank. Yes and no. The difference is explained below.

HISTORY:

To alleviate the problems associated with economic downturns and financial panics, President Woodrow Wilson signed the Congressional Federal Reserve Act on December 23, 1913. To alleviate concerns of some of our citizens, our Federal Deficit of $31.2 trillion is largely an internal debt. Most of the debt is owned by the Federal Reserve System and the Social Security System. Less than $8 trillion is owned by foreign concerns or governments. Eight trillion is a huge amount of money, but compared to 31.2 trillion, it is relatively mild.

The opening paragraph of the act is an introduction: "An act to provide for the establishment of Federal reserve banks, to furnish an elastic currency, to afford means of rediscounting commercial paper, to establish a more effective supervision of banking in the United States, and for other purposes."

STRUCTURE:

Congress structured the Federal Reserve System "to make it autonomous and to isolate it from day-to-day political pressures."

The Federal Reserve System Purposes and Functions best describes the purpose:

"The Federal Reserve System is considered to be an independent central bank. It is so, however, only in the sense that its decisions do not have to be ratified by the President, or anyone else in the Executive Branch of the US government. The entire System is subject to oversight by the US Congress…the Federal Reserve must work within the framework of the overall objectives of economic and financial policy established by the government."

The 12 federal banks operate as any business. Each has its own Board and that Board selects the Reserve Bank President and First Vice President. Those selected must have the approval of the Federal Board of Governors.

The 12 Reserve Banks have bank branches. Most of each Reserve Bank Branches' directors "are appointed by the Branches' Reserve Bank and the others are selected by the Board of Governors." It may be confusing, but it works.

The Boards of Directors of the Reserve Banks and their branches provide the Fed with a wealth of information on economic conditions around the nation. The provided information, along with other sources, is used by the Federal Open Market Committee (FOMC) and the Board of Governors when reaching a decision about monetary policy.

The Reserve Banks each have "independent research staffs that advise their Reserve Bank Presidents on monetary policy and the condition of the regional economy. Each also has regulatory responsibilities including supervision and regulation of their financial institutions. The Reserve Banks also Handle the Feds business operations, in which they act like private businesses, selling services like electronic funds transfers, check processing, and coin and currency services to regional banks.

Congress created the System to be self-funding. It earns revenue on interest-bearing government securities that it holds in its portfolio and sells financial services to banks. The Fed usually has a profit. Using 2002 as an example, the Fed's revenues amounted to $26.7 billion, expenses totaled $2.2 billion and $24.5 billion was paid to the US treasury. In the Federal budget, the line item under income shows "Interest on Federal Reserve Notes."

The Fed does not explain how the dividends to the Regional Reserve Banks are handled other than the fact that they are required by law to be given 6% per year.

BOARD of GOVERNORS: Seven members are appointed to a 14-year term by the US President and confirmed by the Senate. Its staff and the Board members are civil service employees. The terms of office of Board directors "do not coincide with presidential terms."

CENTRAL BANK: The Central Bank is not owned by anyone. It is not a bank at all. The name describes the entire Federal Reserve Banking System. For those interested in a more complete description of the Central Bank, please refer to www.federalreserve.gov.

REGIONAL RESERVE BANKS: There are 12 regional banks in the Fed System and they are located around the country. The regional banks are owned by private banks. The private banks own, but do not necessarily control. Control is with the seven members (or directors) of the Board of Governors. The 12 banks "are chartered as private corporations. Employees are not civil service." Briefly, the Fed's responsibilities include conducting monetary policy, supervising and regulating banking and financial institutions, and providing payment services to the financial institutions.

OWNERSHIP:

When the Fed states that it is not privately owned, that is somewhat misleading. "The Fed is a little defensive about the question of ownership."

"While the Board of Governors (of the Fed) is an independent government agency, the Federal Reserve Banks are set up like private corporations. Member banks hold stock in the Federal Reserve Banks and earn dividends. Holding this stock does not carry with it the control and financial interest given to holder of common stock in for-profit organizations. The stock may not be sold or pledged as collateral for loans. Member banks also elect six of the nine members of each Bank's Board of Directors."

Member banks mentioned above refer to large, private banks. Names of those banks who are members and who own stock in the Fed are almost impossible to find. But according to www.factcheck.org: "The stockholders in the 12 regional Federal Reserve Banks are the privately owned banks that fall under the Federal Reserve System. These include all national banks chartered by the federal government and those state-chartered banks that wish to join and meet certain requirements. About 38% of the nation's more than 8,000 banks are members of the System, and thus own the Fed banks.

The concept of ownership means that the member banks must, by law, invest 3% of their capital as stock in the Reserve Banks, and they cannot sell or trade their stock or use it as collateral as mentioned earlier.

The private banks also have a voice in regulating the nation's money supply and setting targets for short-term interest rates, but it is a minority voice."

FEDERAL OPEN MARKET COMMITTEE (FOMC): Composed of nineteen members, including the seven Federal Reserve Governors and the 12 Federal Reserve Bank presidents. "The FOMC is charged with conducting monetary policy." It is this body that makes the shift in interest rates charged for overnight transactions between member banks. This rate is what makes media headlines.

RESPECT for AUTHORITY:

Respect is a tenuous thing. A lifetime of acting in a responsible manner can be erased in an instant of questionable thinking and acting. That applies to corporations or other institutions as well as individuals. It is rather disturbing to find so many institutions who don't set good examples for following high standards of moral responsibility. America is somewhat different than most countries. We are not a country with citizens whose ancestors have lived within the borders of that country. Instead of historical heritage, our people are immigrants and descendants of those immigrants.

We thus have created a common heritage based, not on blood, but on common values, a common culture created from the mixing of multiple cultures, and the rule of law. The glue is based on respect for our structure, love for the beauty and diversity of our country, and respect for our institutions and our leaders. The more that our leaders and institutions transgress from their moral responsibility, the more our people are disillusioned and lose respect and confidence in our country. Following is a sad listing of institutions that transgressed by various crimes and misconduct. Each example is a story of leadership of companies behaving in a manner that discarded any semblance of providing moral responsibility in the running of their companies. Instead of examples of acting in a moral and ethical manner, they are examples of greed and irresponsibility:

ENRON:

"When energy-trading company Enron declared bankruptcy in 2001, it was the largest bankruptcy filing in United States history. The company's demise was tinged with scandal, as it was revealed that Enron execs were pocketing millions while knowingly overstating the company's earnings to shareholders through fraudulent accounting."

For those living in the West, Enron is often remembered as the company that created "rolling blackouts." Enron wanted to play a major role in California's energy market and was instrumental in the deregulation of the market and they "were largely successful in creating a set of rules that worked to their advantage" in the huge market.

Enron crafted schemes to withhold power from California users of electricity and forced the grid to initiate the rolling blackouts. By withholding power from the California Power Grid, they forced the government to place a cap on the surging prices of energy created by the Enron-imposed shortages. Then Enron purchased power at the capped prices, "sending the power out of state, and then selling it back to California for a lot more when the state was desperate." The power transfer was done so craftily that Enron was able to hide the fraudulent transactions until they were studied and later discovered.

The courts also ruled that Enron's banks involved in the accounting fraud scheme would have to pay out $7.2 billion.

While the abuses of big business has been widespread, it is heartening that our courts are not so tainted that they are still able to dole out penalties to those institutions and individuals who transgress our norms.

ARTHUR ANDERSON:

Arthur Anderson was once one of the "Big Eight" accounting firms in the United States. "In June 2002, the company was convicted of obstruction of justice for shredding and doctoring documents related to the Enron audits" as reported by ABC News. The scandal forced them to close in August 2002.

WORLDCOM:

"At its height, telecommunications company WorldCom handled 50% of all U.S. internet traffic and 50% of all emails worldwide. But in 1999, the company's revenue slowed and its stock price began to fall. To boost earnings, CEO Bernie Ebbers began cooking the books. WorldCom began to classify operating expenses as long-term capital investments and accounted for $500 million in computer expenses as investments without any documentation to back up the claim. The changes made the company appear more valuable than it was by turning its losses into $1.38 billion in profits." After an audit WorldCom admitted to inflating its profits. It filed for bankruptcy at about the same time as their CEO was sentenced to 25 years in prison.

ADELPHIA COMMUNICATIONS:

"Adelphia Communications was one of American's largest cable companies before fraudulent behavior pushed it into bankruptcy." The company CEO John Rigas packed the Board of Directors with his three sons and his son-in-law. The family used Adelphia funds to claim to buy back company stock and then used the funds to purchase perks off the company books. They purchased vacation homes, jet aircraft, and multiple expensive cars. An inquisitive Merrill Lynch analyst questioned how they could buy back over a billion dollars-worth of company stock. The company ended up selling assets to Time Warner and then folding. Two of the Riga's family were sentenced to 15 and 20 years in prison.

E.F. HUTTON:

The well-regarded company ran into trouble in the 1980s when they admitted to "taking part in a check-kiting scheme that involved making bank withdrawals and deposits that gave it illegal access to millions in interest-free dollars. It paid more than $10 million in penalties as a result" and ended up folding.

LINCOLN SAVINGS & LOAN:

According to NBC news, "Charles Keating, a huge political donor and owner of Lincoln Savings and Loan, "made billions by selling Lincoln customers $200 million worth of unsecured 'junk' bonds. Keating was convicted on federal racketeering charges related to defrauding investors." The company went bankrupt, which was the costliest savings and load debacle of the 1980s."

DELOREAN MOTOR COMPANY:

John DeLorean designed a new American sports car and, with the backing of $200 million of investment funding, in 1981 began to produce his gull-wing car in Belfast, Northern Ireland. "Due to rising costs, the highly respected former executive from General Motors, "had to rush the car to market and sold it for more than twice the original asking price. The high price, coupled with bad reviews, led DeLorean Motor Cars to sell only half of what it expected." DeLorean tried to supplement the corporate income with a drug-smuggling scheme and was videoed negotiating with the drug smugglers. DeLorean Motor Cars declared bankruptcy in 1982 with their leader in prison.

STANDARD OIL COMPANY:

Standard Oil "was the most dominant oil company in the world from 1870 to 1911, according to NBC News. The Supreme Court found Standard Oil guilty of violating the Sherman Anti-Trust Act through its practice of using low prices to eliminate its competition. Standard was broken up into separate companies: Chevron, Exxon Mobil, and Conoco Phillips. Texaco was later absorbed into Chevron.

BERNARD L. MADOFF INVESTMENT SECURITIES:

Madoff's name became synonymous with the name Ponzi. Madoff's scheme lost over $50 billion. Business Insider reported that Madoff was charged with 11 counts of fraud, money laundering, perjury, and theft. He was sentenced to 150 years in prison.

CITY of ANAHEIM, ORANGE COUNTY, CALIFORNIA:

When elected representatives betray our trust, it taints many other local representatives. When the betrayal is widespread, voters tend to blame the entire system. The issue is continual. In May of 2022, the Mayor of the "City of Disney," Anaheim, California, Harry Sidhu, resigned in disgrace when the FBI, "in sworn affidavits, agents (accused him) of trying to ram through" a deal to sell the city-owned Los Angeles Angels Stadium in exchange for $1,000,000 in campaign contributions. "Federal agents also alleged Sidhu shared city information with the Angels during stadium negotiations."

BAYOU HEDGE FUND GROUP:

"Samuel Israel defrauded his investors into thinking there were higher returns, and orchestrated fake audits. The Commodity Future Trading Commission filed a court complaint and the business was shut down after the directors were caught attempting to send $100m into overseas bank accounts."

ROMAN CATHOLIC CHURCH:

Sexual abuse is widespread among all religions and denominations. The Roman Catholic Church is singled out for exposure because they are, by far, the biggest example of the violation of codes of decency in the behavior of their priests and the immoral cover up by the Roman Catholic Church authorities. The Church is as guilty as their priests. It is even more abhorrent when one considers that organized religions have portrayed themselves as the standards of moral authority and responsibility.

The scandal was worldwide. "Abuse has been exposed in Europe, Australia, Chile, the United States, and Ireland." To understand the scope of the sexual abuse scandal, over 6,000 priests in the United States alone were found to have committed sexual crimes. The abuses were not only by the priests, but also by nuns and other representative of the Church. The victims were usually between 11 and 14 years old, were both girls and boys, and included girls as young as three years old.

The Church was found guilty of systematic reassignment of accused priests to other parishes where they were not prosecuted and were effectively allowed to continue their practice of sexually abusing those committed to their moral care. The number of lawsuits is very difficult to find, but the total payouts by the Church to victims of its priests amounted to over three billion dollars.

Thus, another pillar of our society and structure came tumbling down. The alleged "House of Our Lord" became a house of cards. The house that had taken 2,000 years to construct, was shaken as if by a violent earthquake. Structural repair will take time, dedication, recommitment, and care.

BOY SCOUTS of AMERICA:

In 1979, the Boy Scouts of America included over 5 million youths. The Boy Scouts, the Girl Scouts, the YMCA, and the YWCA were a large part of America for young boys and girls. For boys, especially in small towns, their first organization ever attended was the Cub Scouts. In thousands of households across America, Cubs met and were introduced to the merits of scouting. Mothers and fathers served as Cub Scoutmasters in leading the teaching of the Cubs. Brownies act in the same capacity for girls between the ages of seven to ten. After that age, they often became Girl Scouts.

Merit Badges were cloth representations of honor for the scouts who mastered a helpful skill. Mastery of many might earn a scout entry into the respected group called Eagle Scouts. The entire process was considered wholesome.

Scouts and members of the "Y" participated in hikes together and summers were filled with trips to camps for stays of up to two weeks or longer. In Southern California, camps, such as Orizaba, existed on Catalina Island, along with a scouting encampment. Mainland camps were many, including Pine Valley in the forested mountains of northern Ventura County.

The Angeles National Forest provided many campsites for scouts and members of the "Y" that lived in Los Angeles County. The camps were spiritual in that they were out among the wildlife and beauty of the mountains and forests. They provided hiking trails that were themselves educators on the world around us.

Scouting and the Christian organizations were a vital part of life and upbringing in our youth. Unfortunately, they too succumbed to the unprincipled acts of some of its adult leaders.

The Boy Scouts still exist, but their numbers are now less than half of what they were in 1979, at 2.3 million with approximately 889,000 adult volunteers. It has been a painful journey for most adult volunteers who were themselves victims of the Scouting Scandals in that they were then looked at as possible predators.

In 2020, the Boy Scouts of America filed for bankruptcy due to the many lawsuits filed against them. According to Wikipedia, "Over 92,000 sexual abuse claims were filed with the bankruptcy court before November 16, 2020."

NEED for ATTITUDE ADJUSTMENT:

The author was once a Rotarian. Rotary is a business-oriented organization that promotes business networking. It also provides investment in the community with donations to charitable causes. Once he heard a fellow Rotarian make the statement that: "I can run any company." He was an accountant and a very good one.

His was a problem of perception and attitude. Because of his comfort with number manipulation, his perception of himself was with extreme confidence. While accountants do provide valuable data that help management in the operation of any company, sometimes all accountants and lawyers do in running a company is run it into the ground. It is essential that any CEO of a company knows his product as well as anyone in the company. Often, engineers become the best company managers of industrial companies because they know about the product or products that are being produced.

Boeing is a company which had a superb reputation for producing a real quality product. Their aircraft are the standard of excellence in the entire world of airplane manufacturing. Their word was always counted on as always being in the best interest of safety and reliability. Their employees took great pride in being from a company that was so known for honesty, integrity, and engineering excellence.

When Boeing encountered two fatal accidents created under the same conditions for the 737-Max, the old Boeing would have immediately grounded its 737s after the first accident to find out the cause. Not the new Boeing. It would have exposed a design defect that was also caused by a management decision based on finance over safety. The top management attitudes caused the deaths of a full load of passengers in the second accident. The cause of the accident would have been found and corrected by the old Boeing.

The FAA believed the comments by Boeing after the first accident. Past practice showed that Boeing was always totally honest. The search for the truth as to the cause of accidents was always a true search. The top management actions, by officers who did not grow up in the Boeing culture, appalled their employees and created a mistrust in those FAA officers who worked with Boeing. It was a huge public relations disaster created by management lies. CEOs who know more about finance, insurance, and accounting than they do about what they manufacture can be a real problem.

Another observation by the author was that the management class often has a disdain for employees and labor unions. The fact is that there are good companies and bad companies. There are good unions and bad unions. It is highly beneficial if managers take interest in their employees and, if their employees are represented by labor union, to try to connect with the unions to work together to better solve company problems. Business management needs to think of companies as teams and not an " us versus them" mentality. That seems to be the norm with new and fast-growing tech companies. Which is a favorable trend.

Some labor unions have caused the entire labor union movement to appear greedy to the American public. Unions need to return to the practices of the old Guilds and be equally concerned with providing union members who are qualified and that work with efficiency instead of just representing laborers in contract negotiations. Unions need to be known for more than always wanting more money and greater benefits.

BOARD of DIRECTORS REFORM:

Proper corporate governance is a matter that is often discussed and legislated by government. There are laws that are intended to provide better representation and protections for stockholders. In an era where the old parameters for a good market investment no longer apply, it is even more important for government to provide proper protections.

Stronger punishment for those who fail to follow guidelines and laws may be an answer. What is important is that government and associations involved in good corporate governance should remain always vigilant to ensure that corporations adhere to their responsibilities to provide for the benefit of their employees, their stockholders, and to the buying public. Often it is the prioritization of those three responsibilities that require oversight.

A truism is that whenever there are large monies at stake, there are threats to acquire those monies in sometimes nefarious ways.

GOLDEN PARACHUTES & ACCOUNTABILITY:

Golden Parachutes are prime examples of the illicit lure of absolute greed and all too often are not an indication of corporate success. They often never tie themselves into the profits or losses of the corporations they represent.

What is a Golden Parachute? It is a series of clauses written into employment contracts for corporate executives. "Usually, (they) stipulate exactly what (an executive) will receive in the event of release from (his or her) contract before it expires. Unlike a severance package, it is not simply a lump sum of money representing gratitude for how long (an executive) had worked in a job; rather, a golden parachute offers significant benefits in addition to cash that can add up to a truly astronomical total value."

Golden Parachute "perks can range from cash payouts to permanent dental insurance, from stock holdings to free lifelong first-class airfare. All things considered; this luxury treatment seems grossly unfair in comparison to the rest of the working world."

HISTORY:

"In the 1980s, the junk bond market grew so popular that no company was safe from takeovers, pleasant or hostile. This made executive jobs more fragile than in previous years, so companies started writing golden parachutes into contracts of high-earning employees in order to guarantee some semblance of a safe "landing, if the company were to be suddenly sold and their jobs were to disappear. Originally, of course, the golden parachute was simply a precaution against total destitution, but the trend took off. After 1990, almost every Fortune 500 company offered golden parachutes to their top earners, and this popularity galvanized companies to offer better and better deals to potential employees. Now, a typical golden parachute includes much more than the money necessary" to keep anyone in the most luxurious of circumstances.

EXAMPLES:

William Agee, Bendix Corporation: "In 1983, this CEO lost his job after a takeover and received a $4 million payout, which is $10 million in today's dollar. This aggressively large reward led to the first big golden parachute scandal, when people began to question why CEOs were being rewarded so highly for failure."

Henry McKinnell, Pfizer: "The pharmaceutical company was having financial trouble in 2005 when McKinnell, the CEO, decided to give himself a 72% pay raise. His greed was met with his own termination, but that included an $ 83 million pension and a plane."

John Hammergren, McKesson: Hammergren is still the CEO of McKesson. "On his termination, he is slated to receive $182.6 million, most of which will be tied up in stocks."

John Welch, General Electric: Welch is a well-known and highly respected, successful corporate leader. If the public knew of his total record, they might think differently. "He spent company money on the purchase of expensive tickets to countless sports stadiums and a New York City apartment with a rent of $80,000 per month. He retired with a whopping $417 million package from the company and a promise of $9 million per year for the rest of his life." Is anyone worth that kind of money?

Ken Lay, Enron: The disgrace of Enron is detailed earlier in this chapter. "Lay was both CEO and Founder of Enron, and ran the company into bankruptcy in 2001. He had a parachute awaiting him that would ensure him over $25 million, but he stayed with the company. He was taken to trial and found guilty of 10 counts of security fraud. He died before he could hear the sentence, which was 45 years in prison."

When considering the depth of greed within these men, consider that the companies they led were public and had stockholders that included pension plans and other group assets. The obscene golden parachutes were literally taking money away from others' retirement plans.

CONTROVERSY:

"It is not surprising that there are many critics of the golden parachute system. Putting aside the illogical nature of profiting from being dismissed from a job, there is a rather cogent argument that the supposed risktakers who companies want at the helm are not actually incentivized to take risks once they have secured their golden parachute. Instead, they can slack off, knowing that the worst outcome of their negligence would be a secured life of luxury. In addition to that, in the event of a merger or takeover, there is a possibility that other company employees may begin to feel hostile toward the exec, whose fate is not decided by the merger, and animosity of that sort in the office can cause bigger problems down the line, with more workers asking for similar benefits.

The most gutting critique of the golden parachute system is the claim that the existence of the parachutes only affirms the fact that the employee is more interested in their individual wellbeing than the wellbeing of the company or its success. The parachute waiting for them ensures that they think of themselves as entirely separate entities from their employers, instead of members of a team.

In the United States, income inequality has grown steadily since the 1970s." The author feels it reflects one of the most dangerous aspects of our present condition. "According to a Brookings study conducted in 2016, the top 1% holds 29% of the country's wealth, a larger portion than the entire middle class. The 1% have been stockpiling wealth, cutting corners in order to ensure that their money does not leave their circles, getting richer and richer as the poorer socioeconomic classes find it harder and harder to survive."

The author feels that the Brooking figures mentioned above are low. Otherwise they don't make sense, unless the difference lies in a better understanding of their definition of what constitutes the upper class that lies under the top 1%., with the assumption that it includes the 2% to 10%?

To ensure that their (the upper class) money is safe and that their investments will earn large dividends, the top 1% make sure that members of Congress are well compensated through donations for listening to and acting on the wealthy's wish list of Congressional actions.

Lincoln's "we, the people" has lost the vote and we must regain it and reinstate a true democracy in one manner or another.

IS OUR NEWS CONTROLLED?

The author and his wife have close friends who were born and raised in Norway. They came to this country as adults and contributed to the well-being of America in several different ways. Representing Hughes and Boeing, coupled with his fluency in seven languages, he often traveled to Europe to negotiate contracts beneficial to America. His engineering skills had him designing the guns used on many American military weapons, including the Navy fighter, the F-4B, the US Army Bradley Fighting Vehicle, and the Army Apache Helicopter.

This accomplished Norwegian loves this new country and has served it well. Yet when it comes to the reading of news, he often chooses to read Norwegian newspapers instead of our own to find out what is really happening in the world. The evidence is anecdotal and not overwhelming, but it seems that reporting is sometimes influenced by those who purchase advertising in the newspapers. Again, when there is money involved, attitudes and actions often are influenced. The adage of "Follow the Money" is always good to keep in mind when questioning things that happen that don't make sense.

OUR HIDDEN OIL RESERVES:

Another example goes back to a newspaper article that appeared in 1985. It involved oil company leases off the coast of California. It was proceeded by events in Southern California that occurred as early as 1969 when the Santa Barbara Oil Spill happened.

Tar on the beaches of Southern California were not a new thing. When many were growing up in Southern California, they swam at the beaches and often had to wash their feet in gasoline to rid themselves of the tar that clung to them. The tar came from the hills behind the beaches. The hills harbored oil springs and seeps where oil literally flowed out of the ground. The oil often flowed into the cold-water creeks to then became tar, which was then washed out to sea to scatter on the local beaches.

Santa Barbara is a lovely beach town of old California money that is framed by the university town of Goleta and the celebrity rich community of Montecito. The oil spill left in its residue an organization called GOO, which stood for Get Oil Out. The spill was caused by leakage from one of the oil platforms that dot the seawater channel between coastal towns, like Santa Barbara, and Channel Islands National Park, created from five of the eight Channel Islands that lie off the coast from Santa Barbara down to San Clemente in Orange County. The oil platforms consist of multiple oil wells harvesting the oil rich channels.

The oil platforms are owned by various oil companies and are on either state or federal leases. The Supreme Court determined that the federal government owned all the seabed off the California coast, but Congress recognized state ownership of the seabed within three nautical miles of shore.

Offshore oil is important to California as well as the rest of the states. State offshore leases produce 37,400 barrels of oil per day and federal leases add another 66,400 barrels per day. The offshore tracts accounted for 16% of state production in November, 2008.

After the1969 oil spill, GOO made life difficult for the oil companies. For a while it seemed that the leases themselves were in jeopardy? The author's opinion of oil company executives is that they seem, by some of their decisions, to be as patriotic as the rest of us. Decisions made overseas were in the interests of the oil companies, but they also always seemed in the best interest of the United States. However, even patriotic oil executives have their limits.

In 1974, America experienced a reported oil shortage. Long lines were seen and experienced in area gas fueling stations. The result was that the influence of GOO rapidly waned. People's attitudes changed when they themselves were inconvenienced by the reported shortages. Interest in closing existing offshore oil wells evaporated.

The validity of the oil shortage is in question. Observations of an airline pilot were mixed. The oil tankage we all see spotted around our country give no external indication of the amount of oil within each tank. But airline pilots can tell.

Tank internal pressure is supplied by movable plates at the top of the tanks. If a tank is full, the top plate is level with the top of the tank. If the oil level is down, that can be seen from above by the lower level of the tank top. No way to hide it. The author noticed that many of the tanks were either full or close to full.

On the other hand, he experienced multiple flame-outs of his jet engines. It was not necessarily a safety problem, as he kept his hand on the igniters and continually restarted engines that might start to spool down. The only likely explanation was that the airline fuel was tainted. The obvious explanation was that it had water in it. Jet fuel is lighter than water. It floats on top of water. If tanks are sucked down to near the bottom of their capacity, then water is possibly sucked in as well. Water vapor can seep in to oil storage tanks due to the space between the tanks and the top pressure plates. That water vapor can then condense and gravitate to the bottom of the tanks. As said, from a pilot's perspective, the observations were mixed but America did have plenty of observable oil during the 1974 fuel crisis.

With the future of existing channel oil wells secured, the oil companies could count on a certain level of production. The 1985 article was illuminating in several ways. It was a comprehensive article on the Channel Island's oil platforms. It stated that the oil reserves under the allowed channel leases were pegged at 5 billion barrels of oil. That is significant.

The article went on to explain that the same subterranean oil and gas reservoir rocks and an anticline structure existed all the way up to Mendocino in Northern California. Anticline traps are subterranean "structural traps formed by the folding of rock strata into an arch-like shape." Within the folds are some oil and gas reservoir rocks and a trap often-filled with water that is topped with sometimes very significant deposits of oil.

The same anticline crossed onshore north of Ventura and was responsible for the Ventura Avenue Oil Field, which was the 4th largest in the United States in the 1950s. The anticline contained and still contains a huge amount of oil. A pro-rated determination of the anticline up to Mendocino, if the capacity is the same as in the existing channel oil leases, shows 40 billion barrels of reserve oil. That figure would make it the largest reserve oil field in the world, over twice the oil reserves of the acknowledged largest field, which is in Saudi Arabia. That information, from the viewpoint of the oil companies, is best left untold. After that article, any information related to the anticline did not get into any known newspaper. Is this an example of controlled news? It appears that it may be.

WHO & WHAT RULES AMERICA?

This is a difficult question to answer. We would like to believe that our democracy is run by the people we elect. In much of what government does, it seems that may be true. But in matters of the economy, it appears that may not be the case.

If the author had an answer, it would be the large banks. Bank employees, at least those we don't see, seem to be exempt from the penalties imposed on the rest of us. Bank excesses were guilty, in the opinions of many, in causing the meltdown of the Great Recession of 2007- 2010. It was a top-down motivation that influenced the financial industry and many related industries, such as that of real property, to claim falsehoods and manipulate so-called facts to the extent that when the truth of many inaccuracies finally surfaced, that the resulting collapse threatened the entire economy.

Falsehoods were apparent to many in related industries that were tied into the need for financing. Examples are many and include the following: Real estate was one of many assets that were "packaged" by financial manipulators. The packages were not for the benefit of the economy but were for the benefit of those packaging. Hedge fund managers, in other countries, abused their

American customers by using investor money to invest for the benefit of the hedge fund, and took the profits but deducted the losses from investor accounts. Uncontrolled investment packages in the US took on a life of their own and investments, which should have been structured for the benefit of the economy as well as the individual investor, were instead strictly for the benefit of the top managers of the banking industry.

Real estate values skyrocketed due to bank manipulation that filtered down to inaccurate valuations of properties that inflated their true value, which enabled financial institutions to broaden their investment bases resulting in the losses of real value for investors who trusted in the inaccurate words of some bank managers.

It was a "house of cards" based on the incessant greed of some in the banking industry. A few top New York based banks were guilty of the creation and presentation of some of the suspect investments, yet they had bank executives that routinely ran the US Treasury and wore the reputation of "too big and too influential to fail." An indication of their strength was that not one of the banking executives who created the Great Recession, were ever sent to prison.

Another example of the manipulative power of the banks is that of Jerry Brown, who served as Governor of California from 1975 to 1983 and from 2011 to 2019. During his second term, from 1979 to 1983, he was deciding on whether to run for President. He had significant backers and momentum, yet he had to make a final stop to gauge interest and support. A small article in the Los Angeles Times managed to slip out. The article said the Jerry Brown was meeting with the bankers in one of the many New York City banking high-rises. The Times said he was trying to solicit the approval of the bankers for his run at the Presidency.

Our banking industry manages to keep a very low profile. They don't seem to like news about themselves. Although searched for, no other article shed any light on what may have transpired at the Brown meeting. Yet, shortly after that purported meeting, Jerry Brown stepped aside and announced he was no longer a candidate and that he had important work yet to accomplish in his home state of California.

The author may be wrong in his assessment, but small signs often are evidence of larger truths.

"Democracy is not the law of the majority, but protection of the minority." — **Albert Camus**

Photo Gallery Four

National Parks in the Rocky Mountains

Colorado, Montana, Wyoming, Utah

Yellowstone National Park, Wyoming

Grand Teton National Park, Wyoming

Mesa Verde National Park, Colorado

Rocky Mountain National Park, Colorado

Great Sand Dunes National Park, Colorado

Black Canyon of the Gunnison National Park, Colorado

Glacier National Park,
Montana

Arches National Park,
Utah

Bryce Canyon National
Park, Utah

Zion National Park, Utah

Capitol Reef National Park, Utah

Canyonlands National Park, Utah

Chapter Eleven

Communications: The Media and Online Democracy
Opinions and Participation

Even true Communism sees the necessity and value of democracy:

"Democracy is indispensable to socialism." — **Vladimir Lenin, who served as first and founding head of government of Soviet Russia**

"Democracy is the right of all peoples, rather than an exclusive privilege of the few." — **Xi Jinping, current President of the People's Republic of China**

Democracy is also indispensable to the American brand of compassionate capitalism. Without it, our destiny will probably be civil war. To keep it, we also must reform our economic structure to make good the compassionate part of capitalism, which Warren Buffet epitomizes. The best form of reform is voluntary, but voluntary reform must not be hollow. Buffet, Bill and Melinda Gates, and others validate the good side of capitalism. It is the process of capturing the rewards of greed and turning them into the needs of the needy. It is also a form of leadership, which reflects a universal satisfaction within our society for the dispensing of compassionate benefits.

<u>ONLINE TOWN MEETINGS:</u>

Our internet age offers a potentially great improvement on prior forms of democratic statement. One can envision the use of the internet to allow virtual town meetings like those held in New England prior to our breaking away from England. It was democracy at its purest and allowed all voices to be heard. While they had far fewer voices, we can still provide voice to those who wish to state their opinions. What better way than from the comfort of our homes.

The internet also allows surveys that can keep a ready tally of community attitudes about a variety of subjects. Voting could also be accomplished with adequate controls to ensure accuracy and accountability. While voting would have to be age-restricted, the voting age could be lowered to build interest in younger age groups. All ages could be encouraged to participate in the meetings. Another thought would be to have meetings occasionally based on age and gender groups. Sometimes young people are reluctant to participate under certain circumstances, especially circumstances involving the opposite sex. Television could be included with a Zoom-like connection. With the rapid increases in communication technology, there will be multiple methods available from which to choose.

THE MEDIA:

"It is not my responsibility to print the truth. It is my responsibility to sell newspapers," a statement made by the editor of a local newspaper during testimony before the Board of Directors of the Thousand Oaks (California) Chamber of Commerce.

There have been increasing indications of multiple methods in which the media are playing soft with the truth. "Fake news" has been mentioned repeatedly of late and some of it is evidently true. Opinions have sometimes been shown as news. More and more news outlets are "reporting" advertisements as news. Larger corporations that purchase advertising in newspapers and magazines often seem to interfere with the reporting of news that might place the corporation in a bad light. The author has witnessed repeated instances of newspapers failing to report both sides of issues if those issues might reflect badly on an advertiser.

Journalists often ask slanted questions that seem designed to elicit inflammatory answers. Journalism is not supposed to create news, it is supposed to report news. All too often aggressive reporters are trying to "enhance" a story to the point where they almost seem to be creating the story or slant the story in a direction designed to "enhance" it.

Sensationalism entices viewers and readers of television and the newspapers. It seems that the only possible way to try to elicit more of the truth goes back to ethical training at universities. With past media owners, such as William Randolph Hearst, and current owners, like Rupert Murdoch, that approach will not work when those directing the journalists want stories sensationalized. The quote from the newspaper editor mentioned on the previous page was witnessed by the author.

Another example where the truth did not win out was witnessed by the author. It involved his union, the Airline Pilots Association, calling a press conference to share the pilot's side of the story in a dispute with the new owners of his airline. At the time, the headquarters for Continental Airlines was in Los Angeles. It was later when the airline decided to move to a more tax-friendly state and transferred their headquarters to Houston, Texas.

The dispute between management and pilots in Los Angeles was big news since the Continental presence at Los Angeles International Airport was large. The pilot's union called the press conference and invited all the local television stations and local newspapers. With one exception, they all thanked the union for the invitation and promised to attend. Yet when the time came, the only media reporter to show up was from the Daily Breeze, which represented the South Bay area and was headquartered in Hermosa Beach. It was later established, in talking with several reporters, that the newspapers and television stations were threatened by Continental to terminate their newspaper advertising with the major newspapers and with the Los Angeles television stations if they showed up at the news conference. Truth again did not win out due to the media valuing revenue over the truth.

It goes back to the introduction to this book. Trust must be reestablished for our nation to get back on track. Chapter 10 dealt with the needed rebirth of trust in organizations. The media in all its forms needs to work to reestablish the trust that is slowly melting away. How that might be accomplished is something that the media industry is better equipped to decide.

"The real safeguard of democracy…is education." — **Franklin D. Roosevelt**

Chapter Twelve
Economic Segregation and Regional Planning
Planned Togetherness

"One thing is sure. The earth is now more cultivated and developed than ever before. There is more farming with pure force, swamps are drying up, and cities are springing up in on an unprecedented scale. We have become a burden to our planet. Resources are becoming scarce, and soon nature will no longer be able to satisfy our needs."
— **Quintus Septimus Florens Tertullianus, Roman theologian 2,222 (2022) years ago.**

Today's problems may seem insurmountable to some, but from the above Roman quote from over 2,000 years ago, there are always those who think the world is coming to an end. It is not and will not. However, we can make the world better, much better, if we make ourselves aware of the problems facing us and the depth of those problems.

Many types of segregation have been evidenced in our society since its inception. Linguistic segregation was voluntary for most of the immigrant groups chose to settle with those who spoke the same language. It created ghettos, which at the time were voluntary and necessary. Later, the various immigrant groups integrated gradually, with public schools playing a large part. Ethnic segregation went hand in hand with linguistic. Religious segregation has never posed much of a problem in America.

Education is another form of division, but that might border on a quality-of-life issue in that people tend to socialize with those of similar education levels. Social and cultural divisions are present in any country. Until recently, that was never a serious problem here as people have tended to be welcoming to those coming from elsewhere.

Racial segregation has been a problem since that day in 1619 when a commandeered ship landed at the docks of Jamestown in the Virginia Colony carrying the first black slaves to what would become the English colonies of the New World. While racial segregation is still a problem, part of it is that of preference. Blacks or any racial group should be free to house themselves anywhere that they can afford, and that includes with other blacks if that is their preference.

Segregation may take many other forms. From the very first years of significant non-English immigration into the United States, newcomers often preferred to live among those with whom they had a cultural affinity or who spoke the same language. Often, they came to live with relatives who lived in ghettos that housed immigrants from the same country. It was segregation, but voluntary segregation.

Integration began to occur in significant amounts when the children of immigrants learned English and started to socialize with locals or other immigrant groups. It has been the story of America repeated many times.

ECONOMIC SEGREGATION:

There is another form of voluntary segregation that is far more insidious. That is the many forms of socio-economic segregation. We see it every day, yet often do not recognize it. Developers of housing tracts usually build similar homes in development areas where homes are priced similarly. Wealthier homeowners often stay hidden behind walls and fences in gated communities. Those same homeowners then send their children to private schools. Both practices, gated communities and private schools are dangers to our national community in that they foster socio-economic segregation. They also foster significant declines in interactions between segregated classes.

Instead of pouring money into bettering public schools, they pour it into private. Public schools are an American invention and it was one of the unifying forces that bonded us as a nation and created a common culture. The predominant English culture was slowly blended into a unique American culture through intermingling with the new immigrant cultures. That American openness acted as a welcome to others who might not speak the same language or live their lives in a similar manner to the predominant English. By welcoming other cultures, newcomers were made to feel at home and did not develop resentments that they might have had if they had encountered blocks against their absorption into the larger culture. The catalyst for that integration were the public schools systems.

While racial segregation became the primary form of separation in America, economic segregation took hold in England long before it ever considered empire. For centuries, England practiced socio-economic segregation and it was exacerbated by their private school system. In India, it was the stratified caste system that rigidly segregated classes. The result in England was a stratification of classes without any clear-cut avenues for lower classes to become upper. America faces development of the same cultural and economic stratification.

Those of us that can remember that far back, can recall towns that had wealthy bankers living side-by-side with lower paid plumbers, electricians, or laborers. Strong parent-teacher associations (PTAs) were common grounds for parents coming from all backgrounds and receiving vastly different pay, that were able to work together and help their children learn their neighbors.

The author's father had a profound personal respect for his neighbors. When asked about why he sent his children to public schools, he replied that it was then possible for his children to get to know their neighbors. It took the rest of his family three years to finally convince him to lock the doors of their home. He felt that locking one's doors was an insult to your neighbors. He had also worked his way up from impoverishment to a measure of wealth through hard work, determination, and education. His was a respect for people from all backgrounds. They were his neighbors and they were fellow Americans.

Another danger of private-school education is that so many of the private schools of today are run by religious denominations. Nothing against them, but they also tend to stratify and segregate ourselves into groups with little interaction with other groups of Americans that come from different backgrounds and that have different beliefs. It is imperative that we mingle with our neighbors to learn their beliefs and their concerns. Gated communities and private schools deny us that privilege.

It has been mentioned in other parts of this book about the dangers inherent in a growing disparity between the management and executive class and the rest of a corporations' employees. These income disparities filter down to housing locations. Supreme Court Justice Louis D. Brandeis was prescient when he coined the following quote: "We may have democracy, or we may have wealth concentrated in the hands of a few, but we cannot have both."

Wealth concentrations often include resentment by those without, if the wealth disparity is significant. Many past civilizations have been destroyed by a resentful "underclass." America became what it has become by allowing lower classes to rise to upper class status through diligence. If those avenues dry up, then resentment will start to build. Private schools, gated communities and other economically segregated housing will only result in America being divided into groups with little communication or understanding between them. It will then only be a matter of time when civil war again will bloody our earth.

REGIONAL PLANNING:

Planning has taken different forms in different parts of our country. In California, underdeveloped counties took over planning until urban areas incorporated, then the counties passed planning to the newly-formed cities. That has been the practice.

In many areas of the country, especially in the greater urban centers, municipal planning has been, either merged into regional planning or had both city and regional planning working side-by-side. That is a beneficial trend, but our cities need to think from a regional, instead of just a city, standpoint.

Municipalities should plan far ahead of urban growth instead of waiting for the urban growth to start the regional planning. They often do in the form of a city's general plan. Why don't we create regional general plans instead of just municipal? The world is getting smaller every day and our neighbor city's issues and problems are often our own.

If the United States ever recognizes the necessity for a Second Constitutional Convention, then regional planning should be on their agenda for investigation and discussion.

Regional planning can at least partially overcome the negative impacts of gated communities and other economically segregated housing. While the author is not suggesting a solution, he is suggesting needed discussions and evaluation of regional planning to overcome regional drawbacks, including segregated communities.

"Democracy is messy, and it is hard. It is never easy." — **Robert Kennedy**

Part 3

Future Visions

Chapter Thirteen
World Survival
and Population Control
Environmental Imperatives

"Overpopulation in various countries has become a serious threat to the health of people and a grave obstacle to any attempt to organize peace on this planet." — **Albert Einstein**

It is a slow process, the transformation of our national parks. The author's first visits to our national parks became trips of wonder. Dedicated rangers of both genders would explain why each park is special and the beauty surrounding the visitors, unmatched. America is a unique area of the world and we possess an abundance of areas that are designated as parks. Other areas of our country are designated national monuments and still others national historical parks. Each is worth visiting. To any visitor, many of the national monuments will someday attain park status. They are deserving.

This book contains six photo galleries filled with one photo each of our 63 national parks. There are some parks with so many excellent views that it was hard to select which photo to choose to represent each park. They are national treasures that also draw attention from those visitors from other continents wishing to share some of our national beauty. The parks are now under threat.

When the author was born, his native state of California contained six million inhabitants. When he was 10 years old, it had expanded by 53.3% in a short decade. Since he was born in a year of national census, the accuracy of the counts did not have to rely on estimations. The following decade saw a 48.5% increase and then witnessed decadal increases of 27.0%, 18.6%, 25.7% 13.8% and 6.1% by the 2020 census. It now stands at almost 40 million. In his lifetime, four Californians now stand where one had stood before. While the migration of humans to California has been historical, the increase is still sobering.

When the author first visited Yosemite National Park, he was amazed at the beauty nature had bestowed on us. The last time he visited Yosemite, he drove from a smog enshrouded city to a smog enshrouded Yosemite. He was forced to park at a distance and the throng of park visitors were much greater than during his first visit, and with the air pollution, they were seeing far less.

If we continue the same insane path we are now traveling, our grandchildren will be forced to purchase a park admission ticket decades in advance. By not corralling our population, we are endangering our grandchildren and, at the very least, ensuring that their quality of life will be much worse than our own. Are we not supposed to prepare our world to be better for those who follow in our footsteps?

In the early times of our national existence, we were far fewer and the people banded together. Now that we are many, we find ourselves shying away from crowds. Current studies find that many of us feel lonely and the trend is significantly upward. While life is precious, the quality of that life is of concern. In the somewhat distant future, will Americans be forced to visit our parks and monuments remotely via virtual visits from our homes?

When our American ancestors strove diligently to develop and populate our lands, they could not have possibly envisioned how numerous we have become. In 1610, three years after the establishment of Jamestown in the Virginia Colony, only 350 non-natives could call our lands home. It took 140 years to reach our first million Americans, although over a million and a half natives lived here before the arrival of the Europeans. Those Indians were first sporadically counted in the 1850 census. It took until the 1890 federal census for a full count of Indians, Eskimos, and Inuit populations to be included in the ten-year counts of blacks and whites.

That first million count (1,170,760) took only two decades to advance to two million (2,148,076) and then to almost four million (3,929,214) two decades later. In another 20 years (1810) it advanced to over seven million (7,239,881). Our population increases accelerated continually thereafter:

1830	12,866,020	1850	23,191,876	1870	38,558,371
1890	62,979,766	1910	92,228,496	1930	123,202,624

From a 1950 count of 151,325,798, we added another 50 million in the 20 years prior to 1970, when we totaled 203,211,926. In 1990, we added another 45.5 million, meaning in only 40 years we were almost 100 million larger at 248,709,873. In 2010, we advanced to 308,745,538 and at the latest census count in 2020, we tallied 331,449,281, which is now estimated to be in excess of 335 million. That is a lot of mouths to feed, houses to build, and cars to fuel.

Has the reader noticed how many American municipalities fail to list the populations of cities or towns on their city limits signs? Most still mention elevations. We seem to be in a period of transition where we formerly prided ourselves in population increases, as it seemed to denote something of worth. Is it now a source of pride when so many cities of the world boast populations in excess of a million and so many live in poverty and hunger?

"Overconsumption and overpopulation underlie every environmental problem we face today."
— **Jacques Yves Cousteau**

Cousteau served a lifetime with concern about the condition of the world in which we all live. We live in a finite world and our resources are finite. Even with the remarkable advances of science and its discoveries, there is only so far that the globe can advance in producing material. Concurrently, there is only so far that the world community can continually find methods to increase the food supply. Cousteau's "overconsumption" meant consumption of material as well as food.

Wikipedia states that "the total number of humans currently living…is estimated to have exceeded 7.9 billion in September, 2022. It took over two million years of human prehistory and history for the human population to reach one billion and then another 207 years to grow to seven billion.

The human population has experienced continuous growth" since the Great Famine of 1315-1317 and the famous Black Death in 1350, when humans numbered 370,000,000. By 1500, there were 585,000,000 humans. By 1700, there were 710,000,000. By 1900, we numbered 1,650,000,000.

YEAR:	WORLD POPULATION:	YEARS COVERED:
1900	1,650,000,000	
1950	2,521,000,000	50

In 50 short years after that, two-thirds of a lifetime for most of us, we went from the 2.52 billion listed above to: 6.14 billion (6,143,494,000) in the year 2000. We almost tripled in 50 years.

2005	6,541,907,000	5
2010	6,956,824,000	5
2015	7,379,797,000	5
2020	7,795,000,000	5

On November 1, 2022, the World Population Clock has us at 7.98 billion.

When the author was born, there were 2.307 billion humans on Earth. We are now more than 8 billion and the author is still alive. The finite Earth cannot sustain a continuation of that level of increase too much longer.

THE BOUNTY of our OCEANS:

We all have read stories about the great abundance of fish available to our early fishermen in the 17th century. Tales of the almost non-stop landing of large fish in offshore fishing boats have been handed down from generation to generation. That abundance almost seems like fanciful tales. They are not. The author has experienced them.

While a teen, the author traveled often to Baja California to hunt and fish. The fishing was all fresh water. In the 1970s, he revisited with his adopted son. They visited San Quentin Bay, shown on the proceeding page, and how it looked in the 1950s and how it looks now. The upper photo shows a current look at the bay without the development that is now around it. When visited in the 1950s and the 1970s, the bay was as it had looked for eternity. It was pristine, only marred by two ramshackle fisherman's shacks on the sand. Other than those two, there was no other habitation or home in sight. There was a small village, but it was located away from the water.

Negotiations netted an agreement for the father and son to ride out with two Baja fishermen on their 11-foot skiff. In return for the fishermen tending their lobster traps that lay on the bottom of the bay, they promised to take father and son beyond the bay to fish. It took about an hour for the two fishermen to lift their traps and harvest their catch, which was not much.

Fishing was extraordinary. More than that, it was epic. At the front of the skiff was placed a gunny sack. Each time a fishing line was dropped, it no more had reached the bottom than when the line bent and another five-to-six-pound cod was lifted out of the water. Halfway through the afternoon, California gray whales surrounded the skiff as they made their way north toward Alaska. When they

Bahia de San Quentin, Baja California Norte. How it looked before.

San Quentin Bay as it looks today.

surfaced, they blew spray all around as they cleared their breathing tubes in preparation to take in oxygen, as they are mammals. It added greatly to the excitement to see them so close. The skiff was no match for them, but the whales knew we were there and avoided us in their passage. They came quite close and the spray from their blows etched the four fishermen in a fine mist.

By the middle of the afternoon, with plenty of daylight left, they all opted to row home. The gunny sack, which stood sentinel at the prow of the little boat, was filled to its capacity of 100 kilos. The bottom of the boat held several lobster and another 40 fish by count. There were no limits on the number allowed to be caught in those days, but the numbers in the boat were enormous. Nothing could ever come close to compare to such fishing. The experience vindicated the stories of old. It also indicated just how much of our local marine fisheries have been depleted.

Scientific American reported in 2015 that the *World Wildlife Fund* (WWF), which studies endangered species and makes recommendations to governments about possible solutions and works in nearly 100 countries, has stated that "the number of fish in the oceans has halved since 1970", (a 45-year period). If they are correct, what happens to those human populations who depend on the revenue from fishing, or much more importantly, those populations that depend on fish for food?" We cannot just ignore those findings. But we do.

THE HARVEST of our LANDS:

According to the Natural History Museum of the United Kingdom, "A third of the world's soil is moderately to highly degraded, threatening global food supplies, increasing carbon emissions, and foreshadowing mass migrations. A change in farming practices has never been more urgent." Some might question why carbon emissions would increase with soil degradation? While the world's forests store 360 billion tons of carbon and the atmosphere contains more than 800 billion tons of carbon, the soils store more than 4,000 billion tons.

Soil depletion has been occurring around the world with haphazard development, with poor farming practices, with elimination of protective jungles and forests, with erosion, and with fires that burn off top cover that then creates floods that carry our fertile soils out to sea. According to Global Agriculture, "Each year, an estimated 24 billion tons of fertile soil are lost due to erosion. That is 3.4 tons of soil lost every year for every person on the planet." In American dollars, the worldwide cost of land degradation reaches about $490,000,000,000 per year, which is far more than the revenue devoted to soil restoration.

Many might believe that we eventually might reverse the continual building of homes, factories, and other structures by tearing them down and returning the soil back to agriculture. It cannot happen. When soil is deprived of oxygen and the addition of natural nutrients, it loses its fertility and that can almost never be replaced. Topsoil is a precious resource. Long before the emergence of mankind on earth, rivers had been depositing fertile alluvial soils on lands and deltas. Trees and plants had been dying and enriching soils for many tens of thousands of years. When we destroy the vitality of that topsoil, it takes a very long time to replenish. "The current high erosion rates throughout the world are of great concern because of the slow rate of topsoil renewal; it takes approximately 500 years for a 2.5-centimeter (.984252 inch) layer of fertile topsoil to form under agricultural conditions." That is 500 years for less than an inch.

The despoiling of the Amazonian forests and jungles by the quest for additional Brazilian farmland has often resulted in the soils losing their fertility after only several years.

The author is not proposing a solution. The UN has a great many competent scientists and agronomists who have ready-made solutions. It is just that governments are unwilling to address the obvious dangers. Since the dawn of man, mankind has waged an untold number of battles and wars over land in which to feed the hungry. With more than eight billion mouths to feed, what may happen?

UNWANTED PREGNANCIES:

Those who have fought for this country often fight for ideals. Their most important ideal is freedom for our people. Free choice is just what it says. It is a woman exercising her right to end an unwanted pregnancy, for whatever reason. It is a freedom issue. What right does society have to dictate what a human being can do or not do with her own body. Those who choose to take a pregnancy to term, for whatever reason, also have every right to make that decision.

There are several other individual issues surrounding this contentious issue: First, forcing a woman to have an unwanted child may be forcing the child into world hunger? We never will know, but with one out of every nine people suffering from hunger, the chances may be significant.

If someone opposing abortion would argue that hunger may not be an issue in this country, the author would ask if morality has geographical boundaries? Besides, many in this country are electing not to have children just because of the population issue. This author has elected that course. No one has any right to deny anyone else his or her free choice not to add to the further increase in world population just as it is a personal right to have children, if wished. While many consider abortion to be a moral issue, is not world hunger an equally moral issue but on a hugely increased scale?

A second and far more important argument in favor of elected abortions, is the probable future of a child who is unwanted by his or her mother. The Washington Post has sponsored discussions on the issue of unwanted children. The paper published a study that states: "that babies born to mothers who do not want them, due to life circumstances, are more likely to grow up neglected and/ or abused, which makes them more likely to turn to crime." Responses to that study mentioned the same conclusions of many studies of children. The author of the Post- mentioned-study, concluded with "fewer unwanted children means reduced abuse and neglect; reduced abuse and neglect means reduced crime."

The author would accuse those who are trying to foist their moralities onto Americans who do not want to be forced, with unknowingly fostering world hunger and with unknowingly forcing an increase in crime. There are consequences for those who would try to limit the freedoms of others by forcing on them their own philosophies of life.

There is another issue regarding those who forced the rescinding of Roe v Wade: They have taken the precious time of all of America to discuss this selfish issue when that time could have been taken up with many of the issues addressed in this book, especially the issue of the population explosion. Of course most who have opposed abortion also, for religious reasons, oppose limiting births.

ENVIRONMENTAL ISSUES:

"Mankind will never truly unite as one unless it is faced with an external threat. Perhaps that threat will be environmental?" — **The author**

We could discuss all the environmental catastrophes facing the world and each must be addressed. Collectively, there are multiple challenges facing us all. Collectively, we have multiple possible solutions to correct our environmental problems. For the short term, no matter what the population, there are real problems needing answers. However, without addressing world population and the potential for world hunger, any solution is only short-term.

Limiting world population will help cure almost all long-term environmental problems. But it will undoubtedly go in-the-face of some church groups. Current Roman Catholic doctrine will not take kindly to the solutions offered here. But our major world religions also elevate the human spirit and sanctify the quality of our lives. If churches really want to elevate our human spirit and sanctify the quality of our lives, then they should support a limitation on our population. Otherwise, some may question church motives to be more political than moral.

How can anyone ever desire human hunger? How can anyone wish for the elimination of the beauty and quiet of our jungles and forests to be replaced with the noise, bustle, and pollution of our cities? Paving over nature will not elevate any of us. We all deserve a betterment of our quality of life and the continuation of the increase in our numbers will only foster a decrease.

CONCLUSION:

The specter of ever-increasing populations will encourage national leaders to explore avenues of territorial expansion and to offer homes for the growing mouths to feed and house. The exhaustion of food resources will exacerbate world hunger. World hunger will encourage world warfare. Isn't it better not to have children than to see those children butchered in battle? Isn't it better not to have children than to see those children suffer and die from malnutrition?

We Americans argue incessantly about abortion. Most arguments against forms of abortion are based on humanitarian grounds and for that are commendable. But is it humane to bring unwanted humans into this world only to see them suffer? This year 7,505,725 humans have died from hunger. "By the end of the year around nine million will have died. This is more than from AIDS, malaria, and tuberculosis combined." A child dies every ten seconds from hunger. Every ten seconds. Is that in any way humane?

One in nine people on this planet go to bed hungry every night. Global warming, largely caused by our population growth, will increase food insecurity. "Of the 822 million undernourished people in the world, 113 million face acute hunger meaning they are in urgent need of food and nutrients. In the 21st century, hunger is still the world's biggest health problem. And it is about to get worse."

Isn't it about time for our Congress to begin to discuss concepts that really matter to our world, instead of what may seem politically expedient?

"To restore the trust of the people, we must reform the way the government operates."
— Arnold Schwarzenegger, former Governor of California

Chapter Fourteen

National Goal Setting
& Investment
Purpose and Objectives

"What you get by achieving your goals is not as important as what you become."
— Henry David Thoreau

THE IMPORTANCE of GOALS in LIFE:

The United States is at its best when confronted with challenge that creates a goal. When the earliest immigrants arrived on our shores, their goals were survival and the creation of a better life for themselves and their families. For the next several centuries, our collective challenge was to win the war with the natives we found, battle the elements to develop the land, and to create a great country. We succeeded in ways that astounded the world. Probably our greatest achievement was to unite peoples from all over the world. We brought together peoples of all races, ethnicities, religious beliefs, and economic status. We did it by uniting our people in a national goal. We did it by striving together to conquer the challenges of reaching that goal.

When confronted with the challenge of a worldwide war, we changed our national objective and, in four short years, became the greatest military power the world had ever seen and in the process, crushed the forces of fascism.

When threatened by the menace of totalitarianism, we stayed strong and resolute. In the process we won the Cold War and exposed Communism for the false hope it projected to the world.

When challenged by President Kennedy, the engineering giant that we had become did what most thought impossible and placed Americans on the moon "by the end of the decade" as Kennedy asked. Confounded by the massive failures of the Apollo 13 spacecraft, we managed to bring three American astronauts home safety. That may have been one of our finest hours.

In the deserts of the Middle East, we defeated the 4th largest army in the world in 100 hours. Just think of that. It had never been accomplished and never even been conceived in the entire history of mankind's conflicts. Total victory in just over four days. We also showed our humanitarian selves by stopping the carnage and saving lives.

The great importance of that short war was that the United States set a goal to drive the Iraqi forces out of Kuwait and when we achieved that goal, we stopped our forces and spared Iraq itself because that was not our objective. Unfortunately, we sometimes make national mistakes and that happened when we later invaded Iraq under false pretenses.

Goal setting is establishing an objective and then planning ways to achieve that objective. Nations as well as people need to have goals and those goals should be "of a higher calling" than just achievement for oneself. National goals should include being for the betterment of mankind. Otherwise, what is our purpose in being?

Our greatest national goals have been when our objectives bettered others and not merely ourselves. Winning World War II, was protecting ourselves, but in the larger context, we were saving democracy for the world. So was the Cold War. We fought it for ourselves, but also for the values that have always guided us. Those values include the betterment of others.

When we landed men on the moon, we did not claim it for the United States. The totalitarian states would have. Russia would have declared that it was part of the Russian Federation. We claimed it for all mankind. The objectives of NASA are not to further enhance us territorially as a nation. Our explorations of the solar system are in the interest of science and to help satisfy our human curiosity. It is not to claim sovereignty over other worlds. Past explorations have been funded by nations that looked to enrich themselves. We have broken that precedent and enriched all of mankind in the process.

We did the same regarding the exploration of Antarctica. Our leadership determined that the frozen continent should not belong to an individual nation or to be split among a handful of nations, but instead belong to all nations. Our navy has helped preserve the notion that the oceans should belong to the world and not part of territorial claims. We continually test the illegal claims of China that their claimed borders extend a great distance from their shores. Our objective is and has been to allow all nations to freely navigate the seas for trade and other beneficial purposes.

Our people have always possessed a pride in what America does, what it stands for, and what it has accomplished. Seemingly, the greatest pride is derived from doing good for humanity and not just ourselves. It is human nature to want to be respected by others. Nationally is no different. We want to be a part of something good and stand for something that is righteous.

SETTING NATIONAL GOALS:

Today, America seems adrift. What is our goal? Other than enriching ourselves, we don't have any goal for which most of us could agree. Self-enrichment is not a worthy goal. We need to be challenged. We need respected leaders who have enough stature to challenge. In Chapter 10, we discussed the need for moral leadership. It is a shame that in our national political campaigns, candidates often use whatever they can use, including lies, to demonize an opponent. In that atmosphere, the creation of a leader with enough stature is almost impossible to achieve. Not only is our government corrupt, but the process of selecting the elected members of our government is also corrupt.

The Hawaiians have a word, "Huipu" that means coming together or uniting. The authors' choice for a national goal, which certainly would be one requiring long-standing, is also a controversial one. It is to establish Huipu between our nation and others. It is to change the method of territorial expansion by making it a matter of free choice. This thought is based on a desire to set in motion a series of events that might eventually end the carnage of war.

Good works and economic opportunity provide incentives for those who wish to emigrate and join with another nation. That has been the case over the entire history of this country. We have provided a relatively free environment to allow our citizens to provide safety, security, and comfort for their families. Many have emigrated from other countries. Let's let countries themselves emigrate to our shores.

The proliferation of countries on our earth has been a catalyst for conflict over the ages. The fewer nations on earth, the greater the possibility of reducing those conflicts. There must be an incentive for nations to unite. If that is provided, then the number of members of the United Nations will be reduced. Granted, if we start that process, other major nations will be hard pressed not to counter the action. They will want to gain strength in roughly the same manner. The process of nation reduction will not be easy and will take many generations to accomplish. The result of the process will likely have all world nations united into three separate countries and it will probably pit those three world nations against one another. Hopefully, international leaders at that time will find ways to unite all our peoples and thus eliminate the scourge of war.

To start the process of Huipu, we need to establish trust between nations just as we need to establish trust between individuals here at home. We need to be truly honest brokers if placed in that position. To establish trust, we need to recognize the legitimate needs and desires of peoples. We need to be fair and honest in our dealings. A case in point is our treatment of the Palestinians. While the establishment of a Jewish state was laudable, the Palestinians also have territorial rights that go back at least 2,000 years. Any visitor to Israel may see that Arabs who practice the Muslim faith are not treated fairly by the State of Israel. Being fair is one of the first steps to being trusted.

Those readers who might take exception to the words printed here, also deserve to be heard. We all do and that is one of the real needs for a second constitutional convention to decide a multiplicity of issues. Another national convention so that we can hash out and decide what we want to accomplish and how we can accomplish. The start of reform must include reforming our political system. The final chapter concludes with the need for a Second National Convention, like the one convened in 1787 that structured our country. Their success is evident in how long our system has lasted.

The author is not recommending elimination of our Constitution. On the contrary, he is suggesting bettering it. Those who fabricated the Constitution could not have envisioned what we have become. We have achieved quantum leaps in so many areas. Could they have seen us flying as a bird? Could they have pictured us viewing moving pictures of others on a screen? The same could be said for computers, the telephone, the internet, the automobile, spacecraft, modern medicine, printers…the list goes on and on. We have created an amazing world through engineering and science. What we have not created is a world of humanity and caring.

The Founding Fathers could not envision advertising and the need for so much money just to win an election. They envisioned common men able to ascend to leadership through the force of their ideas and not on the force of their bank accounts. They could not envision the decline in morals and ethics.

Many profess "If it is not against the law, it must be right." They are totally wrong. Ethical behavior is often absent from our country and it should not be. People don't seem to talk about ethics or ethical behavior anymore. They should. The Golden Rule is a classical example of ethical behavior in our society. "Do unto others as you would have them do unto you." Other examples of societal ethical behavior include: Citizen's respect for the property, choices, and lives of others and people putting the needs of others before their own needs.

The Founders could not envision that cheating and lying would be so commonplace that many now expect it and are surprised when one states an obvious truth that is not self-serving. The national military academies have honor codes that state: "I will not lie, cheat or steal, nor tolerate any that do." There is no gray, only black, and white. Those that transgress and violate the Code are expelled from the academies and the expulsion is not subject to appeal. The academies are announcing: "We have set a high standard and, if you don't comply and conform, you will not be one of us." Nationally, we need to set high standards.

The Founders also could not have envisioned the decline in civility and courtesy that is so prevalent these days in the United States. In the 1700s, Congress was civil, but had lively discussions. They did not lose respect for those with differing opinions .In the 1800s, Congress was known to be uncivil at times. In the 1900s, they again became more civil and respectful. However, the 2000s appear to be a on a path to revisit the near-violence of the 1800s.

Driving used to be a courteous endeavor. The author recalls that people used to wave and smile at others on the roadways. Now, we see drivers racing ahead, often on the side of a highway, simply to cut in ahead of others. The respect for others in waiting for one's proper turn is often absent. Selfishness is too prevalent in our society, and not just in driving.

"How we dress is how we act." What was once a respect for casual, has fallen into acceptance of slovenly appearance. If each of us resolves to dress properly, then we set a standard for all others. If we act with respect for others, then others will likely act with respect in return. When enough act with respect, it forms a standard. The need for change is apparent everywhere. However, our society never seems to stop in the middle when we change. It is like a pendulum. The swing of the pendulum often results in extremes. When we go casual, we end up slovenly. People will someday tire of slovenly and the pendulum will shift to more formal attire, but in the extreme.

Our children witness the extremes and vow to change and thus the pendulum starts to swing. So it is with politics. What was once Goldwater conservatism battled liberalism that was supreme. The pendulum has swung way past Goldwater conservatism and has stopped on extreme radicalization. At least many hope that it has stopped. That too will someday change as we follow the pendulum once again. The question is whether we will survive long enough to see it start to swing?

NATIONAL INVESTMENTS in AMERICA'S ECONOMIC FUTURE:

"The best way to predict the future is to create it." — **Abraham Lincoln.**

Investments can take several different forms: Investment in individual betterment; investment in providing a happier life; investment in the betterment of our world; investment in economic betterment; investment in national betterment. The list continues. This document will investigate only two: Investment in American Values and Investment in America's Economic Future.

NATIONAL INVESTMENT- RESEARCH & DEVELOPMENT (R&D):

"You should set goals beyond your reach so that you always have something to live for."
— **Ted Turner**

Business R&D is necessary if the business product can improve through research.

There is a difference in types of research and an understanding of the differences is important. National commerce needs both Applied Research and Basic Research.

"Based on purpose or utility, a research approach can either be basic or applied. While basic research aims at expanding knowledge by creating new theories and modifying existing ones, applied research is focused on providing practical solutions to specific problems by analyzing empirical evidence."

Basic Research is the type best suited for a national approach. It involves investment in a "research approach that is entirely theoretical and aimed at improving or expanding the knowledge-base of a particular field of study. It focuses on knowledge for its own sake and it is primarily driven by curiosity and the need to explore the unknown.

It is known as fundamental or pure research and it is a systematic investigation set to achieve a better and more detailed understanding of a research subject or phenomenon, not to solve a specific problem.

Applied Research is the type best suited for private enterprise. "In many cases, applied research is follow-up research" to basic research because it further investigates the outcomes of pure research in order to validate their findings and apply them to specific problems.

Government often is the leader in the creation of industries and their expansion. Agriculture was able to harness the investment power of the American government and investigate better methods of crop care and the development of more efficient forms of harvesting and transporting. Government, the university system, and private enterprise united to develop better strains of certain grains and other products.

Examples are many: The US Department of Agriculture developed specific standards for food that enhanced production and, in turn, protected the public. Other departments did the same in their areas of concern.

NASA provided the monetary investment in space that is now being taken over by private industry in the form of companies like SpaceX and Boeing. The Air Force developed the internet for communication in the event of nuclear war and then gave its invention to the world. It is inconceivable that private enterprise would have invested in such an unlikely outcome.

The military has designed and built aircraft that have then become commonplace in civilian airlines. The advent of the jet engine was a product of government. The introduction of rockets was another defense design.

Higher education has also played a very important part. Many universities entice research. Stanford developed computers and the mouse and then provided an introduction for entrepreneurs and Bill Gates, along with Steve Jobs, was listening. It is not happenstance that the Santa Clara

Valley, known worldwide as Silicon Valley, is located so close to Stanford University.

NATIONAL INVESTMENT: ARTIFICIAL INTELLIGENCE (AI):

China is heavily investing in artificial intelligence and that has national security implications. National investment in AI promises many possible peacetime applications that will create whole new industries. The applications for warfare involve national security and the importance to our country in AI research cannot be overemphasized. We need to make this a high priority and government should partner with business to develop, which it seems to be doing.

NATIONAL INVESTMENT: RENEWABLE ENERGY:

Reusable or renewable energy is defined as "energy from a source that is not depleted when used, such as wind or solar power." There are five major renewable energy sources: solar energy, wind energy, geothermal energy (heat from inside the earth), biomass energy derived from plants, and hydropower from flowing water.

Trying to harness the power of heat contained inside the earth presents monumental problems and potential costs, plus dangers. Plant energy is perhaps better studied later, allowing governments and industries to devote limited resources to the development of the more promising: wind, solar, and hydropower.

SOLAR POWER:

Solar is the subject of much research and proposals abound. Several such proposals for solar power are being or have been developed in the Southern California Mojave Desert. The West includes vast territories that have abundant sunlight.

According to the Jet Propulsion Laboratory of the California Institute of Technology, "In September 2013, the largest solar plant of its kind in the world started producing power in Southern California's Mojave Desert. The Ivanpah Solar Generating System uses 170,000 mirrors to focus the sun's heat on giant boilers atop 128 meters high concrete towers, where water is turned into steam to power turbines that generate electricity. The 392-megawatt plant will generate enough electricity to power 140,000 homes."

The Ivanpah facility, shown next page, is one of many different ideas proposed for solar power generation, although Ivanpah is one idea that is proving successful. Another concept proposed by the Australian firm EnviroMission Ltd., is to build a 3,300-foot-high tower, the world's tallest man-made structure, in the southwest corner of the state of New South Wales. The tower will produce 200 megawatts of solar power at a cost of $563 US. It will "stand in the center of a massive glass roof spanning seven kilometers in diameter." The technological process is that the sun will heat the glass roof, which slopes upward from an outer height of 3 meters to a height of 25 meters at the tower base. "As the hot air rises, a powerful updraft is also created by the tower that allows air to be continually sucked through 32 turbines, which spin to generate" continual day and night power.

Solar in the Mojave Desert. Photo by Consumer Energy Alliance.

Ivanpah Solar Energy Facility, Mojave Desert, California. Photo courtesy of Tuck Mapping solutions.

SOLAR-MICROGRID:

In Menifee, California a newly completed housing development is unlike any other. It is the first all-electric, solar, and battery-powered microgrid in California. A microgrid means that the entire development is energy connected with the integrated solar panels and batteries able to protect all the homes in the 200-home community. Each home is equipped with rooftop solar panels, backup battery storage and charging capabilities, a 13KW storage battery, an electric heat- pump and a heat-pump water heater, all electric appliances and components, plus bi-directional charging that

Solar farm in San Joaquin Valley. Courtesy of San Joaquin Valley Sun.

Solar farm in California's San Joaquin (Central) Valley. CNN Photo.

includes battery charging of electric vehicles (EVs).

The project will protect the community from the blackouts that have become more frequent due to higher temperatures and other extreme weather. In the past ten years, the number of blackouts due to weather have increased 78%. The Department of Energy is getting into the act. "Last year, the DOE announced that $61 million in funding has been allocated to created ten connected communities capable of interacting with the grid to optimize energy consumption and reduce carbon emissions." According to the DOE, communities, like that built in Mcnifee with "grid-interactive efficient buildings (GEBs), could save $18 billion in power systems costs while cutting 80 million tons of carbon dioxide emissions each year."

Two communities in Alabama and Georgia were the first in the US to create the energy-efficient microgrid residential communities. Their experience has shown that the individual homes save from "42% to 44% less energy than other all-electric homes."

SOLAR HIGHWAYS:

Germany, Austria, Spain, and Switzerland have all built "so-called" solar highways. In this country, the Sacramento Municipal Utility District "has done a feasibility study on solar highways, but has not built one." In 2008, the nation's first solar highway was completed in Oregon, just south of Portland.

The idea is to utilize the median strips and rights-of-ways of highways for solar panels. Highway rights-of-ways are those areas on either side of major highways that denote various department of highways ownership. The outer limits of highway rights-of-way are usually depicted by barbed wire fences. The distances from paved highways to the fences can often be significant, especially on major highways. The American southwest includes several states that offer over 300 days-per-year of sunshine: California, Nevada, Utah, Arizona, New Mexico, and Texas to name a few. That abundant sunshine will power the illumination of the highways through the solar panels.

Other applications of solar products also seem promising. Solar roof tiles came and went, but the thought was intriguing. Perhaps future homes and offices will be totally energy self-sufficient with the introduction of total insulation, sufficient solar surfaces, and super energy efficient appliances. Government has been good at setting standards for construction as well as products. Standards are needed in any industry. They allow businesses within like industries to be playing on the same page.

WIND POWER:

Wind is being fully investigated and shows promise. Most Americans are fully aware of the vast windfarms that now dot our landscape. Perhaps less is known about advances in wind-power sites off our coasts, like those in the Netherlands.

"Placing (wind) turbines out to sea has multiple advantages. First, the ocean is windy. The National Renewable Energy Laboratory estimates (that) U.S. offshore has the potential to generate up to 2,000 gigawatts of electricity, nearly double the amount the United States currently uses.

Secondly, ocean winds also blow more consistently and tend to peak in the evening, just as power from solar arrays drops. According to John Olav Tande, chief scientist at SINTEF, a Norwegian research institute, "over 80% of the global wind resources are in deep water." Electricity from all wind turbines was 70% cheaper in 2021, than it was in 2009, according to Lazard, a financial advisory firm that publishes annual estimated on energy production costs. Experts told the DOE in 2021 (that) they expect the offshore wind costs to fall by as much as another 35% by 2035, and almost 50% by 2050.

The United States, which has thousands of miles of coastline and world-class offshore wind, is especially well-positioned to capitalize on this energy resource." Norway, which has the world's largest floating wind farm, is now able to ascertain production data and the results are promising.

The Biden administration is investing heavily in offshore wind research. In an effort to propel

Single turbine offshore floating units.

Norwegian multi-turbine floating unit in their world's largest floating wind farm.

America to the forefront of "cutting-edge climate technology," Biden announced an initiative in September 2022, that will invest nearly $50 million to boost floating, offshore wind-turbine technology.

The White House National Climate Advisor Gina McCarthy, stated that the goal of the floating turbines is to provide 15 gigawatts of power by 2035, enough to power 5 million homes. Additionally, the goal by 2035 is to reduce the cost of the electricity produced by the floating turbines by 70% by

2035, which will be less than the cost of fossil fuels.

In February 2022, the United States leased sites off the coasts of New Jersey and New York for the purpose of developing floating wind farms. Six firms paid a net of $4.37 billion, which goes to the US Treasury. Recently, the Supreme Court decided that anything beyond three miles from shore belongs to the Federal government, while less than three miles belongs to the states. The platforms are planned to be about 20 miles offshore and thus often not visible. Those leases went for a larger amount than any energy leases in the history of the United States, including oil and gas leases, which indicates the expected earning power of the floating turbines.

"Floating wind platforms, much like floating oil rigs, are fixed to the ocean floor with mooring lines, much like a ship's anchor." The rigs planned for off the New York and New Jersey coasts are in relatively shallow waters and are thus less expensive to build and maintain than those off the west coast.

"Open-ocean floating turbines can be much larger than land-based ones. The hub of the blades on land is typically about 308 feet. In deep water, it's anticipated the hub could be as tall as 500 feet, the height of the Washington Monument. The blades of these turbines can be up to 360 feet long and produced 15 megawatts of energy, enough to power 5,000 homes."

On December 7, 2022, the first offshore floating turbine leases, off California, were sold for $757 million, which is far less than those leases on the Atlantic coast because the Pacific coast drops off much more rapidly than the Atlantic and the cost to moor and maintain a platform will cost much more. When complete, the wind platforms would provide power to 1.5 million homes. The California platforms will also be 20 miles offshore and be moored as much as a half-mile deep.

The 25-year leases "are only the first part of a relatively long road. Assessment, construction, and planning requirements mean the projects will not likely start for at least five years."

HYDROPOWER:

Hydropower has interesting possibilities. While flowing water on land has been heavily developed, research on harnessing the power of flowing seawater has been limited. Some tidal areas, such as the Canadian Bay of Fundy, have massive amounts of seawater moving rapidly. Could that be harnessed? Should that be harnessed?

The oceans have significant currents that sometimes flow near shores. Could we somehow harness that flow in a manner that is cost effective?

NUCLEAR:

Nuclear is not classified as renewable energy, but it is energy that has no byproducts of production that negatively impact the air or ground around us. It does involve spent radioactive material that must be stored. Research into methods of commercial use of that radioactive material heat might nullify the need for critical storage. Also, needed further research on foolproof and safe methods of nuclear power generation might allow us to build nuclear plants in areas and in ways that are extremely safe and secure. Advanced plant designs have already made nuclear generation construction proposals extremely safe.

In 2021, US energy consumption by source was as follows:

Biomass, 5.0%; Hydropower, 2.3%; Wind, 3.4%; Solar, 1.5%; Geothermal, 0.2%; Nuclear, 8.4%; Coal, 10.8%; Natural Gas, 32.2%; Petroleum, 36.0%. Clearly, we have a lot of work to do to rid us of fossil fuels. The consumption of petroleum and petroleum products has another consideration, other than its negative effect on our environment. Petroleum provides for production of a lot of chemically-based products. If we burn up this resource in our vehicles, we might find that we have destroyed production of needed or even essential products. Oil is not renewable.

HYDROGEN:

Perhaps the most important resource we can use for energy production and other, multiple uses, is hydrogen. "The most important benefit of using hydrogen as a fuel is that when you burn it, the byproduct is just water."

The sun and other stars "generate energy over most of their lives by fusing hydrogen into heavier elements. Such fusion of light hydrogen (protium) has never been successful in the conditions attainable on Earth." But national research is trying in our National Laboratories.

TOKAMAK:

According to Wikipedia: "A tokamak is a device which uses a powerful magnetic field to confine plasma in the shape of a torus. The tokamak is one of several types of magnetic confinement devices being developed to produce controlled thermonuclear fusion power. As of 2016, it was the leading candidate for a practical fusion reactor."

Lawrence Livermore National Laboratory has been working on the Tokamak for decades. Harnessing the power of the sun is no easy task. It was found that the best plasma for use in the Tokamak was that of deuterium. In deuterium, "the thermal insulation layer was found to appear at high density. The plasma density where the thermal insulation layer formed in the deuterium plasma was 1.5 times higher than that in the hydrogen-2 (protium) plasma.

What is a thermal insulation layer? It is a "great solution to reduce energy consumption by preventing heat gain or loss." For the Tokamak, it helps to contain the heat produced. Temperatures up to 40 million degrees have reportedly been successfully contained in the Tokamak. That report has not been verified.

DEUTERIUM:

What is deuterium and how important is it?

Deuterium, or heavy water, is also known as heavy hydrogen. Hydrogen is what powers the sun and gives life to the earth. The sun's heat and energy are supplied by the continual fusion of hydrogen in a process like what happens in an explosion of a thermonuclear weapon.

There are two isotopes of hydrogen, with deuterium, also known as hydrogen-2, being one part or one atom of hydrogen, with the other 6420 atoms in seawater that of hydrogen-1 or protium. It also means that "deuterium accounts for approximately 0.0156% of all the naturally occurring hydrogen in the oceans, while protium accounts for 99.98%."

The process of extraction of deuterium from seawater is time-consuming and thus expensive. Research may find a simpler and less extensive process for extraction. When that happens, deuterium will be as plentiful as the oceans.

Deuterium, used in the Tokomak, is mentioned above, and may become a very vital fuel for energy production if, and when, hydrogen fusion is contained and able to power generators.

Deuterium is also a necessary component of nuclear weapons, but that will not be discussed here. The isotope has been added to drugs and has "significantly lowered rates of metabolism and hence (provided for) a longer (chemical) half-life." Its effect in drugs has only recently been discovered. "In 2017, deutetrabenazine became the first deuterated drug to receive FDA approval." Deuterated polyunsaturated fatty acids slow down the chain reaction of chemicals that damage living cells.

The thermostabilization effect of deuterium has a stabilizing action on live vaccines, such as the oral polio virus vaccine and others. Circadian rhythms that effect test animals such as rats and hamsters, have been slowed by the introduction of deuterium. The same effect may be found when introduced in humans?

"In August 2018, scientists announced the transformation of gaseous deuterium into a liquid metallic form. This may help researchers better understand giant gas planets, such as our Solar System neighbors Jupiter, Saturn, Uranus, and Neptune and related exoplanets, since they are thought to contain large quantities of liquid metallic hydrogen, which may be responsible for their observed powerful magnetic fields."

PROTIUM:

Protium is also as plentiful as the oceans. Protium makes up 99.98% of all ocean waters. Unlimited is therefore an understatement. Different methods are available to separate deuterium and protium from seawater. Most of the costs associated with separation of deuterium is that 0.0156% of seawater is deuterium and that takes a lot of seawater for separation. The opposite is true for protium. After separation, 99.98% of the remaining water is protium and thus the costs are greatly reduced. The advantage of protium is that it is used in hydrogen fuel cell technology and for hydrogen-combustion vehicles. This unlimited source of energy promises an eco-friendly future to us all and should be understood.

NATIONAL LABORATORIES:

Our nation is busy doing desirable basic research in our system of National Laboratories. The fields of their work and the depth of that research would make this book unnecessarily long. But a listing of them will give the reader a sense of just how engaged our country is in needed basic research:

Ames Laboratory, Argonne National Laboratory, Brookhaven National Laboratory, Fermi National Accelerator Laboratory, Frederick National Laboratory for Cancer Research, Idaho National Laboratory, Lawrence Berkeley National Laboratory, Lawrence Livermore National Laboratory, Los Alamos National Laboratory, National Energy Technology Laboratory, National Renewable Energy Laboratory, Oak Ridge National Laboratory, Pacific Northwest National Laboratory, Princeton

Plasma Physics Laboratory, Sandia National Laboratory, Savannah River National Laboratory, SLAC National Accelerator Laboratory, Thomas Jefferson National Accelerator Facility

New discoveries are constantly coming from our National Labs. For example: In 2018, The Pacific Northwest National Laboratory in association with LCW Supercritical Technologies, made "an important breakthrough for the nuclear industry by extracting powdered uranium from ordinary seawater." The new process is inexpensive and "could one day make nuclear energy effectively unlimited."

"The people who are crazy enough to think that they can change the world are the ones who do."
— **Steve Jobs**

FUTURE INVESTMENT- HYDROGEN POWERED VEHICLES:

Most discussions about environmentally friendly vehicles has been about electric cars or hybrids that use gasoline to power the vehicle and to recharge electric batteries that also power the vehicle. The hydrogen option still has development costs to consider, especially regarding the conversion of gaseous protium to liquified, but once inexpensive processes are devised, the future benefits are unlimited. Hydrogen powered cars are not widely available and the infrastructure to support refueling of vehicles is sparse. But that is no reason not to consider hydrogen. It is extremely environmentally friendly as the only byproduct of hydrogen combustion is water and not the noxious tail-pipe emissions common to gasoline-powered vehicles.

Additional benefits include that it is the most abundant element on earth and it "is also very energy-dense: 100 times more energy dense than a typical lithium-ion battery." Production of protium is also environmentally friendly in that "it can be produced from several domestic resources- including bio resources or renewable electricity via electrolysis."

One major benefit of a hydrogen-powered vehicle is that "it can be filled up in a similar amount of time as a gasoline vehicle, roughly five minutes."

DIFFERENT TYPES OF HYDROGEN VEHICLES:

"Hydrogen cars can be roughly divided into two categories: hydrogen fuel cell vehicles (which operate like electric cars) and hydrogen combustion vehicles (which operate similarly to gasoline cars). Both types of vehicles produce zero emissions- but they work in very different ways."

HYDROGEN FUEL-CELL TECHNOLOGY:

Fuel-cell technology pre-dates the automobile. "In essence, a fuel-cell combines hydrogen and oxygen in the presence of an electrolyte to produce electric current. Fuel-cells "were used in America's Gemini and Apollo spacecraft, where they provided crews with electricity and water."

A hydrogen fuel-cell vehicle is an electric vehicle- just without a plug. There is no big battery to recharge. Instead, a driver fills a tank with compressed hydrogen gas. From the pressurized fuel tank, the gas flows to a fuel cell system, which combines the hydrogen with oxygen from the air. A chemical reaction produces the electric current which propels the car. The only thing leaving the tailpipe is heat and water.

Hydrogen fuel-cell vehicles are relatively lighter and less complex than gasoline vehicles, because they don't rely on a huge battery and they are relatively lighter than battery-powered vehicles.

Many who consider hydrogen-powered vehicles think that they must be powered with hydrogen stored in cryogenic fuel cells, which must be kept to a very cold temperature to keep the hydrogen in a liquified state. The latest technology does not require it. Current technology just requires pressurized tanks under enough pressure to keep hydrogen in a liquid state.

The first mass produced fuel cell cars for America, the Hyundai Nexo, and the Toyota Mirai, will be delivered in 2022. Hyundai extols their system and has tested the technology under trying conditions. Being lighter than air, hydrogen will rise if it leaks, but Hyundai feels that would be a rare occurrence. They have crash tested the fuel cell tanks and even shot bullets into the tanks. They do not explode. If leaking from a pressurized tank, the spray of hydrogen would be like that of a propane tank when the liquid propane hits the air and changes to a gaseous state. It is not dangerous, unless there is a combustion source present.

HYDROGEN COMBUSTION VEHICLES:

"Unlike a hydrogen fuel cell vehicle, which creates electricity that powers an electric motor, a hydrogen combustion engine, looks, sounds, and behaves like a gasoline engine- except for the fact that it burns hydrogen and produces no noxious tailpipe emission." It only emits water.

"The advantage of hydrogen combustion engines is faster time to market- because they can adapt existing engineering, including the fuel systems on-board a (gasoline) vehicle. Hydrogen is superior to gasoline because it burns quicker, making powertrains very responsive and exciting."

A disadvantage of a hydrogen combustion vehicle is that it is more complex than a hydrogen fuel cell powered vehicle. It is like a gasoline-powered car and has lots of moving parts, meaning that they have similar maintenance requirements and expenses. Comparatively speaking, the hydrogen fuel cell vehicles will require far less maintenance than combustion vehicles because they rely on a simple electric motor and the fuel cell system. However, the hydrogen combustion engines will require about the same maintenance as the current gasoline combustion engines.

A reader might think that hydrogen combustion sounds very good. What are the drawbacks? While hydrogen performance is superior to gasoline, both hydrogen systems have an expensive pressurized hydrogen storage tank system and there is a lack of refueling infrastructure in the United States. In a vehicle, hydrogen gas tanks take up a lot of space and liquid hydrogen requires a pressurized and cooled container, which is expensive. Hyundai boasts that its hydrogen tankage only requires pressure containment and not cooling, although a cryogenic tank is offered.

Currently, no hydrogen combustion vehicles are on sale and the availability of hydrogen filling stations is limited. "As of early 2022, fewer than 50 publicly accessible filling stations exist in America. However, 40 of them are in California.

Hydrogen fueling infrastructure is bound to improve. Since hydrogen vehicles are so environmentally friendly, the United States government will probably have to do the initial investing to provide a country-wide system of refueling stations. Once established, then the public investment can then be sold to private firms.

Perhaps the greatest advantage for hydrogen fuel cells involves the American semi-truck fleet. To make these heavier vehicles environmentally friendly, will take something other than an electric vehicle because, in order to provide the range and power that long-haul transport requires, "the size of the battery required would be too heavy- massively compromising usable payload,- and would take too long to charge to be practical."

While the fuel cell technology is not new, the application is new. Additionally, hydrogen combustion promises even better performance than fuel cell. New applications require additional technology. In any newly offered vehicle, initial costs fall significantly after challenges have been overcome and mass production takes the place of small unit purchases at the dealer level.

The transformation of long-haul trucks from gasoline or diesel to hydrogen will also increase performance. Since protium is the fuel of choice, production costs will not have to rely on deep-well pumping. They only must rely on our oceans.

HYDROGEN COMBUSTION and ELECTRIC AIRCRAFT:

Brazilian aircraft manufacturer Embraer is developing electric and hydrogen engine powered small and medium range airplanes. In December, 2022, Embraer announced that it is developing four concepts for low-emission aircraft. One concept is a nine-passenger airplane powered by hybrid-electric engines and another with all-electric propulsion. Hydrogen fuel cells will power a 19-seater and hydrogen-burning turbine engines will power aircraft able to carry up to 50 passengers.

Embraer says that "while still in the evaluation phase, the architectures and technologies are being assessed for technical and commercial viability." Two Embraer designs, for 19 and 30 passenger aircraft, "will have a range of about 500 nautical miles. Embraer designs use twin rear-mounted propellers driven by parallel hybrid-electric architectures that maximize the synergies between thermal and electric engines."

The hydrogen fuel cell-powered aircraft will have "twin aft-mounted propellers driven by electric motors. The hydrogen fuel cells will be mounted in the aft fuselage." There are several technical issues that remain to be solved, such as heat dissipation. Embraer proposes using "ram air to the heat exchangers." They believe that the hydrogen fuel-cell technology for aircraft will enable them to manufacture a commercial airplane powered by hydrogen that will carry over 100 passengers with a range of 1,000 miles. They foresee an introduction in the mid-2030s.

Airbus is also interested in the concept of hydrogen fuel-cell powered aircraft. They are in the conceptual development stage and have even proposed installation of hydrogen fueling capacity at the Toulouse International Airport in France. With Europe and Brazil at the forefront of development of aircraft and support infrastructure, America cannot be far behind.

"My philosophy of life is that if we make up our mind what we are going to make of our lives, then work hard toward that goal, we never lose... somehow we always win."
— Ronald Reagan

FUTURE INVESTMENTS- IMPORTED WATER:

With the effects of a possible long-term drought facing the Southwest, and water deliveries literally drying up from reliable sources such as the Colorado River, our nation needs to use the power of mega-investment and find other sources of water that not only replace the existing water delivery shortages, but greatly enhance those deliveries. Large tracts of farmland lie fallow in portions of the Great Central Valley of California due to lack of water. Arizona also faces a reduction of its reliance on Colorado water for its Central Arizona (Water) Project.

Sources for additional water include the huge Columbia River, which has ten times the flow of the Colorado. Currently, Columbia water flows out to sea in massive amounts. That water could and should be corralled and sent east to the scorched areas of Eastern Oregon and Washington and then to the south for an even more parched Nevada, Southern California, and Arizona.

Other rivers farther north also offer promise. The chart below shows water flow in cubic feet per second. The Fraser is one of the largest in North America, but flows out to sea near Vancouver in Canada. The Okanagan and Kootenaii both flow out of Canada into Washington, just as the Columbia. Since planning, property purchase, and development takes at least ten years, the time to act is now. We will have to provide an investment in Canada, but it is past time to worry about such things. It is needed and we should "get it done, whatever the source."

RIVER:	VOLUME: (in cubic feet/ second)
Okanagan	3,039
Kootenaii	27,620
Fraser	122,700
Columbia	264,900

"All successful people have a goal. No one can get anywhere unless he knows where he wants to go and what he wants to be or do." — **Norman Vincent Peale.**

FUTURE INVESTMENTS- GENE THERAPY:

Deciphering the human DNA has opened-up a vast new arena of research. By identifying certain genes, health science has created huge opportunities for doctors to treat diseases by dealing with the genes that have caused the diseases. Research is in its infancy, but government investment in this area would be very "cost-effective" and holds promise for prolonging our lives and making our times on earth much happier and productive. Many biopharma companies are heavily involved currently in such needed research.

In the words of Bayer Global, a large health-care provider: "Health begins with understanding. And in recent decades, science has come to understand a lot about the human body. Particularly, our genetics. This has unlocked promising options for doctors and patients to treat some of the most debilitating diseases. Scientists are looking for answers where biology, chemistry, and data science meet.

Cell and gene therapies offer hope to millions of people living with genetic and some degenerative diseases. These new treatment options are a paradigm shift. They don't treat symptoms; they help the body repair itself from within."

GENE THERAPY—a PREVENTATIVE ANSWER to CURATIVE CARE:

It is reported that sometime in 1910, the healthcare industry opted to provide a system of curative care instead of preventative care. Logically, it did not make sense. Isn't it smarter to prevent illness than to have to diagnose and cure an actual illness? Preventative is far easier and far less expensive. From a doctor's perspective, curative care is much more lucrative. From the perspective of today's overwhelmed healthcare system, that may be changing. Doctors and nurses are overworked and in some cases, overwhelmed.

Some HMOs, like the Kaiser system, are all in on methods of preventative care. From a patient's perspective, it is reassuring. The more people that can be prevented from getting sick, the less patients appear at ERs or clinics and the more care can be given to the doctor's other patients. If preventive care is universally accepted, our enormous national health-care bill will go down, and probably by a great deal.

With the patient's genome figured out, and genes responsible for specific illnesses also found, the healthcare system can then place their money and energy into finding and eradicating guilty genes and those that may cause mutations. Some mutations may be for the good, but gene's that are associated with illnesses can either be eradicated or manipulated.

Gene therapy can then be part of a worldwide data collection system and can be made to eliminate illnesses by working with the affected genes. It promises to revolutionize health care and provide for healthier lives, for happier lives, and for longer lives.

> *"The mystery of human existence lies not in just staying alive,*
> *but in finding something to live for."* — **Fyodor Dostoyevsky**

FUTURE INVESTMENT- SEAWATER INTRUSION:

Seawater intrusion for this discussion involves two types. The first type is subterranean. Fertile agricultural areas that are located near the oceans are threatened by underground seawater intrusion. Once seawater is allowed to enter a subterranean aquifer, it permanently destroys that area for further plantings, especially the planting of trees. This may be a small matter nationally, but it is big in those affected areas. Since we are no longer making any new real estate, unless possibly the big island of Hawaii and Iceland, it behooves our government to work to save what we have, especially if it is fertile ag land.

The island of Lanai is an example: The Dole Food Company used to own Lanai, but it is now owned by Oracle's Larry Ellison, who owns 98% of the island and moved there in 2020. When Dole was in charge, Lanai was a rich island for production of pineapples. While individually, pineapples don't require a lot of water, collectively they can. Dole planted most of the island in pineapples and the drawdown in island water was extreme. The water table kept getting lower and lower until Dole needed over 1,200 feet to pump subterranean water to the surface. At that level, the water became brackish and too impacted with seawater intrusion. It was deemed unusable and Dole had to eliminate its pineapple business on Lanai.

Rising sea levels of the Earth's oceans is well-known and is the second type of seawater intrusion. The United States is the world's primary "have" nation and we have a responsibility. We need to provide help to those Pacific-island nations who are threatened.

The situation of the islands seems ripe for implementation of the author's proposal to extend an offer to others to join our union. In the case of the island republics, most are too small to qualify as individual states. But if they join, and if there were enough of them, they could qualify for the status of an American state and thus subject to the benefits of full citizenship. The process would also support American efforts to contain Chinese expansion.

Citizenship would allow threatened islanders to move to non-threatened areas anywhere in the United States. Currently existing American Pacific territories included in the South and Western Pacific who could also join are: Guam, the Northern Mariana Islands, and American Samoa. It would be a humanitarian gesture to allow all to benefit from full American citizenship.

The proposal does not mean that we should not extend help to any island group that may not want to join. On the contrary, each threatened island deserves our humanitarian help.

Below is a listing of island nations of the Pacific that may be threatened by surface seawater intrusion. The individual American islands included below either have small populations or are unpopulated. Johnston Atoll is military and lies SW of Hawaii. Many American islands are marine or bird sanctuaries.

PACIFIC ISLAND NATIONS:	POPULATIONS:
American Pacific Islands & Territories:	
Palmyra, Kingdom Reef, Johnston Atoll, Midway, Wake, Howland, Baker, Jarvis	
Territory of Guam	170,184 (2021)
Territory of Northern Marianas	57,910 (2021)
Territory of American Samoa	55,103 (2021)
Marshall Islands	59,618 (2021)
Kingdom of Tonga	106,759 (2021)
Solomon Islands	718,737 (2022)
Samoa (formerly Western Samoa)	200,144 (2021)
Palau	18,174 (2021)
Nauru	10,873 (2021)
Federated States of Micronesia (includes Caroline Islands, Yap, and Ulithi Atoll)	116,255 (2021)
Fiji (includes Lau Island Group)	902,899 (2021)

PACIFIC ISLAND NATIONS:	POPULATIONS:
Kiribati	
(includes Gilbert Islands, Phoenix Islands,	
Tarawa, and some Line Islands)	121,388 (2021)
Tuvalu	11,925 (2021)
Vanuatu	314,464 (2021)
Total:	**2,864,433**

Many Pacific islands are mountainous, created by volcanic activity. The low-lying atolls are what is left of volcanic islands that collapsed. Those atolls are in danger of being submerged.

FUTURE INVESTMENT—MINING THE OCEAN FLOOR:

"The ocean floor holds vast deposits of ores containing sought-after metals. Companies are exploring the potential to mine three types of deposits in the deep sea: ferromanganese nodules, metal-rich crusts o seamounts and sulfide deposits near hydrothermal vents along the mid-ocean ridges. Most commercial attention is focused on the nodules in the Pacific Ocean's Clarion-Clipperton Zone (CCZ)." Estimates suggest the astounding fact that the CCZ holds a greater quantity of certain metals than do all land deposits combined.

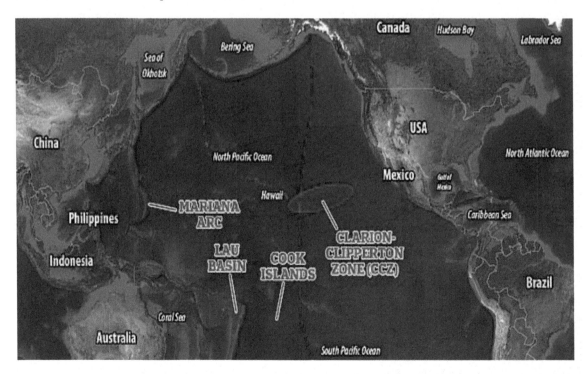

The Clarion-Clipperton Zone (CCZ) lies next to the American State of Hawaii. The Cook Islands belong to New Zealand. The Mariana Arc is next to the American Territory of the Northern Marianas. The Lau Basin is next to the Lau Islands, part of Fiji. Map courtesy of the Daily Mail.

The United States had better consider mining of the ocean floor as not only a desirable option, but a necessary option and one that involves national security. Currently, China is the world's foremost provider of rare earth metals. The U.S. requires rare earths for a variety of applications. "Rare earth elements are used as components in high technology devices, including smart phones, digital cameras, computer hard disks, fluorescent and light-emitting diode (LED) lights, flat screen televisions, computer monitors, and electronic displays."

MINERAL: **CCZ RESERVES:**   **TERRESTRIAL RESERVES:**

Numbers listed below are estimates only and come from only one source. They have not been confirmed from other sources. Minerals colored in red have more in CCZ reserves than terrestrial reserves. (Reference: mt = million tons)

	CCZ Reserves (mt):	All Land Reserves (mt):
Manganese	5,992	5,200
Nickel	274	150
Tellurium	0.08	0.05
Thallium	4.2	0.0007
Yttrium	2	0.5
Cobalt	44	13
Copper	226	>1,000
Titanium	67	899
Rare-earth Oxides	15	150
Vanadium	9.4	38
Molybdenum	12	19
Lithium	2.8	14
Tungsten	1.3	6.3
Niobium	0.46	3
Arsenic	1.4	1.6
Thorium	0.32	1.2
Bismuth	0.18	0.7
Platinum	0.003	0.08

Nature (www.nature.com) has provided a comparison between just the small portion of the Pacific designated as the CCZ, and total land-based mining. If Nature is right, then we have a problem. While the United Nations is attempting to control the awarding of leases within the CCZ, the potential for riches and the virtual control of rare earth metals, means that totalitarian states like Russia and China might try to extract the metals while bypassing the controls.

While looking over the chart (above), keep in mind that the CCZ, located southeast of Hawaii, is just a small part of one ocean. What do the other oceans and the rest of the Pacific also hold in the way of such metals?

"The economy is the start and end of everything. You can't have successful education reform or any other reform if you don't have a strong economy."
— **David Cameron, Prime Minister of the U.K. from 2010 to 2016**

Photo Gallery Five

National Parks on the Atlantic Coast
Maine, Virginia, North Carolina, South Carolina, Florida, United States Virgin Islands

Acadia National Park, Maine

Shenandoah National Park, Virginia

Great Smoky Mountains National Park, North Carolina

Congaree National Park,
South Carolina

Biscayne National Park,
Florida

Everglades National Park,
Florida

Dry Tortugas National Park, Florida

Virgin Islands National Park, United States Virgin Islands Territory, Atlantic & Caribbean Sea

Chapter Fifteen
Criminal Punishment, Swift Justice, & Judicial Reform
Defining Consistent & Fair Rules

"A people that values its privileges above its principles soon loses both."
— **Dwight Eisenhower Inaugural Address, Washington DC 1-20-1953**

THE BILL OF RIGHTS to the UNITED STATES CONSTITUTION:

Amendment I: "Congress shall make no law respecting an establishment of religion, or prohibiting the free exercise thereof, or abridging the freedom of speech, or of the press, or the right of the people peaceably to assemble, and to petition the government for a redress of grievances."

Amendment V: "No person shall be held to answer for a capital, or otherwise infamous crime, unless on a presentment or indictment of a grand jury, except in cases arising in the land or naval forces, or in the militia, when in actual service in times of war or public danger, nor shall any person be subject for the same offense to be twice put in jeopardy of life or limb, nor shall be compelled in any criminal case to be a witness against himself, nor be deprived of life, liberty, or property, without due process of law, nor shall private property be taken for public use without just compensation."

Amendment VI: "In all criminal prosecutions, the accused shall enjoy the right to a speedy and public trial, an impartial jury of the state and district wherein the crime shall have been committed, which district shall have been previously ascertained by law, and to be informed of the nature and cause of the accusation, to be confronted with the witnesses against him, to have compulsory process for obtaining witnesses in his favor, and to have the assistance of counsel for his defense."

Our original, written Constitution and the amendments included in the attached Bill of Rights, have provided us with adequate judicial protections. The provision of Amendment VI stating that "the accused shall enjoy the right to a speedy and public trial" is being abused by our American judicial system. In no way can our criminal trials be considered speedy. In fact, intentional or not, the trial system that has evolved in the United States provides excessive compensation to judges and attorneys that benefit from a "stretching out" of the time required to conduct a trial. When the appellate process is included in the time required to conclude a trial, it seems that someone who has been criminally accused only has a right to a slow and costly trial. The judicial system and its members are thus in direct violation of the very Constitution they are obliged to protect and adhere to its provisions as well as pledging an oath to defend.

The United States Code Title 28, Part I, Chapter 21, page 453 requires the following oath to be spoken by any judge or justice before assuming office: "I do solemnly swear that I will administer justice without respect to persons, and do equal right to the poor and to the rich, and that I will faithfully and impartially discharge and perform all the duties incumbent upon me under the Constitution and laws of the United States. So help me God."

Chief Justice John Roberts of the Supreme Court, commented on judicial extremes: "Judges have to have the humility to recognize that they operate within a system of precedent, shaped by other judges equally striving to live up to the judicial oath."

While most judges seem to act with fairness and justice to those accused of crimes, far too many of them act as though they are omnipotent and that they have the right to act as law instead of acting in behalf of legislated law. The Constitution clearly gives to the Congress the sole right to make law. Judges are entrusted to judge on those legislated laws. Often, they do not.

While the Constitution protects the rights of the accused, it is also, indirectly, protecting the rights of the public. The public has a right to protections under the provisions of the Constitution when those provisions are abused for monetary reasons. The system that the lawyer class has created abuses the right of the public to be protected from the excesses and greed of the lawyer class. Judges, being lawyers, are also part of the lawyer class that has acted as a form of oligarchy in that they have created a structure that only lawyers can interpret and administer. The Constitution not only protects the rights of all individual Americans, it also protects the rights of the general public.

Judicial activism began early in our republic. Jefferson observed in 1821: "The great object of my fear is the Federal Judiciary. It is a misnomer to call a government republican in which a branch of the supreme power is independent of the nation." In that, he seemed to anticipate the Supreme Court's striking down Roe v. Wade, when the public overwhelmingly disagreed.

Alexis de Tocqueville (1805-1859) was a French aristocrat, diplomat, political scientist, political philosopher, and historian. He served as Minister of Foreign Affairs in France as well as serving in the French General Council, the French National Assembly, and the French Chamber of Deputies. He is probably best known for his travels in and observations about the United States. His *Democracy in America* is a classic and considered by many to be the best foreign assessment of America in existence. He observed that: "There is hardly a political question in the United States which does not sooner or later turn into a judicial one."

IN DEFENSE of a SECOND CONSTITUTIONAL CONVENTION:

In chapter 18, the final chapter, the arguments for the proposal for a Second Constitutional Convention are developed. That proposal is one of many that have been offered, almost from the beginning of our republic. While Thomas Jefferson had a strong hand in the framing of our Constitution and spoke at length about the virtues of the Constitution, he felt that it might, of necessity, be changed sometime in the future. In 1812 he wrote: "Unless the mass retains sufficient control over those entrusted with the powers of their government, these will be perverted to their own oppression, and to the perpetuation of wealth and power in the individuals and their families selected for the trust. Whether our Constitution has hit on the exact degree of control necessary, is yet under experiment." In that, he implies that future American societies may need to revise our Constitution if future American publics' cannot control excesses wrought by power and wealth. The necessity for the use of excess wealth to influence elections would be cause to consider Congressional revision.

The recommendation to convene a Second Congressional Convention is predicated on the premise that there are too many needed changes to be made that would overwhelm the amendment process. In 1801, Jefferson seemed to envision the accession to power of Donald Trump when he wrote: "I sincerely wish we could see our government so secured as to depend less on the character of the person in whose hands it is trusted. Bad men will sometimes get in and with such immense patronage, may make great progress in corrupting the public mind and principles. This is a subject with which wisdom and patriotism should be occupied." Our Constitution must protect us from would-be demigods like Trump, who famously wanted to be President for Life in total violation of the provisions in the Constitution specifically designed to protect the public from just that type of action. If that is not a danger to our democracy, the author is unaware of what internally has transpired from the birth of our republic that would equally qualify.

Jefferson also stated a case for the active change of the Constitution through the amendment process: "The real friends of the Constitution in its federal form, if they wish it to be immortal, should be attentive, by amendments, to make it keep pace with the advance of the age in science and experience." His case for a possible second convention: "Our children will be as wise as we are and will establish in the fullness of time those things not yet ripe for establishment. Laws and institutions must go together with the progress of the human mind. As that becomes more developed, more enlightened, as new discoveries are made, new truths disclosed, and manners and opinions change with the change of circumstances, institutions must advance also and keep pace with the times. It is more honorable to repair a wrong than to persist in it."

THOMAS JEFFERSON & the CONSTITUTIONAL CONVENTION:

Thomas Jefferson was one of three Virginians who were instrumental in the First Constitutional Convention. Many Americans think that we first declared our independence from England and then started our revolution with a first battle at Lexington-Concord. That was not the case. Lexington-Concord lit a fire, but identities are hard to change. At the time of Concord, many Americans still identified with England. It took over a year for Jefferson to write the Declaration of Independence and have it presented to England. Concord was on April 19, 1775. The United Colonies declared their independence from England on July 2, 1776, over 14 months later than Concord, and then debated the formal, written declaration.

Five prominent patriots: John Adams, Benjamin Franklin, Thomas Jefferson, Robert Livingston, and Roger Sherman were entrusted with writing the Declaration. Jefferson took it upon himself to write a first draft and, with few changes, that became the actual document that was passed by Congress on the 4th of July.

"On November 15, 1777, Congress adopted the Articles of Confederation, which served as the first American constitution and came into force on March 1, 1781, lasting until 1789 when the present-day Constitution went into effect."

The 1780s proved to be critical in the initial development and transition of the United Colonies to the United States. In 1781, with considerable help from the French Army, Marines, and Navy, Washington, Lafayette, and Rochambeau captured Yorktown. Actual combat after Yorktown ceased from 1781 to 1783. On September 3, 1783, the United States signed, along with France and Great Britain, the Treaty of Paris that formerly ended the conflict and turned the United Colonies into the United States with a territory extending from the Atlantic to the Mississippi and from the border of northern Florida to Canada.

The Articles proved to be too weak and poorly structured to properly govern the various states. "Each state had only one vote in Congress, regardless of size. Congress did not have the power to tax or to regulate foreign and interstate commerce. There was no executive branch to enforce any acts passed by Congress." Basically, it was unworkable. However, it also proved to be an education in how not to structure their country. Smaller states might not have agreed with the Constitutional provisions without the experience of working under the Articles.

On May 25, 1787, the First Constitutional Convention convened in Philadelphia. At the time, it was called the Federal Convention or the Philadelphia Convention. George Washington, the winning General in the Revolutionary War, presided over the convention as he did for the Articles of Confederation convention. The Constitutional Convention completed their deliberations and signed the new Constitution on September 17, 1787.

The Constitution provided for a Presidential election and that election was held in 1789. George Washington won the election and was inaugurated on April 30, 1789. He served for two terms, followed by his Vice President, John Adams, who served one term to be followed by Thomas Jefferson.

Jefferson was the leader of the Virginia delegation to Congress and was held in high esteem by the rest of Congress and the public. Benjamin Franklin, who saved the Revolution with his work with France, served as Ambassador to France and negotiated the saving French loans to the Continental Congress as well as influencing the French Navy to intervene in the conflict. Franklin was replaced by Jefferson in Paris and he returned to the U.S. in time to participate in the Constitutional Convention. Therefore, Jefferson did not participate in and did not sign the document. He was, however, extremely influential in its construction. Jefferson was brilliant and he was quite a writer. He communicated his thoughts by letter to many before the Convention and during the progress of negotiations.

The three influential Virginians mentioned included Jefferson, the presiding officer George Washington, and perhaps the most important signer, James Madison. One of the great benefits of the Virginian plantation system was that it provided free time for owners and lots of it. Jefferson was no exception. Providence provided and Jefferson's plantation was within a days horseback ride (30 miles) to the plantations of both James Madison and James Monroe, both later presidents of our republic. That allowed many evenings of discussion over dinners that were often held. Jefferson and Madison forged a close friendship. Madison is acknowledged as the most influential of those attending the convention. His insights often formed the basis for enacted decisions. With the continual exchange of letters between Paris and Philadelphia, Jefferson's influence cannot be overestimated.

JUDICIAL REFORM:

Recent changes in the degree of the actions taken by the Supreme Court have lessened the respect shown by the public for an institution that has such power, yet rules on issues in the face of public condemnation. There is just too much power in single, unelected people in the form of federal judges. Judges should judge based on laws enacted by the legislature and not make laws on their own. There is just too much power in the hands of the lawyer class. Judicial activism has fostered the necessity for judicial reform.

One of the problems with the current governmental situation in the United States is the politicization of parts of government intended to remain independent. The Supreme Court has been politicized and radicalized. New member candidates lied to members of congress during the confirmation process, and thus were admitted as Justices. Past justices, from any political persuasion, were distinguished enough that they managed to be independent. The Founding Fathers allowed that by making the position of Supreme Court Justice as a lifetime appointment.

The Justice Department of the Executive Branch had also been politicized under Trump. It is imperative that it remain independent of any outside influence, including that of the Supreme Court and the Executive itself. This argument does not propose making the judiciary any less independent. It needs to remain totally independent as envisioned by George Washington. Ariel Sharon, former General of the Israeli Army who served as the 11th Prime Minister of Israel, perhaps said it best in a promise to the Israeli people: "The government, under my leadership, will act to implement the rule of law and to maintain the independence of the judicial system, which is one of the pillars of maintaining a democratic system." The judiciary must remain independent, but is still in need of reform.

CONSISTENT RULES:

Those waiting punishment for the conviction of a serious crime should be facing the same penalties regardless of the state in which the conviction was decided. Federal Judges do have online guidance under the Judiciary Sentencing Information platform. The guidance data presented is recommended and does not require compliance. Any judicial reform should look at the variances in sentencing for the same type of crime. Any guidelines should be provided with more "teeth" and federal judges should be held accountable for large deviations from the sentencing norms.

CRIMINAL PUNISHMENT:

A reform of the judiciary should include a reduction of punishment for certain crimes and misdemeanors to lessen the load on the court system, but also to increase punishment for more serious offenses. Recidivism is a problem for many of those sentenced to prison for crimes. If the prison sentences did not cure the criminal tendencies, then we need to find sentences that do minimize their needs to reenter a life of crime.

Those who might evaluate the judiciary might consider elimination of any jail time for victimless crimes. Some victimless crimes might deserve to be removed as crimes altogether. For sentencing, community service is a much better approach.

The punishment and conviction rate needs to be sufficient to cause those considering crimes to reconsider. With strong enough punishments, the drop in crimes should lessen the pressure on the court system.

Consideration should also be given to limiting the time allowed for the appellate process. The overall time allowed between indictment and punishment should be reduced to finally comply with the Constitutional requirement for swift justice.

CRIMINAL JUSTICE SYSTEM STATISTICS:

The RAINN organization states that they are the "nation's largest anti-sexual violence organization." They maintain the national sexual assault hotline, with confidential 24/7 support. They also collect statistics on the national criminal justice system.

A reprint of their data might surprise some and perhaps might lead to system-wide improvements:

SEXUAL ASSAULTS: Out of every 1,000 sexual assaults, only 310 will be reported. Of those, 50 will lead to an arrest with 28 leading to a felony conviction and only 25 out of the 1,000 assaults will lead to incarceration. That is a 3% jailing rate.

ROBBERIES: Out of every 1,000 robberies, 619 will be reported; 167 will lead to an arrest; 22 will lead to a felony conviction and only 20 robbers will be jailed. That is a 2% jailing rate. Are these rates enough to deter criminals?

ASSAULT & BATTERY: Out of every 1,000 crimes, 627 will be reported to police, leading to 255 arrests, which will result in only 41 felony convictions with 33 going to jail. Another 3% jailing rate.

For sexual assaults, "the rape-kit backlog is currently one of the biggest obstacles to persecuting perpetrators of sexual violence." That is a system fault. That only 31% of those assaulted are reported, is of additional concern. The reasons of not reporting are like those of other crimes: 20% feared retaliation; 15% did not believe the police would or could do anything to help; 13% said it was a personal matter; 8% deemed it unimportant; 7% did not want the criminal to get into trouble, and 30% gave other reasons.

Incarceration rates of 2%, 3% and 3% are atrocious. Clearly something needs to be done to fix a broken system. With all the time and money spent on adjudicating crime, the results are not "cost-effective" at all. It speaks to a failure of the entire system.

That known guilty, such as O.J. Simpson, can go free by virtue of having more money to afford the best legal counsel, means that we have a long way to go to resurrect a system that boasts fair and swift justice.

"Our ability to reach unity in diversity will be the beauty and the test of our civilization." — **Mahatma Gandhi**

"The mystery of human existence lies not in just staying alive, but in finding something to live for." — **Fyodor Dostoyevsky**

"Goals determine what you're going to be." — **Julius Erving**

Chapter Sixteen
Universal Government Service
Obligation of Citizenship

"The best way to find yourself is to lose yourself in the service of others."-
— **Mahatma Gandhi**

Many Americans have become soft. Many also have minimal interest and knowledge of American history and worldwide geography, all needed to properly evaluate what is happening in our world. They do not understand what it took to establish and maintain our freedoms and our thriving economy. It took the sacrifices of millions and the death of hundreds-of-thousands in both war and peace to establish and maintain this country.

Over the years, many have proposed a Universal Military Service. It was and still is a valid concept. However, to honor the wishes of those who do not believe in military service, the author is proposing an alternate plan: Universal Government Service. There are many possible avenues of service that could be considered.

Americans could also use a little discipline. To participate in the physical sacrifice endured by so many who voluntarily enter our military services would benefit the individuals in so many ways.

PROPOSAL for UNIVERSAL GOVERNMENT SERVICE:

The proposal is for mandatory service to our government for a period of two years. It would include both men and women 18 years of age. University educations and jobs would have to wait until the age of 20.

The first three months of service would be required training for all. In those three months would be the time that discipline was taught, just as it is for military personnel. It would be conducted along with those who chose to enter the military, so that period of training would also be universal. It would also get participants in physical shape to endure some of the service options that would be available to them.

One of the options that should be available for those entering Universal Service, would be the military option. Universal Military Service, under the control of the Department of Defense would offer the country several beneficial options. It would complete the members military requirement and eliminate the member from any draft list. A trained class of military volunteers who selected the military option would be a wonderful reserve for the United States to call up in the event of an all-out war.

Another option for those selecting could be the Peace Corps. Currently, the Peace Corps is comprised of 7,000 volunteers. Their assistance programs were interrupted by COVID and all volunteers were returned to the United States to wait out the pandemic. They are slowly being reassigned under safe conditions. It is proposed to integrate the Peace Corps into Universal Service. Since water is such an important worldwide consideration, an option for service could include a Water Service Corps, with Africa being a primary target. It could be assigned to a designated Africa Corps, not to be confused with Rommel's corps in WWII.

Newly arrived immigrants requesting asylum, green-card status, or permanent residency status, could also be given an option to enter service. After the initial 3-month training, indoctrination classes could be given to them on Civics, American history, American laws, driver's education, and English, after which they could then be allowed to enter the military along with other volunteers in the Universal Military Training option.

For others who finish the initial military-style training, their next step after selecting their desired option would be to enter training for that option. An incomplete listing of training options might include: water resources, languages, farming, health care, construction, teaching, etc. They would then be sent out to teach others.

The Pacific islands are a special case and another option might be a Pacific Corps. Our government considers China and not Russia as are biggest long-term threat. The Pacific region, including Western Pacific has been an important geopolitical area for the United States since the days of sailing exploration and discovery.

China has recently made headway in trying to sway Pacific-island governments to ally themselves with China instead of their long-term alignment with Pacific nations including France, the U.K., the United States, Australia, and New Zealand. Those Chinese inroads recently have included the Solomon Islands and Vanuatu.

It is imperative that we maintain our current rapport with the island nations. We can maintain it if we continue to offer free infrastructure maintenance in the form of the Pacific Seabees. The immediate concern of many in the Pacific is global warming and its rising sea levels. Those islands that are atolls are vulnerable and even now experiencing inundation and the requirement to relocate.

In another chapter, we have dealt with the potential for offering a form of political union with the United States. That would allow offering relocation within this country for island citizens. It would also allow a solidification and expansion of the current defense treaties and agreements. Since they would attain territorial status, our defense would be their defense. America can also gain great advantage by offering support in other areas, such as that provided by volunteers.

UNIVERSAL MILITARY SERVICE:

"There is nothing stronger than the heart of a volunteer" — **General James H. Doolittle, commander of the Doolittle (Air) Raiders of Tokyo during WWII**

"No man is entitled to the blessings of freedom unless he be vigilant in its preservation." — **General Douglas MacArthur, commander of American Army forces in the Pacific during WWII**

THE PRICE of FREEDOM. For those of us who may object to the idea of universal military training and service, it is time to reflect upon past sacrifices to protect America. Americans tend to forget those past sacrifices made in behalf of a free America. We are currently experiencing an internal threat to our democracy and it may require sacrifices by ourselves to protect our freedoms. The strength of our military is awesome to those who are or have been part of our military structure. Because of that strength, the greatest threat to our democracy is internal, not external.

Since World War II, a great number of Americans have traveled to Europe. Those who chose to visit the Normandy American Cemetery have been awed by the beauty of and care given to the hills overlooking Omaha Beach, where so many American soldiers died storming the beaches on "D Day." Many would be surprised to know that the rest of France and Europe are covered with American cemeteries containing the remains of soldiers, sailors and airmen who died in two world wars. Normandy is not even the largest at 9387 graves. That honor belongs to the Meuse-Argonne American Cemetery honoring 14,246 dead and 3,724 missing-in-action.

Seventy percent of American families chose to have their son's bodies sent back to the United States. Those remaining bodies were buried in many of the cemeteries listed below. For those who might wonder why we have chosen to fight and give up the lives of so many of us overseas, consider that it is far better to fight on foreign soil than to fight on American soil with its associated damage and destruction of our own country.

"The object of war is not to die for your country, but to make the other bastard die for his."
— General George S. Patton

AMERICAN FOREIGN CEMETERIES (22):

Cemetery Name & Location:	War Dead:	Missing:
Ardennes American Cemetery, Ardennes, Belgium	5,329	
Three-fifths were airmen. The rest: Battle of the Bulge, Assault on Germany		
St. James American Cemetery, Brittany, France	4,410	545
Containing those killed at Normandy and Brittany Campaigns		
Suresnes American Cemetery, Suresnes, France	1,541	974
Containing soldiers from both World Wars		
St. Mihiel America Cemetery, Thiaucourt, France	4,153	284
Died in the WWI Battle of St. Mihiel		
Somme America Cemetery, Bony, France	1,844	333
Died in the assault on the Hindenburg Line during WWI		
Sicily-Rome American Cemetery, Nettuno, Italy	7,861	3,095
Died in the liberation of Sicily and during the Anzio landing		
Florence American Cemetery, Florence, Italy	4,402	1,409
Contains graves of those killed after the capture of Rome, during the fighting around Florence, and in the Apennine Mountains.		

Cemetery Name & Location:	War Dead:	Missing:
Rhone American Cemetery, Draguignan, France	861	294
Died during Allied invasion of Southern France		
Brookwood American Cemetery, Brookwood, Surrey, England	468	563
Most of missing were in the US Navy and Coast Guard and were lost at sea.		
Cambridge American Cemetery, Cambridge, England	3,812	5,127
Graves include airmen who died in European bombing and sailors who were killed in North Atlantic convoys. Missing were from the Battle of the Atlantic or in the strategic bombing of northwest Europe during WWII.		
Henri-Chapelle American Cemetery, Liege, Belgium	7,992	450
Died during Allied advance into Germany during WWII		
Oise-Aisne Cemetery, Fere-en-Tardenois, France	6,012	241
Died during World War I in area 70 miles Northeast of Paris		
Aisne-Marne American Cemetery, Belleau, France	2,288	1,060
Resting place for those killed in the Battle of Belleau Wood during WWI		
Epinal American Cemetery, Dinoze, France	5,255	424
Soldiers killed in fighting through the Heasbourg Gap & invasion of Germany		
Normandy American Cemetery, Normandy, France	9,387	1,557
Contains the graves of those killed during the Normandy Invasion. Includes airmen shot down over France and the graves of two sons of Theodore Roosevelt.		
Flanders Field American Cemetery, Waregem, Belgium	411	
Graves of those who fought in the Ypres Campaign at the end of WWI		
Netherlands American Cemetery, Margraten, Netherlands	8,301	1,722
Died liberating the Netherlands from Nazi occupation		
Meuse-Argonne Cemetery, Meuse, France	14,246	3,724
Largest number of American war dead in Europe; Contains graves of those killed during the WWI Argonne Offensive		
Luxembourg American Cemetery, Luxembourg	5,076	370
Graves of those killed in the nearby Battle of the Bulge		
Lorraine American Cemetery, Moselle, France	10,489	450
Died during drive to the Siegfried Line. Soldiers of General Patton's Third Army		
Manila American Cemetery, Manila, Philippines	17,206	32,520
Also contains 3,762 Philippine Nationals who fought alongside Americans Largest number of graves of any WWII cemetery. Includes those killed in New Guinea and during the Battle of the Philippines (1941-1942)		
Mexico City National Cemetery, Mexico City, Mexico	813	750
Graves of those American killed in 1847 during the Mexican-American War		

At the end of the Cold War, America did not march its troops into the Soviet Union as they had told their people we would. Instead, we sent a group of 500 lawyers to Moscow to assist them in their transition to a democratic state. We also sent other groups to assist. Moscow would have sent troops to occupy us as they did in Eastern Europe at the end of the Second World War.

AMERICAN LANDMARKS in WASHINGTON D.C.:

Washington National Monument honoring the Commanding General of the Continental Army in our Revolutionary War and the First President of the United States. Photo courtesy of Wikivoyage.

The Lincoln Memorial honoring the 16th President of the United States, who held the Union together during the devastating American Civil War. Photo courtesy of Encyclopedia Britannia.

"The legitimate object of government, is to do for a community of people, whatever they need to have done." — **Abraham Lincoln**

The massive Pentagon, control & nerve center for the American military and its worldwide deployments. Photo courtesy of <u>VeteranLife.</u>

The Federal Reserve Building, meeting place for the Governors of the Federal Reserve and nerve center for the American Federal Reserve System. Photo courtesy of Freepik.

At the end of World War II, the Soviets moved their western borders, including Poland, 500 miles further west. They then moved the Polish western border 500 miles into defeated Germany. They sent troops and occupied Eastern European nations creating Soviet client states in Bulgaria, Rumania, Poland, East Germany, Hungary, Albania, and what was then Czechoslovakia. When citizens of Hungary, Poland, and Czechoslovakia demonstrated, wanting to establish more democratic governments, the Russian troops drove their tanks and brutally crushed the "rebellions," killing thousands of their client state citizens. When given their free choice, every one of those former client states have become democratic members of NATO.

World War II Memorial, Washington D.C. Photo courtesy of Adobe Stock.

Korean War Memorial. Photo courtesy of the Wall Street Journal.

Vietnam War Memorial, Photo courtesy of WorldStrides.

Arlington National Cemetery. Photo courtesy- the National Park Service. Burial ground for notable Americans and for members of the military.

Jefferson Memorial honoring the 3rd President of the United States and the architect of the American Declaration of Independence from Great Britain. Photo courtesy of Encyclopedia Britannica.

Franklin Delano and Eleanor Roosevelt at the FDR Memorial. Photos courtesy of Dreamstime.

President Roosevelt rescued the United States from the Great Depression by greatly expanding the size and mission of the federal government, thereby providing jobs for the unemployed. He presided over our involvement in World War II.

With German being the largest ethnic minority in the United States, it took years for Roosevelt to finally convince Americans of the necessity of countering the Nazi menace in Germany. He also worked wonders by convincing American industry to get behind the war effort and changed our industrial base from a peacetime commercial base to a warfare-based economy.

Eleanor advocated for women, for the civil rights of African & Asian Americans, for the rights of war refugees, for the rights of union laborers, for the power of labor unions, and for the ease of laborers joining the unions.

National Parks in the American Heartland

Arkansas, North Dakota, South Dakota, Tennessee, Kentucky, Missouri, Michigan, Minnesota, Indiana, West Virginia, Ohio

Great Smoky Mountains National Park, Tennessee

Mammoth Cave National Park, Kentucky

New River Gorge National Park, West Virginia

Cuyahoga Valley National Park, Ohio

Theodore Roosevelt National Park, North Dakota

Badlands National Park, South Dakota

Wind Cave National Park,
South Dakota

Indiana Dunes National
Park, Indiana

Hot Springs National Park,
Arkansas

Gateway Arch National Park, Missouri

Isle Royale National Park, Michigan

Voyageurs National Park, Minnesota

Chapter Seventeen
American Disaster Response
Helping Others in Need

"Rising sea levels, severe droughts, the melting of the polar caps, the more frequent and devastating natural disasters, all raise demand for humanitarian assistance and disaster relief."
— **Leon Panetta, former California Congressman, Secretary of Defense, CIA Director, White House Chief of Staff, and Director of the Office of Management & Budget. Currently head of the Panetta Institute of Public Policy and Distinguished Scholar for the California State University System. He serves as professor of public policy at Santa Clara University.**

One of the hallmarks of American history is that our people have always come to the aid of those suffering from natural disasters. Twice we came to the aid of European democracies to help them fight totalitarian states bent on world domination. We established the Peace Corp to help others. We created the Alliance For Progress (Allianzo Para Progresso) to help Latin America. Countless efforts, both public and private, are giving humanitarian assistance to African nations suffering from malnutrition, health emergencies, and the scarcity of water. Privately-funded organizations, similar-to the Bill and Melinda Gates Foundation, are busy committing resources to the solving of world problems and providing for world needs.

PROPOSED DISASTER RESPONSE TEAM:

All too often, American aid to those countries less fortunate takes the form of money spent. While often of utmost need, the projects, supplies, or equipment that money provides is then controlled by others. That has been the norm for disaster responses for many years, and it is needed, beneficial, and welcomed help to others.

There have been instances when American provided food and other supplies have been confiscated by lawless groups or misappropriated by foreign governments who then take credit for the provided aid.

In-person, face-to-face, human-to-human response is always welcomed and seeing the American flag on uniforms or the clothing of aid workers leaves no doubt as to who and what is providing the assistance. We are in a global struggle with China to influence others. While it should never be the primary reason to offer assistance to others, which is humanitarian aid, it can only help that global struggle with China if we do what we have always done best and that is showing our caring and altruistic side.

TOTALITARIAN versus DEMOCRATIC RESPONSES:

China, as Russia, is a totalitarian state. It is Communistic in name only. As is often said, "absolute control is absolute." If China wins in its global struggle with America, its dictatorial response is not likely to be what the United States has done in past struggles. We can never afford to lose and become subjects of a foreign power.

At the end of World War I, when we lost 116,000 dead soldiers, America did not ask for the "spoils of war" in its aftermath. We did not try to expand our territorial control. We only wanted to establish a League of Nations to offer an alternative to war. World War II was no different. We were primary in establishing the United Nations. The only territorial control we established was temporary and meant to help and not control. While we could easily have made the Ryukyu Islands, of which Okinawa is a part, an American state, we chose to give it back to Japan even after waging the greatest fight in American history to conquer.

After World War II, we gave the Philippines their independence on July 4, 1946. We gave the Pacific-island United Nations trust territories their choice of independence or a territorial status with America. Palau, the Caroline Islands, and the Marshall Island chose independence while the Northern Marianas chose to become a territory of the United States. We gave several Line Islands owned by America to the new island republic of Kiribati. We still support the independent states with infrastructure maintenance at America taxpayer expense. We have provided American Samoa citizens with a per-capita income of $11,522 in 2018, while that of the independent State of Samoa was $6,300 as of 2021. The difference is the result of American assistance.

At the end of World War II, the Soviet Union entered the war one week before the surrender of Japan in August, 1945. America had fought since December 7, 1941, yet we asked for no territories. Instead, we provided assistance for rebuilding and wrote the Japanese Constitution that provided for labor unions and gave the vote to women, both non-existent prior to the war. The Soviet Union, on the other hand, demanded and received from Japan in defeat, the Kurile Island chain, and Sakhalin Island. All that for one week of declared warfare in which it did not fight.

The postwar American response in Europe was to create the Marshall Plan, which was a multibillion-dollar commitment to the rebuilding of Europe, including sufficient funds devoted to the economic revival of Germany. In 1949, we created NATO, which included Belgium, Canada, Denmark, France, Iceland, Italy, Luxembourg, the Netherlands, Norway, Portugal, the United Kingdom, and the United States. This, the most successful military alliance in world history, now has 30 member states.

To help ensure Europe would never again engage us in war, the United States of America conceptualized a United States of Europe, which led to our creation of the European Common Market, also called the European Economic Community (EEC), consisting of France, West Germany, Italy, the Netherlands, Belgium, and Luxembourg. It has since morphed into the European Union which now consists of 27 countries.

THE DISASTER RESPONSE TEAM:

The idea for a disaster response team is that it be a standing asset capable of coming to the aid of any area or country suffering from a major natural disaster. It would also be of use in the event of an American disaster.

Rescue teams that react in response to earthquakes always state that the first 24-48 hours is critical for rescue. After that, it becomes more of an issue of the recovery of bodies. Quick response time is critical.

Much of the world is housed in old-world construction, which often consists of brick, rock or some type of mortar or cement. None of that material gives during the shock waves of a major earthquake. Japan and America, especially California, have advanced research into the effects of quakes and the types of structures best able to handle severe shaking. Wood-frame construction is the best because it gives. Each moderate to severe earthquake is evaluated from a construction standpoint and improvements are made to the California Building Code.

Most countries that have structures constructed of non-giving material, suffer severe damage and loss-of-life in even moderately-sized quakes. Thus, the need to aid many impacted countries. The proposal is to have a Disaster Response Team on standby alert to offer such assistance.

The need is to be able to move rescue personnel (capable of speaking the languages of those affected) and equipment to most world areas within a short enough time to be able to rescue. To do that, we would need to establish forward supply depots and forward encampments of needed personnel, with only enough personnel needed for an extremely quick response. Others could be flown in quickly. Prepositioning would be needed for equipment and most medical and other supplies.

For very quick responses, the U.S. Air Force could be employed for cargo transport using its C-5, C-17 and C-130 cargo aircraft. Aircraft could be utilized from the Civil Reserve Air Fleet (CRAF), under the control of Air Mobility Command. According to the Air Force, CRAF is "a unique and significant part of the nation's air mobility resources. Selected aircraft from United States' airlines (are) contractually committed." They are to "augment Department of Defense airlift requirements in emergencies when the need for airlift exceeds the capability of military aircraft. The CRAF has two main segments, with one being international, which is further divided into short range and log-range sections. Aircraft assignment depends on the nature of the requirements and the performance characteristics needed."

C-130 Cargo Plane flown by the USAF. Wikipedia photo.

Disasters are certainly classified as emergencies and the C-5s and C-17s are military long-range units that could easily be used for disaster response. These monster aircraft also have the capability of moving heavy construction equipment of the type that could be used in rescue. The C-130s have special capabilities to land on short, dirt runways and can be sent overseas with buddy tankers as well as the cargo jumbos.

Author's Note: *I flew as pilot aboard the Continental Airlines cargo version of the DC-10 on Central and South Pacific strictly cargo routes. It is classified as a jumbo and can carry an extraordinary weight for extended distances. Many cargo aircraft are equipped with in-flight refueling capability. The Air Force tanker version of the DC-10 is the KC-10 Extender, which can fly buddy with cargo aircraft and extend their range significantly. Non-stop flights around the world with tanker support have been flown.*

The massive C-17 flown by the USAF. Air Force photo.

The C-5M Super Galaxy. Business Insider photo.

Envisioned capability of the Disaster Team would be Equipment Ships, Personnel Ships, Helicopter Rescue Ships, and Hospital Ships. Currently, the US Navy had two operational Hospital Ships. If we are not engaged in war, those could be used to anchor near disaster locations and care for the injured.

Helicopter Rescue ships could be converted America Class or Wasp Class, diesel-powered aircraft carriers. Currently in the U.S. Navy fleet are nine Conventionally Powered (diesel) aircraft carriers. Most have been converted to helicopter carriers. Two are classified as LHA, which stands for Landing Helicopter Assault. Seven are LHDs, which means Landing Helicopter Dock. Docking ships can carry other types of equipment and can offload them directly to a dock.

Equipment (Cargo) Ships: The United States Navy currently has 12 Spearhead-class expeditionary fast transport ships (EPF). Another 16 are planned. Those ships can travel up to 45 knots (52 mph), which could quickly access overseas areas by traveling round-the-clock. They could also be located at forward operating bases.

Converted fixed-wing, Essex-Class, WWII helicopter aircraft carrier. Wikipedia photo

Spearhead Class expeditionary fast cargo transport ship. Defense Brief photo.

The United State Navy has a similar capability to that of the Air Force. They are called the United States Navy Reserve Fleets and there are six of them:

James River Reserve Fleet: Consists of six decommissioned warships anchored near Newport News in Virginia.

Suisun Bay Reserve Fleet: Located at Benicia, California. Unknown number of ships that include the *Glomar Explorer*, former Howard Hughes ship for submarine rescue.

Beaumont Reserve Fleet: Located near Beaumont, Texas, contains several transports ships.

Philadelphia Inactive Ship Maintenance Facility: Holds several dozen inactive warships, including the aircraft carriers *USS John F. Kennedy* (nuclear) and the *USS Ticonderoga* (conventional)

Bremerton (Washington) Inactive Maintenance Facility at Puget Sound Naval Shipyard: Holds two dozen decommissioned submarines, numerous supply (cargo) ships, amphibious transport dock ships, including the amphibious transport dock ship *Dubuque*. Bremerton houses seven decommissioned aircraft carriers, including the *Kitty Hawk*.

Pearl Harbor (Hawaii) Inactive Ship Maintenance Facility: Holds logistic support ships.

Humanitarian hospital ship Mercy. US Navy photo.

These ships could be recommissioned and retrofitted for disaster transport.

The idea of a Disaster Response should be considered by the American government. It would mark a first for the world and potentially be of enormous public relations benefit worldwide, in addition to the obvious benefit of saving lives, treating injured, and clearing the debris of tragedy.

"Democracy is an unfinished experiment." — **Walt Whitman**

Chapter Eighteen

National Reform: Territorial & Constitutional

Decentralization, Welcoming Others, and Rewriting the Constitution

"And if we cannot end now our differences, at least we can help make the world safe for diversity. For in the final analysis, our most basic common link is that we all inhabit this small planet. We all breathe the same air. We all cherish our children's future. And we are all mortal."
— **John F. Kennedy, Commencement address at American University in Washington DC, June 10, 1963.**

GEOPOLITICAL CONSIDERATIONS IN QUEST OF WORLD UNITY:
THE BRUTALITY of RUSSIA:

The United States is the world's best hope for peace through unity. After World War II, we sponsored unity in Europe through the creation of the Common Market. For nations of all the continents, we sponsored the United Nations and established its permanent headquarters in New York City. Later, we sponsored the creation of NATO. The current iterations of NATO and the European Union are the direct results of our efforts. Both have achieved peace through unity and the EU is creating wealth through working together.

Russia's invasion of Ukraine is a prime example of violent quests for territorial expansion. It is hard to figure how the Russians expect to endear themselves to Ukrainians and have Ukraine accept Russian domination, when Russia keeps pounding Ukraine with bombs, missiles, and artillery.

Their European legacy is a Europe united against them. Heretofore, Sweden and Finland have remained neutral, even during World War II. Russian aggression has convinced both Sweden and Finland to join NATO. The Baltic States of Lithuania, Estonia, and Latvia were once part of the Russian Soviet Union. The Russians so endeared themselves to those states that all three are now independent parts of NATO and their armies face the Russians across what once was a border between Russian states.

At the end of World War II, the Russian (Red) Army was in control of much of Eastern Europe after the surrender of Germany. The Russians created client states of seven occupied nations: German Democratic Republic (East Germany), Poland, Hungary, Romania, Bulgaria, Albania, and Czechoslovakia. They created the Warsaw Pact in opposition to NATO and the seven client states, under duress, were forced to join the Soviet Union. The Russians, under the guise of the Soviet Union, brutally suppressed rebellion in their "client" states of Hungary in 1956, Czechoslovakia in 1968, and Poland in 1981.

Today, Czechoslovakia has been split in two, with the Czech Republic and Slovakia both members of NATO. East Germany reunited with the rest of Germany, which was already a member of NATO. Albania, Poland, Hungary, Romania, and Bulgaria are all now members of NATO. Such is the lesson of being partners of Russia, either voluntarily or involuntarily. All are now united in opposition to the aggressive Russian Federation. Will other members of the Russian Federation follow in the footsteps of the former members of the Warsaw Pact?

In 1991, the former Soviet Union dissolved. It could not keep up the military costs of a sustained Cold War competition with the United States. It is instructive to learn of what has happened to the former Soviet states: The five countries of the so-called Stans have remained independent and several have provided airfields and encampments for American pilots and soldiers during the American wars in the Middle East. They are: Kazakhstan, Uzbekistan, Turkmenistan, Kyrgyzstan, and Tajikistan. Each country is Muslim and each is tribal. All are still suffering the effects of the invasion of the Mongolian Genghis Khan in the 1200s. None of them show signs of any willingness to reunite with Russia.

Armenia, another former member republic in the Soviet Union, is a largely Christian country and has resisted Russian efforts to enlist its support in Ukraine. Azerbaijan has openly opposed Russian's invasion of Ukraine. Lithuania, Estonia, and Latvia, as mentioned above, are independent and members of NATO. Moldova is also independent. Moldova is not a member of NATO, but are participating in the NATO peacekeeping force in Kosovo. They are members of the Euro-Atlantic Partnership Council, which works closely with NATO, and they host a NATO Liaison Office. Moldova does have an area on its east side, Transnistria, which has a common border with Ukraine and has a population consisting of roughly 50% Russian.

The remaining three Soviet Republics are Georgia, which Russia also invaded, and still partially occupies under Red Army control. Ukraine, and Belarus. Russia is named after the Rus tribe which has inhabited Russia for many centuries. Belarus is also named after the Rus tribe. The citizens of Belarus are also Russian and they are the only ally of Russia among all the other 14 prior Russian-allied Soviet Republics. One out of 14 is another example of why the Russian habits of heavy-handedness and brutal repression does not win friends. There is also ample evidence that Belarus is desperately trying to avoid involvement in the Ukrainian War, despite excessive Russian attempts to involve it militarily.

Belarus is also called White Russia and the name Belarus is also White Russia in the Russian language. In the Middle Ages, the vast area controlled by the Rus tribe was given many different names to describe regions. Those regions were the locations of the different subgroups of the Rus Tribe: Red Rus, Galician Rus, Black Rus, Great Rus, Little Rus, and White Rus. Thus, Belarus has many ties to "Mother Russia" which include common language, common ancestry, and common culture. With the financial support given Belarus over the years by Russia, it is surprising that it has managed to avoid entanglements to-date in what has become a protracted war in Ukraine. If Belarus eventually joins Russia in its brutal suppression of Ukraine, it will endanger the entire world as the NATO nation Poland is not likely to continue to stand by without outright intervention.

With its abortive invasion of Ukraine, Russia has placed itself on a rocky road to potential oblivion. Its naked aggression exposed it for being a tyrant and the reaction of the world will drive its economy to ruin or next-to-ruin. Even now, the economies of the American states of California ($3.56 trillion), Texas ($2.35 trillion) and New York ($2.03 trillion), each are superior to that of Russia ($1.78 trillion USD (2021). The International Monetary Fund (IMF) expects Russia's GDP to fall 3.4% in 2022 and 2.3% in 2023. With the current loss of Russia's European petroleum customers, those figures are undoubtedly very low.

The bedrock of Russian economic success has been its significant resources of oil and natural gas. Those fossil fuels are still critical for Europe, but are becoming less critical for it and the rest of our world as the movement away from fossil fuels and toward environmentally friendly sources of power accelerates. Russia's invasion created the European need to convert the source and types of its fuels more rapidly. Many NATO countries, such as Germany, are rushing construction of port facilities to handle natural gas loaded ships which will replace the needed pipeline-supplied oil and natural gas that Russia has formerly supplied. Russia's intentional withholding of needed fuels, in a blatantly stupid attempt to force Europe to accept its will, further alienated Europe, further accelerated Europe's move away from Russian fuel, and further united the wavering rest of Europe. Putin's attempts to bludgeon his way will eventually result in one of the most epic downfalls of a major power in world history. Either that or Russia, under Putin, will use nuclear weapons in Europe. Putin cannot continue to stay in power in the face of such monumental misjudgments.

In a way, Putin's exposure of the true Russia could possibly be a strange blessing for the environmental movement in that it has forced European governments, especially that of Germany, to reevaluate its dependence on fossil fuels.

It is trending that Russia will need Western Europe more than Western Europe needs Russia. It is almost probable, post Putin, that it will eventually become part of the EU to recover its economy and that it also will become part of NATO to protect it from an expansionistic China hungry for its own living room and resources. To qualify for memberships in the European Alliances, Russia would have to prove it has become a true democracy, which may be very difficult to achieve.

THE THREAT of CHINA:

The true world enemy of the United States is China, yet China incorporates the seeds of an eventual unity with the West. That unity will be a long time in coming and the years until it comes will be filled with uncertainty and tragedy. We can live together in peace but our path to peaceful unity must be marked by our standing fast against the Chinese quest for world domination. China is now recognizing its potential to become a world giant, both economically and militarily.

The true danger in trying to forge a working relationship with China to thwart its quest is that the Chinese People's Liberation Army is fiscally independent of the Chinese Central Government and the Chinese Communist Party. It has its own sources of revenue from its owned network of independent companies that are part of the burgeoning Chinese economy. The Army does not need to depend on the Central Government for revenue and often does not pay heed to the dictates of that government. Perhaps Xi Jinping, the President of the People's Republic of China, will attain enough power to actually, instead of nominally, place the Army under the authority of the Central

Government? He has been in power since 2013 and was recently reelected to a third term as General Secretary of the Chinese Communist Party. That election affirms that he will remain as chief of state for the foreseeable future.

Former American Secretary of State John Foster Dulles (1953-1959) proscribed a policy of containment of Communist Russia, which was very successful. America must once again formulate a policy of containment against another powerful Communistic state. The major areas of world conflict will be in the Pacific and in Africa. Only the conflict will probably not escalate to open warfare other than possibly on a small scale, but will instead consist of a battle for influence over those primary areas.

China is and has been working to extend its influence in Africa and has been marginally successful in its efforts. It has been providing needed development financing to several impoverished African nations. But its help is not given without cost. For Africa, dependence on China means giving up a measure of control. A great danger lies in the enormous natural resources of the huge African continent. The West cannot afford to allow China unlimited access.

Healthy competition between the United States and China over influence in Africa, if handled properly, could result in monies spent for mankind instead of spent in warfare, which only results in losses of life, property, and the squandering of resources. Our efforts in Africa should be with consideration for what is in the best interests of the Africans. Showing a true caring for others, in this case other nations, often results in returned benefits, the result of gained trust. That approach will have limited success in those countries under authoritative rule.

While influenced by a quest for power, our mutual efforts could fuel the needed progress necessary to allow the African nations to properly join the world economy as equal partners and, in the process, provide health and wealth to its citizens as well as improve its world trade. The United States started out as a Christian nation. We are still largely Christian. Isn't it Christian to strive for the benefit of others?

CHINA—a MERCANTILE COUNTRY:

When the author commented that China has within it the seeds to be allied with the United States, he was referring to the fact that China is a mercantile country just as the United States. Both countries have had to fight to throw off the oppression of colonial rule. What China has accomplished in a few short years to explode its economy is several steps above amazing.

For some reason, the author also feels that China's leaders are not nearly as brutal as Russian leaders, apart from Mao. They certainly are much smarter leaders than the Russian, who are not mercantile. China made the decision to keep its politics totalitarian, yet create a free-enterprise system within its economy. It has worked wonders. Russia opted to change both the politics and its economy at the same time and it has been a disaster. If not for their enormous fossil fuel resources, they would have been "deep sixed" long ago. While Chinese merchants have accepted the challenge of manufacturing in the 21st century, Russian merchants are severely impacted by the high incident rate of Russian alcoholism and its negative effect on productivity. .

The United States has been the leading industrial nation in the world since 1870. In other words, we have been for the last 153 years. Up until the prelude to World War II, around 1939, the Americans used their industrial muscle to provide for their citizens. Starting in 1939, we slowly transitioned to a wartime industrial base. Since then, we must deal with, as Eisenhower called it, the Military-Industrial Complex. We are still somewhat a warfare economy. It has helped us conquer would-be dictators and has helped to keep us out of major war for most of the post-WWII period.

China, at about $13 trillion GDP, is not threatening the US at over $21 trillion, but they are starting to get close. Evidence of the Chinese mercantile prowess abounds throughout Asia. Their population has spread throughout its neighbors and has been a catalyst for economic growth. Success sometimes has negative consequences, which was shown in 1965 when Indonesia reacted violently to the Chinese success within its borders. In a self-defeating move, the Suharto regime sponsored a genocide among its own Chinese population and killed so many that rivers were tainted with their blood and bodies floating downstream were common sights.

The mass killings were ostensibly against the Communists, but killed mainly Chinese. The killings were done by the Indonesian Army and reportedly eliminated up to a million Chinese. The killings adversely affected the Indonesian economy and, in some ways, it has never totally recovered. The following chart shows the extent of Chinese involvement in other Southeast Asian nations:

MERCANTILE CHINESE POPULATIONS of SOUTHEAST ASIAN COUNTRIES (2021-2022):

Country:	Population:	Chinese:	Percentage:
Vietnam	98,186,856	749,466	0.7%

Chinese are not well regarded by the Vietnamese people. There is enmity between both groups going back many hundreds of years.

Indonesia	276,400,000	2,833,000	1.0%

Chinese have difficulty assimilating into this Muslim country and are persecuted. Muslims account for 86.7% of the population, with an overwhelming number of them, Sunni Muslim.

Philippines	113,022,606	1,350,000	1.2%
Laos	7,535,505	150,710	2.0%
Myanmar	54,179,306	1,626,000	3.0%
Cambodia	16,832,327	700,000	4.2%
Thailand	70,213,017	7,100,000	10.1%

Up to 14% of Thai blood is Chinese who have intermarried and assimilated with the Thai and consider themselves Thai. Chinese assimilate easier in Buddhist countries, such as Thailand, than in Islamic areas like Indonesia. The Thai, being progressive, work well with the ethnic Chinese.

Brunei	447,350	46.077	10.3%

Brunei is a repressive monarchy located on the Malaysian island of Borneo.

Malaysia	32,700,000	7,455,600	22.8%

Malaysia is a predominantly Muslim country with 63% of its population practicing Muslims. It is the official religion in Malaysia. Chinese have a difficult time assimilating into Muslim cultures, but have managed to help create a vibrant small business merchant's economy here.

Country:	Population:	Chinese:	Percentage:
Singapore	5,640,000	4,280,000	75.9%

> *The vibrant economy of Singapore is a testament to the influence and productivity of its Chinese mercantile population. Singapore and Hong Kong, other than Taiwan, are the most predominately Chinese populations outside of mainland China. Before its political reintegration into mainland China, Hong Kong was an economic powerhouse like that of Singapore, with a like-sized population.*

BENEFICIAL TERRITORIAL EXPANSION:

When the idea of territorial expansion is discussed, it usually brings up thoughts of one nation fighting against another to take over that nation's territory. American peaceful territorial expansion could and should be considered a national goal and a needed item of national security. Instead of expansion through military conquests or the threat of conquest, our expansion should be one of a welcoming offer to nations that they could evaluate the pros and cons of joining our union and then making their independent choice of whether they would want to amalgamate into a joint union, as have all our American states.

Any offer should be a blanket offer and any interested nation should be evaluated by the United States before acceptance. The entire idea, other than the military imperatives mentioned here, is with the eventual unity of more and more nations. The goal is the elimination of war and the objective is unity to eliminate that threat.

PACIFICA, an IDEA with PROMISE:

The threat posed by China poses a second area of conflict: that of the Pacific islands. The populations of the Pacific island nations have been previously discussed. Collectively, they have few people and even fewer natural resources. What they do have are vital locations in the Pacific.

China now has what is widely considered the second most powerful navy in the world. Without the preponderance of American nuclear submarines and massive nuclear aircraft carriers, the People's Liberation Navy would be first. Their fleet is much newer and more modern than that of the United States. While the Chinese ships themselves are more modern, the United States still possesses better onboard electronics and weapons systems.

Current Pentagon planning has cargo and both tactical and strategic bomber capability able to overfly vast distances with the advantage of in-flight refueling. However, even though American cargo aircraft are huge in comparison to past cargo planes, maritime transport of equipment and supplies is still far superior to airborne. While cargo ships do not travel at anything but a probable one-tenth of the speed of cargo aircraft, the differences in the amount of cargo carried is huge. We must be able to have open shipping lanes for that necessary cargo transport as well as the equally necessary and important transport of soldiers. America has a need to quickly transport large army formations supported by heavy tanks, howitzers, armored personnel carriers, Apache helicopters, and other needed weapons of war. We need that shipping.

The Pacific covers one-third of the surface of our planet. That is a lot of surface to cover with our needed shipping. Any future military conflict with China will occur in the Pacific and possibly Africa. The Korean War (1950-1953) saw American troops fighting China. Korea sits on the western edge of the Pacific. The Vietnam War saw America fighting China in the air and on the ground in a nation that borders the South China Sea, an extension of the Pacific.

Recent Chinese warlike advances onto both natural and man-made islands in the South China Sea are evidence of their appreciation of what island fortresses have to offer. Since World War II, America and its Pacific allies, France, New Zealand, Japan, Taiwan, Philippines, the United Kingdom, and Australia have exerted control and influence over the entire Pacific and especially the vitally important Western Pacific.

A MILITARY NEED:

Shipping is helped with ports along its routes. Island fortresses provide warehousing that will shorten the distance that some cargo may need to be transported to areas of conflict or potential conflict in the Pacific. Consider warfare in the Western Pacific: Needed supplies will need to be transported by ship from America, with the closest American islands: Guam, Tinian, Saipan, the Hawaiian Islands, and the Japanese island of Okinawa within easy reach of areas of potential conflict. Eventually our bastion in Okinawa will need to be ceded to Japan in fact as well as legally. Okinawa is our location for the storage of nuclear weapons for the Western Pacific as well as holding many assets of our Army, Navy, Air Force and Marines. It is by far the largest concentration of American military might west of Hawaii in the Pacific. It will need to be replaced.

Guam is a candidate, but Guam is only 212 square miles large and already has a significant military presence. The twin islands of Saipan/Tinian in the Northern Marianas are only 85.41 square miles large, while Okinawa is 463 square miles. We will need additional islands to properly support a future war with China. We will need additional islands for ports to house needed naval warships. Ulithi Atoll in the Caroline Islands housed, at one time, up to 722 American warships ships prior to the WWII battle of Okinawa. Ulithi is in danger of being swallowed by rising seas, but does offer a possible anchorage if built up to levels out of reach of rising seas.

If we don't create an island fortress in the North and Central Pacific, we may be facing a China that has established the same islands as military strongholds that are allied with China and have provided China with military airfields, supply depots, army camps, and naval ports.

A HUMANITARIAN NEED:

The chart in Chapter 13 showing the populations of many of the Pacific island groups lists a total of only 2.86 million inhabitants of all the island groups surveyed. Those groups represent almost all the non-aligned island republics. Many islands belong to and are territories of established nations: New Zealand has many island territories and was recently in control of Samoa and established good relations with that independent nation. It also owns the large Cook Islands, plus many individual islands. Australia owns Lord Howe and Norfolk Islands as well as the islands in the Coral Sea, plus several in the Indian Ocean.

Japan owns outer islands and the Eastern Pacific finds ownership with Chile, Ecuador, Columbia,

Costa Rica, Mexico, as well as the UK and France. France is the largest owner of Pacific islands which attests to its extensive voyages of European discovery. The largest island holding by France is French Polynesia, consisting of the Society Islands, the Austral Islands, the Marquesas Islands, and the Tuamotu Archipelago. France also has several islands in the Eastern Pacific plus the large New Caledonia in the west. France also owns Wallis and Futuna Islands, just west of Samoa, which is west of American Samoa.

Many of those islands are atolls which are very low-lying and thus subject to being submerged by rising seas. Their populations need help. America should supply that assistance and planning. Help that is needed include transport from the islands and a destination. By virtue of its military capabilities, America is better suited than any nation to move those populations. Providing that it should be a given if welcomed.

The evacuations have just begun. The future promises to have an increasing number of islands threatened and requiring that needed help. The question is where the island populations could be moved. Due to lifestyle, it might be better to relocate islanders to other islands? However, if the American experience with American Samoa is any indication, islanders may be willing to locate elsewhere?

The economic opportunities for Samoans in America is considered far greater than those in American Samoa. The only industry in American Samoa, other than individual fishing, is a fish cannery located on Tutuila, the capitol island. They have been emigrating to the United States in increasing numbers. Any glimpse of the roster of players on a great many American university football teams will show many are Polynesian. A few of those Polynesians are Hawaiian, but almost all are considered Samoan. The Samoans are the biggest race on earth with consideration of individual size. For takeoff on a powerful DC-10 with a full load of Samoans, pilots would add another 2,000 feet onto the takeoff charts for normal loads.

The entire population of American Samoa is 55,103. The estimated population of Samoans living in the Unites States is 200,000, including 37,453 in Hawaii. However, that is not the entire story. The only true Polynesians are from Samoa, American Samoa, and Tonga. It is very common that Tongans and Samoans from Samoa proper move to American Samoa and thus pass themselves off as Americans. Samoa has 200,144 people and Tonga consists of 106,759. Many of the Polynesian-Americans originated in either Tonga or the former Western Samoa, neither belonging to the United States. The lesson learned is that at least three island groups have sizable populations with many that preferred to move to the United States instead of staying on their paradise islands in the Pacific.

Another lesson learned is that it is costly for the US to make massive investments, as we did on Okinawa, only having to give those investments up to another entity. The suggestion for the establishment of the American territory of Pacifica involves offers to impacted islands to move their threatened populations and allow them to move anywhere in the United States, including our Pacific island territories and states.

Invitations to join in our Union could include a common defense and government provided infrastructure provision and maintenance. Of all the island nations that are unaligned, Fiji, consisting of 305 islands, would probably qualify for immediate statehood. With the inclusion of Guam, the

Northern Marianas, and American Samoa with those island groups that might desire to join, the ability to attain statehood status might occur rather quickly.

In any event, the humanitarian need is enough for the US to provide the necessary aid so that island residents could be comfortably relocated. If we can bring those islands under the umbrella of American military protection and be able to use those locations in common defense, all the better. Currently, the Marshall Islands and the Carolines are under our umbrella of protection. The Philippines are also under our protection as affirmed by recent treaty.

The Chinese have been reinforcing South China Sea atolls so that the elevation is safely above any threat of sea-level rise. On those man-made islands, they have been placing airfields, naval port facilities and they have filled the islands with soldiers, sailors, airmen and deadly surface-to-air missiles. The threat is real and the concept of Pacifica should be considered.

NEEDED INCOME REDISTRIBUTION:

American wealth is becoming more and more concentrated. Many evaluators have long considered that the definition of our American upper class includes the top 10% of holders of wealth. The chart below show just how concentrated it has become. The chart shows the top wealth groups, the number of Americans within that group and the wealth share as a percentage of total wealth share in the entire United States:

Wealth Group:	# of Americans:	Wealth Share:
Top 0.1%	238,700	15.7%
Average net worth of $50 million; Average annual wage of $3.21 million		
Top 1%	2,386,600	33.7%
Average net worth of $11,099,166; Average annual wage of $823,763		
Top 10%	232,866,300	68.6%
Average net worth of $854,900; Average annual wage of $173,176		

The chart above shows that the bottom 90% of Americans only hold a wealth share of 31.4%. That is unacceptable and the trend is toward a further concentration of wealth. If Americans feel that the system is fair, they have always supported the system. If, on the other hand, wealth is unfairly distributed and that their portion of wealth is continually eroding, no matter how hard they work or how ingenious they create, then the unity will be broken.

If the author was in that top 1%, he would be alarmed by the above figures. America may not endure for long the disparity that currently exists. Either the 99% will change the distribution through Congress or the 99% will change it through other means. The problem is that Congress is so much under the control of the top 1% as to make any evolutionary change very difficult. The alternative to evolutionary change, which is the hallmark of truly democratic societies, is of course revolutionary change.

There are more important values than the value of money. America should reward the creation of money and the beneficial redistribution of money, never for the mere existence of money. Our estate taxes, as currently written, are of immense benefit to those families who have accrued great wealth. Those laws should be changed. While there are other forms of wealth redistribution, estate taxes are legal and effective. Too many of the super wealthy class use wealth that was previously created by ancestors. Let them use their purported ingenuity at creating wealth and our society should confiscate most of accumulated wealth at the death of the creator.

Author's Note: *My next-door neighbor was born and raised in Rhodesia. His family had lived for many generations in Rhodesia, having originally emigrated from England. He owned a 3,000-acre farm in Zimbabwe, which is the name of the former Southern Rhodesia. Land redistribution in Zimbabwe took the form of the black taking of white properties without any form of compensation. He was forced to walk away from his ancestral farm without anything other than the clothes on his body and whatever investments he was able to sequester overseas. That is what unjust and illegal re-distribution looks like. However, illegal is just a concept. In the former Southern Rhodesia, the confiscation of white land was not illegal, just immoral.*

"Unity is strength, division is weakness." — **Swahili Proverb**

THE NEED for a SECOND CONSTITUTIONAL CONVENTION:

"For the strength of the Pack is the Wolf, and the strength of the Wolf is the Pack."
— **Rudyard Kipling**

"Even the weak become strong when they are united." — **Friedrich von Schiller**

To remain united in purpose as well as fact, we need to do some changing. This document includes many suggestions. Far too many than can be accomplished in any form short of a second constitutional convention. Strong consideration by our government should be given to such a conclave.

The author has a suggestion on a possible process and structure for such a convention:

The first step should be to select participating members in an Advisory Council. That process could be conducted by the President selecting five qualified candidates. One of those selected by the President would be the presiding officer for the convention. The Chief Justice of the Supreme Court could select four and each house of Congress could select three from among their members. Three of the five members selected by the president should not be members of government. Two of the four selected by the Chief Justice should not be members of the Supreme Court. The resulting group would consist of 15 qualified delegates. The method for each selection should be left up to the governmental branch selecting, with a suggestion that listings of qualified candidates be selected by appointed committees with the power to vest and to meet with candidates.

The Advisory Council would then be tasked to select the Constitutional Convention Delegates and the agenda of the convention. The convention delegates would number 101 and include the 15 members of the Advisory Council. The Council would have six months to prepare the delegate listing and the convention agenda items to discuss. Additionally, the Advisory Council would prepare rules for guiding the convention. Some of the selected delegates should come from academia, plus knowledgeable men and women from different disciplines that would have relevance to discussions. Constitutional scholars should be included. No more than fifty of the 101 delegates should be lawyers, with a definition of what constitutes a lawyer decided by the Council.

The actual Constitutional Convention would convene in Philadelphia three months after the termination of the time allotted to the Advisory Council. They would have to sign a pledge to adhere to the rules during any debate and during the time when the convention was in session. There should be no time limit on any debate and the presiding officer should have authority to conduct each debate in a manner that is fair and equitable for all delegates. Rules for debate termination should be decided by the delegates.

The convention should have the right to include additional items to debate and include in a future constitution. The time and manner of conclusion of the convention should be up to a vote of the delegates but in no case should it be less than six months from the start date of the convention.

The above items are just a suggested "first draft," Elected officials of government should decide the process, rules, and structure. Ideas are assets and any convention structure should incorporate processes that incorporate as many beneficial ideas as possible

FURTHER SUGGESTIONS:

Suggested items to discuss are listed throughout this book. An additional suggestion regards trying to avoid the excesses and misrepresentations of the media. That is going to be extremely difficult as we cannot dictate to the media on what they state or print. Additional problems exist due to the scattered nature of our current media with so many voices present on the internet.

However, we need to legislate curriculum in our schools. Not only should we require several additional courses to qualify for a degree in journalism, we should require those courses for any degree given. In the case of the media, degree requirements should include courses on history, geography, ethics, morals, and journalistic responsibilities. Emphasis should be on the requirement that journalists and all reporters should not make news, but only report on the actual news and not suggestive reporting that changes the nature of the news. As mentioned, that might not be possible and would be extremely difficult to provide. It would also be beneficial for journalists to be conversant in geography, American and world history.

In the introduction to this book, the need for the reestablishment of trust is mentioned. A recommitment of reporters to responsible journalism and professional conduct would be helpful. This discussion in no way is a blanket condemnation of the journalistic profession that has so many dedicated and professional members.

DECENTRALIZATION:

Just as stronger penalties for crimes coupled with much higher conviction rates should lower crime rates, so should decentralization of much of central government, lower costs and shift authority and responsibility to state and local governments.

One of several needlessly costly efforts by government is the duplication of effort. Consider environmental regulatory authority: City, county, state, and federal agencies make rules and oversee some of the same conditions and situations. While some rules and regulations are not duplicated, many are and they pose a nightmare for affected businesses. A convention could write constitutional rules that mandate non-duplication, which would have the effect of lowering overall governmental agency costs. The problem with our present setup is that agency employees will fight to keep their jobs even though keeping them creates duplication.

Decentralization would have the effect of transferring authority and responsibility from federal to state, and then by state to county or city as needed. To make the individual states perform in a manner common to other states, laws could and should be enacted to ensure a unified compliance.

Congress would then still have the authority to control national issues, but the staff handling of the issues could then be conducted at state level.

CONGRESS- THE POLITICAL CLASS:
TERM LIMITS & LONGER TERMS:

With the continual expansion of what is considered the campaign season, the two-year terms for all congressmen and women leaves less and less time devoted to the people's business and more and more spent on the representative's business. Thought should be given to extending Congressional Representatives terms from two years to four and those of senators from six to eight. Term limits should be installed giving 16-year-limits for all members of Congress. That would limit senators to two terms and representatives to four. That would allow a congressman to serve four terms and then run for the Senate for an additional two terms, for a collective term of 32 years in both houses of Congress.

PART-TIME CONGRESS:

It used to be that members of Congress were part-time and had full-time jobs back in their districts. They were citizen representatives instead of full-time politicians like we have today. Consideration should be discussed on this subject. The following listing shows how many state legislatures currently have part-time legislatures.

FULL vs. PART-TIME STATE LEGISLATURES:

According to the National Conference of State Legislatures (7-28-2021), the following is the current status of the various state legislatures:

States with legislatures that are **full-time,** well-paid and with large or intermediate sized staffs: Average time on job 84%, Compensation $82,358, Total Staff 1,250.

Legislatures in this category "require the most time of legislators, usually 80% or more of a full-time job. Legislators are paid enough to make a living without requiring outside income. They generally spend more time on the job because their sessions are longer and they have large districts and the states are usually with large populations. These legislators are very similar to Congress."

California, New York, Pennsylvania, Michigan, Alaska, Hawaii, Illinois, Massachusetts, Ohio, and Wisconsin.

Part-time with low pay and intermediate sized staffs: Average time on job 74%, Compensation $41,110, Total Staff 469.

Legislators in this category "typically say that they spend more than two-thirds of a full- time job being legislators. Pay is usually not enough to allow a living without having other sources of income. States are usually in the middle of the population range."

Alabama, Arizona, Arkansas, Colorado, Connecticut, Delaware, Florida, Georgia, Indiana, Iowa, Kentucky, Louisiana, Maryland, Minnesota, Missouri, Nebraska, Nevada, New Jersey, North Carolina, Oklahoma, Oregon, South Carolina, Tennessee, Texas, Virginia, Washington

Part time with low pay and small staffs: Time on job 57%, Compensation $18,449, Total Staff 160.

Idaho, Utah, New Mexico, Kansas, Mississippi, West Virginia, Maine, Montana, North and South Dakota, Wyoming

These figures are significant. Fully 80% of states have part-time legislatures. Full-time legislatures, such as our own Congress, have developed a sort of "New Political Class" that is less beholden to the people. Gerrymandering makes representatives even less beholden. The new Political Class even considers itself above those that it purportedly represents. Consider this: Congress, who votes on our Social Security and Medicare and has members who have even voiced their elimination, is not even tied into the Social Security and Medicare Systems. They vote on both but they have their own separate health and retirement systems. They also have provided for themselves a lifetime pension after the completion of only one term in Congress. Think of that: a pension for life after working for two years. Those are not examples of a representation of their constituents. Instead, it is a blatant representation of themselves.

The need for our Congressmen and women to solicit donations on an almost non-stop basis, not only deprives our country of their full-time devotion to their duties, but also makes them beholden to their donors at the expense of their constituents. It goes beyond that. The need for money to win re-election requires candidates to request money from their party. That additionally makes the candidate beholden to the mainly unelected "power brokers" of their respective parties. The result is that there is little "beholden" left for those that elected them.

Former Louisiana Republican Governor Bobbie Jindal was a respected representative of his people. He was elected as the Chairman of the Republican Governor's Association. Governor Jindal wrote a book titled: *Leadership in Crisis* (Regnery, 2010). The following is excerpted from his book: "Americans don't have a high opinion of Congress right now. Polls show that only 21% of Americans believe Congress is doing a good job." That was written in 2010, but the 21% approval has held through 2021. "When it comes to ethics and morality, studies show Americans rank congressmen

213

barely above a car salesman, an unfair comparison, at least most states have lemon laws to protect you from dishonest car salesmen.

Believing they are unpopular because Americans 'just don't understand the great job they're doing, congressmen send out more letters, fight for more pork and earmarks, and make more TV appearances'. But the American people dislike congressmen precisely because they know what they are doing—they are spending our country into oblivion. Congress has lost touch with the people they are supposed to serve."

When those whom Americans elect to Congress can just sit in Washington and not regularly return to their districts, they lose touch. They then become part of the ruling Political Class that is beholden only to themselves and the rest of their class, which includes their party manipulators and their donors. Continuing with excerpts from Jindal's book:

"Our country is in terrible financial shape, as we compile a massive debt for our children and grandchildren to pay. Right now, each American "owes" $45,000 on the national debt, and that figure is set to rise much higher. What we need to do is institute a series of radical changes that I would call the "Saving Our Grandchildren's Inheritance" package.

We start by restructuring Congress and there are several vital steps America needs to take: The first: make being a congressman a part-time job. We used to pay farmers not to grow crops so maybe we should pay members of congress not to pass laws. It would fundamentally change Washington, forcing congressmen to spend much more time back in their districts interacting with regular people. It would also encourage greater independence by young members of Congress. Most crucially, under a part-time Congress, congressmen would no longer regard politics as their career.

Plenty of solid research shows Congress feels the need to do something when it is in session. Looking at Congress over a 25-period, Professors Mwangi Kimenyi and Robert D. Tollison, discovered the more time Congress spends in session, the longer and more complex laws become, and the more money Congress spends.

We also need a series of what I would call Fiscal Sanity initiatives. For example:

(1)   We need a federal balanced budget (constitutional) amendment. Most states already must abide by these limits, and Washington should do the same.

(2)   We should adopt a constitutional amendment to require a supermajority in Congress to raise taxes, along with a pay-as-you-go rule to help enforce a balanced budget amendment.

(3)   A supermajority should also be required for government spending that exceeds historical norm as a percentage of GDP.

Serving in Congress used to be just that--an act of service, not a financially lucrative ground for lobbyists." It is interesting that Jindal mentions service. Does the reader remember when gas stations used to be called service stations? They no longer service. The same is with Congress. We used to call serving in Congress as governmental service. No longer. Does the reader consider that his or her Congressman or woman is serving them?

We still refer to service in the military as military service. We seem to consider that our military people still serve us. The difference is stark. Refer to the Gallup Poll results printed in another chapter. The difference in confidence in and respect for both is stark.

"Our Founding Fathers envisioned that being a member of Congress would be a part-time job. Pennsylvania's state constitution even had a provision calling for members of the Legislature to 'have some profession, calling, trade, or farm, whereby he may honestly subsist.' Otherwise, they feared legislators would come to rely on politics as a career, and they would be unable to 'preserve (their) independence.' Back then, farmers would literally leave their fields and go to legislate in our nation's capital.

For almost 200 years, being in Congress meant holding down another job. As recently as the 1950s, Congress was still largely a part-time institution. Aside from extraordinary times, such as World War II, members arrived in Washington by train in January and left in the summer. Granted, a part-time Congress would face its own ethical issues. How can we avoid conflicts of interest when people simultaneously run a business and pass laws? How can we prevent businesses from hiring congressmen just for the sake of influence? The answer is simple: full disclosure. Let the voters know everything, and they can then render their judgment at election time."

CONCLUSION—MEMORABLE QUOTES:

In the author's words: *"When viewing the Republicans, I have noticed that they often display the American flag. Independent voters and Democrats also proudly honor the flag.*

Long ago, when participating in the Vietnam War, an airman from Tarzana, California came to my fighter aircraft as I was about to climb into my cockpit for a Mig Cover mission to the North. He gave me a California flag and asked me to fly with it into combat. One month later, the base gave me an American flag to lay on my lap as I again ventured North. That American flag is now in my home, packaged inside its original plastic cover. I cherish that flag and all it represents. When most Americans cherish our flag, there is hope."

The following quote is famous and oft-repeated. It is an important reminder that all citizens have an obligation to our community, both national and local. Obligations often require sacrifices. The author asks the reader to please consider what he or she may do to help the difficult process of getting America back on track to once again be a beacon of hope to many and a force to stand against those who would enslave the world's people.

"Ask not what your country can do for you...ask what you can do for your country."
— **President John F. Kennedy** (1961- 1963) in his Inaugural Address, January 20, 1961

"Cautious, careful people, always casting about to preserve their reputations...
can never effect a reform." — **Susan B. Anthony,** Champion of women's suffrage, temperance, abolition of slavery, the rights of labor, and equal pay for equal work.

"It is time to fundamentally change the way that we do business in Washington. To help build a new foundation for the 21st century, we need to reform our government so that it is more efficient, more transparent, and more creative. That will demand new thinking and a new sense of responsibility for every dollar that is spent." — **President Barack Obama** (2009-2017)

President Calvin Coolidge (1923-1929) suggested the below quote. His important message is placed in parchment on the walls of many American homes:

"Nothing in the world can take the place of persistence. Talent will not; nothing is more common than unsuccessful men with talent. Genius will not; unrewarded genius is almost a proverb. Education will not; the world is full of educated derelicts.
Persistence and determination alone are omnipotent."

America needs a Second Constitutional Convention to right the many wrongs that have marred our governance and negatively affected who and what we are as a people. We need a national rebirth. It will take commitment from all of us. It will take determination from all of us. If we are determined and persist in that determination, we can accomplish wonders.

Visions of a Just & Reformed Union
Supporting Documents Section

Bibliography

BOOKS, MAGAZINES, NEWSLETTERS, NEWSPAPERS, & DICTIONARIES:

"World Languages and Cultures Courses Descriptions".... Los Angeles Unified School District

"Estimated Student Enrollment (in)
        LA Unified Boundaries?" .... Los Angeles Unified School District

Definition of "Golden Goose"..............................Merriam-Webster Dictionary

"Ethics and Virtue" ....Santa Clara University

"Future Humans: Inside the Science of Our Continuing Evolution"
        Scott Solomon - 2016 .... aeon Newsletter

"The Future is Mixed-Race"..
        Scott Solomon .... aeon Newsletter

"What Jefferson Said" .... The New Republic

"The Genetic Ancestry of African Americans"
        The National Center for Biotechnology Information,
        part of the NIH. January 8, 2015 .... NIH - National Library of Medicine

"Genetic Study Reveals Surprising Ancestry of Many Americans"
        Lizzie Wade, December 18, 2014 ....Science

Definition of "Gerrymandering" .... Oxford Dictionary

"George Washington: On Religion and Government"
        Thomas V. DiBacco, American University historian
        - September 17, 1984 .... Christian Science Monitor

"Americans Divided on how the Supreme Court Should Interpret the Constitution"
        Jocelyn Kiley, July 31, 2014 ....

"Founders Spoke Out on Church/State"
        Rebecca R. Bibbs, July 22, 2017........................... The Herald Bulletin

"List of 63 National Parks by State"
        Julia Jennings - updated September 14, 2022.............. Well Planned Journey

"Constitutional Revisionism" Harvard Civil Rights - Civil Liberties
        W. Pengine, October 28, 2010......................... Harvard Law Review

"Comparing Practices of U.S. and Japanese Companies"
        James R. Martin, PhD .... Management and Accounting Web

"US Total Factor Productivity Growth; 1948-2017" ....Research and Science

"The Largest National Parks in the World"............................ Safaris Africana

"The 10 Most Important Moral Values"...................... Invictus International School

"Californio to American: A Study of Cultural Change" .... National Park Service

"Los Angeles Area Television Stations" .... Los Angeles Almanac

"Facts on US Immigrants, 2018"................................Pew Research Center

"Evolution of Pneumatic Tube Transportation" .... Tomorrow's World Today.com

"On Campaign Finance Reform: The Root of All Evil is Deeply Rooted"
    Daniel Hays Lowenstein, 1989 . . . . Hofstra Law Review
"Lorraine American Cemetery" . . . . American Battle Monuments Commission
"DARPA Looks to Microbes to Process Rare Earth Elements"
    C. Todd Lopez, DOD News . . . . .US Department of Defense
"California Business Exits Soared in 2021, and There is No End in Sight" . . . . . Hoover Institute
"19 Corporations & Businesses Fleeing California for Texas" . . . . Concordia University
"Taxes in California for Small Business: The Basics" . . . . Investopedia
"Special Taxes and Fees" . . . . California Department of Tax and Fee Administration
"Discretionary Spending Options" . . . . Congressional Budget Office
"Fuel Cells" . . . . US Department of Energy
"How Do We Use Rare Earth Elements" . . . . American Geosciences Institute
"What is the Judiciary Sentencing Information Platform?" . . . . U.S. Sentencing Commission
"Nonrenewable Resources" . . . . National Geographic Society
"Sources of Energy" . . . . US Energy Information Admin.
"Discretionary Spending Options" . . . . Congressional Budget Office
"Hydrogen Fuel Cell Technology" . . . . US Department of Energy
"Articles of Confederation" . . . . .National Archives
"What were the Drawbacks of the Articles of Confederation" . . . . .National Archives
"What Have Anaheim Investigators Found in the City Hall Corruption Probe?"
    Spencer Custodio, October 24, 2022 . . . . Voice of Orange County
"Committees" . . . . California State Senate
"Confidence in Institutions" . . . . Gallup
"Establishing a Federal Republic" . . . . Thomas Jefferson
"What is Monetary Policy" . . . . .The Economic Times
"Who Owns the Federal Reserve Banks?" . . . . Federal Reserve Bank of St. Louis
"Is the Federal Reserve a Privately Owned Corporation?" . . . Fed Reserve Bank of San Francisco
"The Constitution of the United States" . . . . .National Archives
"The Warsaw Treaty Organization" . . . . Office of the Historian of the US
"NATO Relations with the Republic of Moldova" . . . . North Atlantic Treaty Organization
"Top Wealth in America: New Estimates and
    Implications for taxing the Rich" . . . . Princeton Economics
"Are Texas Republicans Serious About Secession"
    Peter Holley, November 2022 . . . . Policy and Politics
"Prehistoric DNA Reveals Two Groups Migrated to the U.K. After the Last Ice Age"
    Will Sullivan, November 2, 2022 . . . . .Smart News
"The Mueller Report"
    Scribner . . . . .The Washington Post
"The First All-electric Community Powered by a Solar and Battery Microgrid Launches
    in California" - Peter Johnson, November 2, 2022 . . . . www.elektrek.com

BIBLIOGRAPHY

"First Offshore Wind Power Sites Auctioned Off California's Coast"
Elizabeth Weise.. Ventura County Star

INTERNET / WORLDWIDE WEB:

"The History of "My Country, Right or Wrong!" .... www.ThoughtCo.com

"Fuel Cell Electric Vehicle (FCEV)".................... www.tech.hyundaimotorgroup.com

"House of Representatives" .... www.senate.gov

"Purebred Dogs May Face Health Challenges"..................... https://caes.ucdavis.edu

"Can You Really See Russia from Alaska?" ....https://slate.com

"Ancient DNA Puts a Face on the Mysterious Denisovans" ....www.science.org

"Multiple Lines of Mysterious Ancient Humans Interbred with Us".... nationalgeographic.com

"Oaths of Justices and Judges"..............Legal Information Institute, www.law.cornell.edu

"Immigrants in California" .... www.ppic.com

"Treaty of Paris" ....www.archives.gov

"The Value of Goal Setting"...............................www.findyouranswers.com

"Bill of Rights".. www.billofrightsinstitute.org

"GDP Ranked by Country - 2022" ....www.worldpopulationreview.com

"U.S. States Ranked by Population - 2022" ....www.worldpopulationreview.com

"Bankruptcy - United States Courts" .... www.uscourts.gov

"The Judicial Branch" .... www.whitehouse.gov

"Independence and Accountability" .... www.lawfareblog.com

"Small Claims Court" ....California Department of Consumer Affairs, www.dca.ca.gov

"Small Claims General Information" ....Superior Court of California, www.sb-court.org

"How Courts Work" .... www.courts.ca.gov

"2012 Republican Party Platform" ....www.presidency.ucsb.edu

"Bible Verses About Tolerance"............................. www.openbible.info.com

"Factory Worker Salary in Japan............... Economic Research Institute, www.erieri.com

"Chief Executive Officer Salaries in America" .... www.salary.com

"Chief Executive Officer Salaries in Japan"
Abby Budiman, August 20, 2020 .... www.salary.com

"Health of Black or African-America non-Hispanic Population"
Center for Disease Control - Health Statistics ....www.cdc.gov

"Declaration of Independence"............................... www.bensguide.gpo.gov

"Jefferson's Quotes"...www.famguardian.org

"Health of White non-Hispanic Population"
Center for Disease Control - Health Statistics...................www.cdc.gov

"Health of Asian or Pacific Islander Population
Center for Disease Control - Health Statistics...................www.cdc.gov

"Key Findings about U.S. Immigrants" .... www.pewresearch.org

"White Deaths Exceed Births in a Majority of U.S. States," Applied Population Laboratory
　　　Rogelio Saenz and Kenneth M. Johnson.....................www.apl.wisc.edu
"The Battle of San Pasqual"
　　　California Department of Parks and Recreation...................www.ca.gov
"The Zeppelin Aircraft"...www.britannica.com
"Hydrogen Vehicle Overview".......................................www.greencars.com
"Hydrogen Storage"...www.energy.gov
"Cryogenic Hydrogen - An Overview"..........................www.sciencedirect.com
"The History of Transportation"..................................www.twinkl.com
"Was America's Aurora Hypersonic Aircraft Real?"...................www.sandboxx.us
"How Does the Federal Reserve Affect Inflation"
　　　Board of Governors of the Federal Reserve System.......www.federalreserve.gov
"Edwards History"...www.edwards.af.mil
"Population of Counties in California"...................www.worldpopulationreview.com
"System Map - BART"...www.bart.gov
"Where Will BART take us 50 years from now?"....................www.sfchronicle.com
"China High Speed Railway Network"...........................www.travelchinguide.com
"California Budget: Big surplus, big differences".....................www.calmatters.org
"Peace Corp During COVID".......................................www.peacecorps.gov
"Getting Big Money Out of Politics"...........................www.elizabethwarren.com
"H.R. 2356 - Bipartisan Campaign Reform Act of 2002"..............www.congress.gov
"Democrats election Reform Bill Failed in the Senate.
　　　What's Next for Campaign Finance Reform"
　　　Jimmy Cloutier, January 27, 2022......................www.opensecrets.org
"California's shrinking population has big impacts".................www.calmatters.org
"Declaration of Independence"..................................www.bensguide.gpo.gov
"Special Taxes and Fees"...www.cdtfa.ca.gov
"Civil Reserve Air Fleet"...www.af.mil
"Guide to US War Cemeteries Located on Foreign Soil"..............www.vereranaid.org
"World War I American Cemeteries in Europe"...................www.pritzkermiitary.org
"What is a Fuel Cell"..www.climable.org
"Debunking Four Myths about the Federal Reserve"......The Federal Reserve, frbservices.org
"Seabed Mining is Coming - Bringing Mineral Riches and Fears of Epic Extinctions"
　　　...Nature, www.nature.com
"Rewriting the Future of Healthcare"....................Bayer Global, www.bayer.com
"California Budget"...www.ebudget.ca.gov
"Who Owns the U.S. National Debt"..........................www.thebalancemoney.com
"What is the National Debt".............................www.fiscaldata.treasury.gov
"The Criminal Justice System: Statistics".............................www.rainn.org
"Quotes from experts on the future of Democracy"...............www.pewreasearch.com

"Judicial Sentencing" . . . . www.ussc.gov

"Institute for the Study of War". . . . . www.understandingwar.org

"United States Sentencing Commission". . . . . www.ussc.gov

"National Laboratories" . . . . www.usa.gov

"Cost-Effective method of extracting Uranium from Seawater" . . . . .www.newatlas.com

"Fuel Cells" . . . . .www.climable.org

"2022 Nexo Fuel Cell" . . . . www.hyundaiusa.com

"Cryogenic Hydrogen". . . . . .www.sciencedirect.com

"Who Owns the US National Debt". . . . . www.thebalancemoney.com

"Confidence in the U.S. Institutions Down; Average at New Low," Gallup Poll. .news.gallup.com

"Forum on Crime and Society". . . . . www.unodc.org

"A look at Thomas Jefferson's constitutional legacy" . . . . www.constitutioncenter.org

"Thomas Jefferson and the Constitutional Convention". . . . . www.study.com

"Bill of Rights". . . . . www.billofrightsinstitute.org

"Oath of Justices and Judges- Title 28- U.S. Code p463". . . . . .www.lawcornell.edu

"Sixth Amendment to U.S. Constitution" . . . . .www.lawcornell.edu

"Unwanted Children, Unwanted Crime" . . . . www.washingtonpost.com

"Swift Justice Authorization Act" . . . . www.justice.gov

"Soil Degradation - The Problems and How to Fix Them"
                British Natural History Museum. . . . . www.nhm.ac.uk

"Soil Fertility and Erosion" . . . . www.globalagriculture.org

"The Problem of Monopolies and Corporate Public Corruption"
                American Academy of Arts and Sciences . . . . www.amacad.org

"Top Five Large Corporations Sued for Sexual Harassment". . . . . . www.caemployeelawyer.com

"Enron and the 24 Other Most Epic Corporate Downfalls of All Time" . . . .gobankingrates.com

"Analyzing the Department of Education's final Title IX rules on Sexual Misconduct"
                . . . . www.brookings.edu

"About the Fed," Board of Governors of the Federal Reserve System . . . .www.federalreserve.gov

"Is the Federal Reserve a Privately Owned Corporation?"
                Federal Reserve Bank of San Francisco . . . . www.frsf.org

"Federal Reserve Bank Ownership". . . . . www.fastcheck.org

"The Legacy of Enron in California's Power Challenges" . . . . www.marketplace.org

"Anticlines" . . . . .www.sciencedirect.com

"Golden Parachutes". . . . . www.farygodboss.com

"All of Robert Mueller's Indictments and Plea Deals in the Russia Investigation". . . . . . . vox.com

"Texas Secession was a Key Theme in Russian Disinformation
                Campaign During the 2016 Elections, Report Says" . . . . www.texastribune.org

"Texas GOP Votes Down Controversial Secession Proposal" . . . . www.texastribune.org

INTERNET / GOOGLE:

"The United States Minor Outlying Islands"...................................Google

"Definition of a Subculture" ....Google

"What Island Groups make up the Marianas islands?".........................Google

"What is Rainn Organization"..Google

"How Large is Yellowstone National Park"....................................Google

"First Amendment to the United States Constitution" ....Google

"Opinions of Thomas Jefferson"...Google

"The Promise of Gene Therapy"..Google

"How Fast do French Trains Go"...Google

"Definition of Tolerance"...Google

"Exchange Rates - Japanese Yen to American Dollars..........................Google

"Muroc" ....Google

"Average American Corporate Worker Salaries" ....Google

"Births and Deaths for Hispanic Population in the U.S.".......................Google

"Per Capita Income of Western Samoa"...Google

'What is Open Secrets"..Google

"Basic vs Applied Research" ....Google

"Byproducts of Nuclear Energy"..Google

"Byproducts of Hydrogen Combustion" ....Google

"Per Capita Income of American Samoa" ....Google

"Bering Strait"...Google

"First Arrival of the Dutch in America"..Google

"When was the Declaration of Independence Presented to England" ....Google

"Bremerton's Mothball Fleet" ....Google

"When did the US first count Indians in the census?"..........................Google

"Member countries in NATO" ....Google

"First Arrival of the French in America".......................................Google

"Breakdown of Who Pays the Most in Taxes"...................................Google

"Lawrence Livermore National Laboratory".....................................Google

"The French in New Orleans" ....Google

"The Treaty of Guadalupe Hidalgo" .... Google / National Archives

"How many nuclear power plants in France" ....Google

"What is BART" ....Google

"Just How Big are Federal Interest Payments" ....Google

"Treaty of Paris" ....Google

"Do all Federal Courts have Common Sentencing Guidelines"...................Google

"What is the percentage of convictions for capital offenses in the United State".........Google

"When did the first Continental Congress convene"............................Google

"What were the drawbacks of the Articles of Confederations" ....Google

"Importance of the Insulation Layer"..Google

"Corruption in the military."..Google

"What is the Oath of Office required of Judges"...............................Google

"Copy of each amendment to the Bill of Rights".............................Google

"Are Unwanted Children More Apt to Commit Crimes".....................Google

"Facts About the Decline of Ocean Fishing"...................................Google

"How many Die in the World from Malnutrition".............................Google

"Growth of World Population Since 1400".......................................Google

"Ways in Which Our Soil is permanently Depleted".........................Google

"Organizations that Have been Tainted with Scandal?".....................Google

"Catholic Church Abuse Scandal Statistics"....................................Google

"Scandal at the Boy Scouts of America"..Google

"What American Institutions Have been Accused of Wrongdoing
        and Sexual Abuse or Harassment".......................................Google

"Management Corruption in Large Corporations".............................Google

"Large Corporations that Went Bankrupt Due to Corruption".............Google

"Scandals Involving the Police"..Google

"What are the Most Highly Respected Institutions in America".............Google

"Large Corporations and Sexual Misconduct that Led to Failure".........Google

INTERNET- WIKIPEDIA:

"Virtues"   ....Wikipedia

"Juan Bautista Alvarado"..Wikipedia

"Alta California"...Wikipedia

"History of the Acadians"..Wikipedia

"European Economic Community"................................Wikipedia

"Xi Jinping"..Wikipedia

"United States Navy Reserve Fleets".............................Wikipedia

"List of Aircraft Carriers in Service"............................Wikipedia

"Spanish Colonization of North America".......................Wikipedia

"Dutch Colonization of the Americas"...........................Wikipedia

"Landing Helicopter Assault".....................................Wikipedia

"Landing Helicopter Dock"..Wikipedia

"Edwards Air Force Base"..Wikipedia

"The Republic of Palau"..Wikipedia

"Bipartisan Campaign Reform Act"..............................Wikipedia

"Open Secrets"...Wikipedia

"US Constitutional Convention"..................................Wikipedia

"Vanuatu"   ....Wikipedia

"Spearhead-class Expeditionary Fast Transport"..............Wikipedia

"FEC v. Wisconsin Right to Life, Inc. .... Wikipedia

"Bantu Expansion" .... Wikipedia

"List of United States presidential elections by popular vote margin".............. Wikipedia

"Lonely Planet Publishing" .... Wikipedia

"List of U.S. States and Territories by GDP" .... Wikipedia

"No Religious Test Clause" .... Wikipedia

"List of Largest Producing Countries of Agricultural Commodities".............. Wikipedia

"Aurora (aircraft)".. Wikipedia

"Metrolink (California)" .... Wikipedia

"Economy of Texas" .... Wikipedia

"California High-Speed Rail" .... Wikipedia

"Open Source".. Wikipedia

"Constitutional Convention".. Wikipedia

"Alexis de Tocqueville" .... Wikipedia

"Ariel Sharon" .... Wikipedia

"Deuterium" .... Wikipedia

"Demographics of California"... Wikipedia

"World Population"... Wikipedia

"Catholic Church Sexual Abuse Cases" .... Wikipedia

"Boy Scouts of America Sex Abuse Cases" .... Wikipedia

"Category: Law Enforcement Scandals".................................... Wikipedia

"Catholic Church Sexual Abuse Cases" .... Wikipedia

"Catholic Church Sex Abuse Cases in the United States" .... Wikipedia

"Boy Scouts of America Sex Abuse Cases" .... Wikipedia

"List of Corporate Collapses and Scandals" .... Wikipedia

"Oil and Gas in California" .... Wikipedia

"1969 Santa Barbara Oil Spill".. Wikipedia

Photo & Map Credits

The author is grateful to those providers of included photos.

This book contains information and concepts that have not been previously published. Since any profits from book sales of any kind will be donated to a non-profit, and that the purpose of this book is to make public those heretofore unpublished concepts to provide a better understanding of America and its history, this document, and its included photos and maps, is protected under the Fair Use Doctrine of the United States Copyright Act.

BOOK COVER PHOTOS:

Front	Mount Rushmore	www.canstockphoto.com
Back	American Flag (retrieved from 9/11 WTC site)	smithsonian.org

NATIONAL PARK PHOTOS:

National Parks in the Pacific Southwest:

Channel Islands, California	www.californiacrossroads.com
Death Valley, California	www.istockphoto.com
Joshua Tree, California	www.standard.co.uk
Kings Canyon, California	www.peakvisor.com
Lassen Volcanic, California	www.lonelyplanet.com
Pinnacles, California	www.insidehook.com
Redwood, California	www.selectregistry.com
Sequoia, California	www.aspeckintime.com
Yosemite, California	www.cntravelor.com
Haleakala, Hawaii	www.pinterest.com
Hawaii Volcanoes, Hawaii	www.earthtrekkers.com
American Samoa, American Samoa	www.theactivetimes.com

National Parks in the American Heartland:

Hot Springs, Arkansas	www.youtube.com
Theodore Roosevelt, North Dakota	www.stepoutside.com
Badlands, South Dakota	www.u.s.-parks.com
Wind Cave, South Dakota	www.KatieWanders.com
Great Smoky Mountains, Tennessee	www.nationalparks.org
Mammoth Cave, Kentucky	www.nationalpark.org
Gateway Arch, Missouri	www.greatriverroad.com
Isle Royale, Michigan	www.matadornetworks.com
Voyageurs, Minnesota	www.minnesotamonthly.com

Indiana Dunes, Indiana . . . . www.aroundindy-wordpress.com

New River Gorge, West Virginia. . . . . www.wvexplorer.com

Cuyahoga Valley, Ohio. . . . . www.theculturetrip.com

National Parks on the Atlantic Coast:

Acadia, Maine . . . . www.en.wikipedia.com

Shenandoah, Virginia. . . . . www.roadtrippers.com

Great Smoky Mountains, North Carolina . . . . www.tripsavey.com

Congaree, South Carolina . . . . www.meanstoexplore.com

Biscayne, Florida. . . . . www.wanderu.com

Dry Tortugas, Florida. . . . . .www.gettyimages.com

Everglades, Florida . . . . www.dirtinmyshoes.com

Virgin Islands, US Virgin Islands . . . . .www.npca.org

National Parks in the Pacific Northwest:

Denali, Alaska . . . . .www.wildnatureimages.com

Gates of the Arctic, Alaska. . . . . .www.rvshare.com

Glacier Bay, Alaska . . . . www.britannica.com

Katmai, Alaska. . . . . www.istockphoto.com

Kobuk Valley, Alaska . . . . www.pictoram.com

Lake Clark, Alaska . . . . .www.gonorth-alaska.com

Wrangell - St. Elias, Alaska . . . . www.gonorth-alaska.com

Kenai Fjords, Alaska. . . . . www.onlyinyourstte.com

Mount Rainier, Washington . . . . www.treehuggar.com

North Cascades, Washington . . . . www.bearfoottheory.com

Olympic, Washington. . . . . www.ourdoorphotographer.com

Crater Lake, Oregon. . . . . www.togetheranywhere.com

National Parks in the American Southwest:

Grand Canyon, Arizona. . . . . www.cntraveler.com

Petrified Forest, Arizona . . . . www.parksandtrips.com

Saguaro, Arizona. . . . . www.travelandleisure.com

Red Rock State Park, Arizona . . . . www.travellers.com

Great Basin, Nevada . . . . www.hikeitbaby.com

Carlsbad Caverns, New Mexico . . . . www.sahahmartinhood.com

White Sands, New Mexico. . . . . www.apertureandlight.com

Big Bend, Texas . . . . .www.en.wikipedia.com

Guadalupe Mountains, Texas . . . . www.britannica.com

National Parks in the Rocky Mountains:

Black Canyon of the Gunnison, Colorado . . . . www.en.wikipedia.com

Great Sand Dunes, Colorado. www.bearfoottheory.com

Mesa Verde, Colorado www.5280.com

Rocky Mountains, Colorado . . . . www.bouldercoloradousa.com

Glacier, Montana. . . . . www.nps.gov

Yellowstone, Wyoming. . . . . www.moon.com

Grand Teton, Wyoming . . . . www.en.wikipedia.com

Arches, Utah . . . . www.amtrakvacations.com

Bryce Canyon, Utah . . . . www.nm.utahparks.com

Canyonlands, Utah . . . . www.lonelyplanet.com

Capitol Reef, Utah. . . . . www.washingtonpost.com

Zion, Utah . . . . www.outsideonline.com

Grand Escalante Staircase National Monument, Utah . . . . . www.nationalparkreservations.com

CHAPTER PHOTOS & MAPS:

Chapter Six:

Map showing Bering Strait. www.ibtimes.com

Photo of man standing, looking at Russia . . . . www.drivinvibin.com

Chapter Seven:

Artist conception of Aurora . . . . Wikipedia

Map of Southern California. www.enwiivoyage.com

Map of Los Angeles Metrorail . . . . www.pinterest.com

Map of the BART transportation system . . . . Bay Area Rapid Transit

Map of California high-speed rail lines . . . . www.hsrail.org

Photo of HyperloopTT test track in France. . . . . HyperloopTT

Photo of HyperloopTT levitated train . . . . www.newcivilengineer.com

Chapter Eight:

Photo of U.S. Capitol building . . . . www.disolve.com

Photo of U.S. Supreme Court building. . . . . www.wbur.org

Chapter Thirteen:

Photo of Bahia de San Quintin . . . . Wikipedia

Chapter Fourteen:

Map of the Clarion-Clipperton Zone (CCZ). . . . . Daily Mail

Chapter Seventeen:

Photo of the C-130 . . . . Wikipedia

Our Natural Wonders

Whatever America hopes to bring to pass in the world must first come to pass in the heart of America." — **General of the Army and President Dwight David Eisenhower Inaugural Address, Washington DC, 1-20-1953**

NATIONAL PARKS:

The United States invented the National Park system. Yellowstone became the first park in the 1800s followed by the establishment of a greater park system than found anywhere in the world.

"Thirty states in the United States have national parks. In addition, two American territories, the United States Virgin Islands and American Samoa, also have national parks. In total, these states and territories protect 63 national parks."

The states and territories without national parks are Alabama, Connecticut, Delaware, Georgia, Illinois, Iowa, Kansas, Louisiana, Maryland, Massachusetts, Mississippi, Nebraska, New Hampshire, New Jersey, New York, Oklahoma, Pennsylvania, Rhode Island, Vermont, and Wisconsin. Territories without national parks include Puerto Rico, Guam, and the Northern Mariana Islands.

To give an idea of size and location, the following listing is provided. Several of the parks also include ocean area, which is shown in purple:

Park:	Country:	Size in km^2:
(1) Paphanaumokuakea Marine	Hawaii, USA	1,510,000
(2) Northeast Greenland	Greenland (Denmark)	972,000
(3) Kavango Zambezi Transfrontier	Zambia, Botswana,Namibia, Zimbabwe, & Angola	519,912
(4) Phoenix Islands (Pacific)	Kiribati Republic	408,250
(5) Great Barrier Reef Marine	Australia	344,400
(6) Galapagos Marine Reserve	Ecuador	133,000
(7) Great Limpopo Transfrontier	South Africa, Mozambique, Zimbabwe	99,800
(8) Arctic National Wildlife Refuge	Alaska, USA	78,051
(9) Yukon Delta Wildlife Refuge	Canada	77,538
(10) Queen Maud Gulf Migratory Bird Sanctuary (Canada)		61,765
(11) Selous Game Reserve	Tanzania	54,600
(12) Wrangell-St Elias Park & Preserve Alaska, USA		53,321
(13) Central Kalahari Game Preserve Botswana		52,000
(14) Namib-Naukluft	Namibia	49,768
(15) Wood Buffalo	Canada	44,807
Yellowstone	Wyoming, USA	8,991

The author has chosen to honor the beauty and diversity of our National Parks by including photos of them all within the text of this book.

NATIONAL MONUMENTS:

"Additionally," as of January 2021, there are 130 National Monuments that are managed by various federal agencies. National Monuments are located in 32 states, the District of Columbia, the Virgin Islands, American Samoa, the Minor Outlying Islands, and the Northern Marianas. From New York's Statue of Liberty to the Muir Woods of California, these monuments are as diverse as they are beautiful.

The federal agencies that manage the vast National Monument system are almost as diverse as the system itself: The National Park Service (NPS) manages 85 of the monuments, one of which is co-managed with the Fish and Wildlife Service (FWS), and two with the Bureau of Land Management (BLM).

The Bureau of Land Management manages 28 monuments, five of which are co-managed with the National Park Service. Both agencies, along with the FWS, are under the Department of the Interior. The FWS manages 9 monuments, five with the National Oceanic and Atmospheric Administration (NOAA), one with the NPS, and one with the Department of Energy (DOE).

The United States Forest Service (USFS), which is under the Department of Agriculture, manages 14 monuments, five which are co-managed with BLM. The NOAA manages five, which are all co-managed with FWS. The DOE only manages one and that is co-managed, also with the FWS. The NOAA is under the Department of Commerce.

The final two monuments are under the Department of Defense: The United States Air Force manages one and the Armed Forces Retirement Home manages the other.

LISTING OF NATIONAL MONUMENTS BY STATE OR TERRITORY:

AMERICAN STATES with NATIONAL MONUMENTS: (listed by number)

CALIFORNIA (18): Berryessa Snow Mountain, Cabrillo, California Coastal, Carrizo Plain, Cascade-Siskiyou (with Oregon), Castle Mountains, Cesar E. Chavez, Devil's Postpile, Fort Ord, Giant Sequoia, Lava Beds, Mojave Trails, Muir Woods, Saint Francis Dam Disaster, San Gabriel Mountains, Sand to Snow, Santa Rosa and San Jacinto Mountains, Tule Lake

ARIZONA (18): Agua Fria, Canyon de Chelly, Casa Grande Ruins, Chiricahua, Grand Canyon-Parashant, Hohokam Pima, Ironwood Forest, Montezuma Castle, Navaho, Organ Pipe Cactus, Pipe Spring, Sonoran Desert, Sunset Crater, Volcano, Tonto, Tuzigoot, Vermilion Cliffs, Walnut Canyon, Wupatki

NEW MEXICO (13): Aztec Ruins, Bandelier, Capulin Volcano, El Malpais, El Morro, Fort Union, Gila Cliff Dwellings, Kash-Katuwe Tent Rocks, Organ Mountains - Desert Peaks, Petroglyph, Prehistoric Trackways, Rio Grande del Norte, Salinas Pueblo Missions

UTAH (9): Bear Ears, Cedar Breaks, Dinosaur (with Colorado), Grand Staircase-Escalante, Hovenweep (with Colorado), Jurassic, Natural Bridges, Rainbow Bridge, Timpanogos Cave

COLORADO (8): Brown's Canyon, Camp Hale--Continental Divide, Canyons of the Ancients, Chimney Rock, Colorado, Dinosaur (with Utah), Florissant Fossil Beds, Hovenseep (with Utah), Yucca House

NEW YORK (6): African Burial Ground, Castle Clinton, Fort Stanwix, Governors Island, Statue of Liberty (shared with New Jersey), Stonewall

ALASKA (5): Admiralty Island, Aleutian Island World War II, Aniakchak, Cape Krusenstern, Misty Fjords

OREGON (4): Cascade-Siskiyou (with California), John Day Fossil Beds, Newberry Volcanic, Oregon Caves

WASHINGTON (3): Hanford Reach, Mount St. Helens Volcanic, San Juan Islands

WYOMING (3): Devil's Tower, Fossil Butte, Pompeys Pillar

VIRGINIA (3): Booker T. Washington, Fort Monroe, George Washington Birthplace

ALABAMA (3): Birmingham Civil Rights, Freedom Riders, Russell Cave

TEXAS (3): Alibates Flint Quarries, Military Working Dog Teams, Waco Mammoth

NEVADA (3): Basin and Range, Gold Butte, Tule Springs Fossil Beds

IDAHO (2): Craters of the Moon, Hagerman Fossil Beds,

GEORGIA (2): Fort Frederica, Fort Pulaski

NEBRASKA (2): Agate Fossil Beds, Scotts Bluff

MONTANA (2): Little Bighorn Battlefield, Upper Missouri River Breaks

MINNESOTA (2): Grand Portage, Pipestone

KENTUCKY (2): Camp Nelson, Mill Springs Battlefield

MARYLAND (2): Fort McHenry, Harriet Tubman Underground Railroad

FLORIDA (2): Castillo de San Marcos, Fort Matanzas

OHIO (1): Charles Young Buffalo Soldiers

MISSOURI (1): George Washington Carver

IOWA (1): Effigy Mounds

SOUTH DAKOTA (1): Jewel Cave

MAINE (1): Katahdin Woods and Waters

LOUISIANA (1): Poverty Point

ILLINOIS (1): Pullman

MISSISSIPPI (1): Medgar and Myrlie Evers Home

HAWAII (1): Papahanaumokuakea Marine (with U.S. Minor Outlying Islands)

AMERICAN TERRITORIES, DISTRICTS, & OUTLYING PACIFIC ISLANDS:
U.S. MINOR OUTLYING (Pacific) ISLANDS (3):

The Minor Outlying Islands consist of eight islands or island groups: Baker Island, Howland Island, Jarvis Island, Johnston Atoll, Kingman Reef, Midway Atoll, Palmyra Atoll and Wake Island, Northeast Canyons and Seamounts Marine, Pacific Remote Islands Marine, Papahanaumokuakea Marine (with Hawaii).

DISTRICT of COLUMBIA (2): Belmont-Paul Women's Equality, President Lincoln & Soldier's Home

UNITED STATES VIRGIN ISLANDS (2): Buck Island Reef, Virgin Islands Coral Reef

AMERICAN SAMOA (1): Rose Atoll Marine

MARIANAS ISLANDS – Consisting of the Northern Marianas and Guam (1): The Northern Marianas include 14 islands with the main islands being: Saipan, Guguan, Tinian, Rota, and Pagan. The Marianas also include Guam and the Yap Island Group, but Yap is administered by the Caroline Islands: Marianas Trench Marine, (the Marianas Trench is the deepest point of all the oceans).

America–An Exceptional Country
Listing of American Accomplishments

"A lot of different flowers make a bouquet." — **Islamic Proverb**

<u>**THE GOOD SIDE of AMERICA:**</u>

    <u>**Authors Note:**</u> *Throughout this book, I refer to American faults. It sometimes helps to remember that America is a good country. We have many things to be proud of. I have tried my best to find out and print the truth about our faults and with what is printed below, our strengths and virtues as a people. Sometimes that truth can shed our great country in bad light. That is not my purpose. Our country has always been unafraid to criticize itself, and that is one of our many virtues. Criticism is necessary for us to grow in our ever-changing culture and society.*

    Below, I will point out many of the things we have done that have improved our world and our innovation and generosity have been, and are, rather amazing. It is meant to shine a light on our bright side, which far outshines our dark side. The listings of our discoveries and inventions are both very long. Our collective accomplishments have provided most of what we use in our everyday lives. Read them. They are also what the rest of the world uses in their everyday lives. It makes one proud to be a citizen of an America that has been so generous to, and beneficial for, our world community.

<u>**AN EXCEPTIONAL COUNTRY:**</u>

    Throughout the history of any country there are myths and hidden truths, and ours is not excepted. My research has illuminated several things that the history of our country has chosen not to emphasize. It is better to emphasize good things, rather than bad, but the bad have to be understood in order for the good to be better understood and appreciated.

    A diverse culture is often at cross purposes. The New England churches preached for generations against the evils of slavery, yet our ancestors participated by buying, using, and selling humans. Sometimes under the cloak of national security, our motives are more skewed to profits than the national good. Yet, we are the world's greatest donor nation.

    While we may be imperfect, the good far outweighs the bad. We are an exceptional country by almost any evaluation. Consider what we have accomplished: Instead of being a tribe of common blood, we are an amalgamation of many tribes and diverse bloods. Yet, we have united under a banner of community that adheres to the rule of law, to democratic principles, and to basic human rights.

<u>**AMERICAN EFFORTS to END COLONIALISM:**</u>

    Prior to World War II, victorious nations always claimed properties belonging to the defeated nations. It was the case in World War I, when Britain and France punished Germany by exacting monetary and territorial sacrifices as spoils of war. At the end of World War II, the United States and the Soviet Union were clearly victorious. America claimed nothing, yet the Soviets moved their western borders 500 miles farther west, forcibly occupied its so-called Warsaw Pact neighbors, and wrested the Kurile Islands and the rest of Sakhalin Island from a defeated Japan, even though the Soviet Union only entered the war against Japan one week before its defeat and never fired a shot against Japan. Instead of claiming spoils of war, we spent part of our national treasure to help our former enemies recover from their wounds of war. That is the action of a good and caring country.

A reported 1943 meeting in London between the British military and the U.S. Army Air Corp, resulted in an agreement for the British to accomplish a final dismantling of their colonial system after the end of the war in return for American help in defeating Nazi Germany. With consideration that there is more German-American blood than English-American blood in America, our help for Britain against Germany was not a given.

HONORING OUR PROMISES and COMMITMENTS:

Prior to the 20th century, America was interested in territorial expansion. The result was a sad tale of not honoring many agreements and treaties signed with the various Indian tribes throughout our land.

Since the start of the 20th Century, we have never coveted the lands of others and have only administered lands temporarily at the conclusion of world wars. We offer lands to join us by choice, as the Northern Mariana Islands have recently done, rather than by force-of-arms.

The Federated States of Micronesia, were Pacific trust territories of the United States after World War II. We administered them under a United Nations mandate until we deemed it right to release them back to their own control. Yet we have treaties with the Republic of Palau and with the Caroline and Marshall Islands to protect and defend them. At our own expense, we have entrusted the care of their infrastructure to our Pacific Seabees, which is the popular name given to our Pacific Naval Construction Battalion based in California.

Before Jamestown and the *Mayflower*, countries often based their claims on foreign lands on the basis of voyages sailed. The United States "sailed" to the Moon and planted its flag, but it was in behalf of our effort and, instead, claimed the Moon for all mankind. Think about that. We were establishing that space was not to be a continuation of past claims by individual countries.

NASA (National Aeronautical and Space Administration) has launched multiple space probes that were the first visits to planets and moons within our Solar System. (See the discoveries portion of this section). Yet we did not claim them for America. If the Soviet Union had been the first to visit the Moon, do you think that they would have claimed it for all mankind? Would any other nation have done what we did?

During World War II, we promised to waive our claim on the Philippine Islands and grant their independence. We honored that promise and they now celebrate July 4, 1946 as the birth of their nation.

In 1999, we honored our commitment to independent Panama by turning over the Panama Canal, which American funding, ingenuity, and the enormous efforts of the United States Army Corp of Engineers, had built for the significant betterment of worldwide trade. We did it after France was unable and after the expenditure of 22,000 French lives.

Our goal with the Canal was never to enrich ourselves. That was always evident in that we hardly raised our transit prices that we put in place just after completion of the Panama Canal, almost a hundred years before revision of control to Panama. Our goal was to vastly shorten the distances needed to travel for trading ships, to enrich world trade, and thus bring richer lives to those living within the trading nations.

MEETING & DEFEATING OUR CHALLENGES:

Our nation has continually met and conquered our challenges.

We were challenged by a hostile environment and hostile natives, yet we were able to conquer the land and create a great nation based on enduring values and a stable, long-lasting   structure.

We met the challenge of a dictatorial Britain and defeated it militarily, twice.

We met the challenge of dissolution by defeating the forces that tried to separate us in a tragic Civil War.

We met the challenge of our fast-disappearing natural wonders by creating the National Park System. We were the first nation in the world to establish National Parks.

We met the challenge of an authoritarian Germany by defeating it militarily, twice.

We met the challenge of a worldwide depression by changing the structure of our government, changing the authority of our government, and changing its relation to our industries.

We met the challenge of an expansionist Japanese Empire and defeated it militarily.

We met the challenge posed by the multiplicity of nations by creating the United Nations, fostering the creation of the Common Market leading to the European Union.

We met the challenge of expansionist Russia by creating NATO to stop the relentless spread of Russia in the aftermath of World War II, and in the old and new Cold Wars, that have made the 21st century as dangerous as the 20th.

We met the challenge, posed by President Kennedy, of sending a man successfully to the moon and returning him successfully back to earth, within the decade of the 1960s.

We have met the multiple challenges posed by nations trying to expand their control in: Korea, in Vietnam, and in Kuwait.

We are meeting the challenge posed by a worldwide pandemic. We will defeat it.

Through dedication, determination and diligence, we have met and defeated all our challenges. We have often led the world in great efforts. It is the nature of our people, who in our infancy as a nation, grew their character by always reaching for the goal of the frontier. Always striving to achieve, America needs a goal.

Perhaps the greatest challenge to face us is that of a changing environment. Our number one goal should be to save our world as we know it. It will take total dedication and a commitment like no other. We have to change our long-standing dependence on fossil fuels and find ways to work in concert with our environment and not against it. To do that, we have to convince other nations to work together. To do that, we must be willing to give up some of our cherished national sovereignty. It will not be easy. It will be the hardest things we have ever done, both individually and collectively.

But we have shown we can successfully weather the coming storm and create a better world, a sustainable world, in the process.

We need only look back at what we have accomplished. Prior to this, our greatest goal and challenge of the past was the creation of a great nation and then spreading that nation westward in a manner as shown within this book.

WHAT WE HAVE DONE and WHAT WE DO:

We are often the first to rescue in times of peril.

We have created, through our Constitution, a nation dedicated to rule by the majority with protections for the minorities.

Our soldiers, sailors, airmen and civilian governmental workers, swear allegiance to our Constitution, not to any leader.

We created three branches of government under law, with one branch dedicated to making the laws, another to enforcing the laws, and a final branch to interpreting the laws.

We were the first to have public schools.

We were the first to have free public libraries and have built a university system that is the envy of the world.

While it is imperfect, we built a national health-care system that has foreigners flocking to our hospitals, just as they flock to our universities.

We sponsor global research.

We delegate decision-making to our states more than ever practiced in our world.

With government help, we established our farms to be the breadbasket of the world and have never used food as an instrument for forcing our national policies, or as a tool to raise export prices as have other countries who control a needed product, such as petroleum.

We built an economy so vast that it staggers the rest of the world in comparison.

We built a Navy that is able to project national power to all corners of the world, with nuclear-powered aircraft carriers that exceed the numbers of the rest of the world, combined.

We invented the airplane and have perfected its use by setting production, safety, and performance standards emulated throughout the world economies, airlines, and governments.

We have created a world order based on common needs and values, with the idea that we can make ours a better world by working together and preventing wars, rather than being separate and creating wars.

Instead of the world practice, in vogue before Jamestown and the *Mayflower*, of creating alliances to further war, we sponsored NATO to prevent war and sponsored the United Nations to encourage peace.

We encouraged unity by establishing the European Common Market, which has developed into the European Union.

We encourage world democracies.

We have also sponsored other worldwide organizations to bring together like-minded people from throughout the world to help solve mankind's problems such as hunger, disease, lack of water, and poverty.

We became the first to have a governmental agency dedicated to protect Americans, as well as the entire world, from the ravages of disease and pandemics.

Through science and innovation, we have created farming practices and new or changed plant species that have greatly lessened world hunger.

Our scientists have enriched the world's collective knowledge and made our lives better.

Our industries have designed products to make all of our lives easier.

We launch space probes and satellites that provide, without charge, knowledge and capabilities for the entire world.

Our Air Force gave to the world: the internet, without charge or contract, devised the wind-chill factor for better evaluation of temperature-wind effects, created PERT (Program Evaluation and Revue Technic), which revolutionized methods and almost cut in half the time necessary for the development of large-scale, multi-subcontractor, weapon systems and aircraft. The method was adopted by industry.

We proposed, funded with three billion dollars, and sponsored the Human Genome Project which, with its development of DNA, is continuing to revolutionize the health-care industry and holds promise of amazing, future gene-therapies.

We proposed, funded, and sponsored a worldwide navigation system

We proposed, funded and sponsored a worldwide weather satellite system.

We did the same for a global communication system and a Global Positioning System

We devised, helped fund, and helped build a worldwide air traffic control system.

We proposed and sponsored Interpol, which is a worldwide system for reducing crime.

We created and provided initial funding for the World Bank, which provides worldwide loans for needed projects.

We proposed, sponsored and funded the World Health Organization (WHO).

We were the first to provide street lights for cities.

We wrote the Japanese Constitution, which, for the first time, gave equal rights to women, structured a democratic system, and allowed labor to unionize.

We have repeatedly come to the aid of Africa by providing: food for its famines, Peace Corps help for its villages, capital for its major projects, and personnel and supplies for its epidemics. We were a major factor in the elimination of Apartheid in South Africa.

Our inventors, universities, and innovators have given the world personal computers and super-smart phones that have changed how we communicate, how we access knowledge, and have literally changed our lives.

Our athletes have defined the meaning of good competition and have continually set Olympic standards.

We were victorious when we met the challenge of the worldwide depression by revamping how our government operates with relation to the scope of its efforts and its relation to our industrial base. We built a better, fairer system, and recovered.

We met the challenge of a colossal world tyrant in Hitler, by expanding our peacetime military, numbering 139,000 in 1938, to more than 11 million at the conclusion of World War II in 1945. We were victorious.

We have built the largest air force in the world (USAF).

We have built the 3rd largest air force in the world (USN).

We have built the 4th largest air force in the world (USA)

We sponsored the international use of Antarctica, instead of claiming it as a territory of the United States, when we established the first scientific station on Antarctica at McMurdo Sound in February, 1956.

We honor our commitments, by funding organizations intent on the good.

We answer the call of famine, by providing food for the hungry.

We commit American troops for the protection of others.

We fund research to better the lives of the entire world.

We sponsor construction standards that save lives.

We often give our creations and discoveries to the world without charge of any kind.

We are among the first to always offer aide to those in need or suffering from disaster.

The list goes on.

AMERICAN DISCOVERIES:

Even though America was created after much of the physical part of our globe had been discovered, we still managed to find a few places on earth and about our earth: The Jet Stream and the Gulf Stream, Johnston Atoll, Fanning Atoll, Teraina Island, Palmyra Atoll, Kingman Reef, South Orkney Islands, Howland Island, Baker Island, and Midway Atoll, the process of Seafloor Spreading.

We managed to get in on the ground floor of discoveries in our Solar System and the Universe in which we live: Deimos and Photos (moons of Mars), Amalthea, Sinope, Carme, Lysithea, Ananke, Leda, Themisto, Metis, Thebe (moons and satellites of Jupiter), Phoebe, Pandora, Prometheus, Atlas, moons of Saturn, Miranda, Puck, Portia, Juliet, Cressida, Rosalind, Belinda, Desdemona, Cordelia, Ophelia, Bianca, Mab, Perdita, Cupid, moons and satellites of Uranus, Nereid, Larissa, Proteus, Despina, Galatea, Thalassa, Sedna, Psamathe, moons and satellites of Neptune, Pluto, Charon, Hydra, Nix, moons of Pluto, Seyfert Galaxies, elliptical galaxies, Van Allen Radiation Belt, Lucifer (main belt asteroid), Barium Stars.

Pulsating white dwarf stars, Binary pulsar stars, 1983 Bok-minor planet, Rings of Uranus, Rings of Jupiter, Rings of Neptune, Comet Shoemaker-Levy 9, Comet Hale-Bopp, dwarf planet in Kuiper Belt, Makemake (3rd largest dwarf planet in Solar System), Eris (largest dwarf planet in Solar System), Dysnomia (moon of Eris), Barnard's Star, Orcus (trans-Neptunian dwarf planet and its moon Vanth.)

Dinosaurs: Torosaurus, Tyrannosaurus, Oviraptor.

Health & Biology: the smoking-cancer link, Embryonic stem cells, Heparin, Aspartame, Vitamins A & E, Niacin, homeostasis, Warfarin, Serotonin, Tetracycline, polio vaccine, DNA structure, and drugs too numerous to count or mention. Particles, Waves, Atomic structures.

Electron diffraction, heavy hydrogen, cosmic radio waves, positrons, deuterium (heavy water).

Elementary Particles: (Muons, Neutrinos, Tau leptons), Antiproton, Antineutron, Kaon (mesons), Quarks, Eta Meson, Xi baryon. The list goes on and on.

Synthetic chemical elements: (Plutonium, Streptomycin, Americium, Curium, Promethium, Berkelium, Californium, Einsteinium, Mendelevium, Seaborgium, Di-positronium),

Polymers: Fluropolymers, Teflon, and many others.

This listing is incomplete.

AMERICAN INVENTIONS:

Americans have always been an inventive people.

Electric cars, plastics, the telephone, microprocessors, lasers, the zipper, lightbulbs, artificial hearts, pacemakers, fire alarm systems, hearing aids, dental floss, the phonograph, electro-magnetic motors, sewing machines, motion picture projectors, nylon, nuclear reactors, microchips, mobile phones, e-mail, video games, chemotherapy, light-emitting diodes (LEDs), assembly lines, microwave ovens, traffic lights, cardiac defibrillators, radiocarbon dating, weed whackers, universal product codes, anti-lock brakes, magnetic resonance imaging, cellphones, aircraft, voicemail, digital cameras, electronic spreadsheets, we discovered electricity and created DC and AC current, Space Shuttle, graphical user interface, 3-D printing, contact lenses, nicotine patch, stealth technology.

Hubble space telescope, Photoshop, smart pills, drones, propane, computer operating systems, Wi-Fi, iPod, bio-artificial liver, Facebook, YouTube, Twitter, iPhone, Fitbit, 3-D ocean farms, COVID vaccines, catheters, lightning rods, swivel chairs, flatboats, bifocals, cotton gin, wheel cipher, cupcakes, suspension bridges, fire hydrants, amphibious vehicles, refrigeration, coffee percolators, circular saws, milling machines, multiple coil magnets, doorbells, , combine harvesters, solar compasses, electrical relays, gridirons, circuit breakers, morse code, steam shovels, corn shellers, sleeping railroad cars, vulcanized rubber, trusses, grain elevators, inhalational anesthetics, ice-cream makers, rotary printing presses, gas masks, printing telegraph machines, baseball, basketball, donuts, jackhammers, dishwashers, safety pins, inverted microscopes, burglar alarms, potato chips, breast pumps, egg beaters, condensed milk.

WD-40, toilet paper, mason jars, vacuum cleaners, escalators, electric stoves, dustpans, ironing boards, electronic pencil sharpeners, pencil erasers, postcards, machine guns, breakfast cereals, jelly beans, ratchet wrenches, urinals, motorcycles, paper clips, barbed wire, paper bags, vibrators, tape measures, pipe wrenches, clothes hangers, can openers, sandblasters, feather dusters, earmuffs, grain silos, jeans, fire sprinklers, mimeographs, synthesizers, airbrushes, cartons, cash registers, fuel oil burners, metal detectors, clothing irons, electric fans, solar cells, thermostats, dissolvable pills, skyscrapers, popcorn machines, cooking mixers, fuel dispensers, filing cabinets, screen doors, induction motors, drinking straws, revolving doors, ballpoint pens, payphones, space observatories.

Tupperware, credit cards, diapers, transistors, supersonic aircraft, hair spray, cable television, satellite television, video games, atomic clocks, heart monitors, aerosol paint, teleprompters, artificial hearts, heart-lung machines, voltmeters, cardiopulmonary resuscitators, synthetic diamonds, radar guns, nuclear submarines, hard-disk drives, videotapes, Fortran programming language, skid-steer loaders, integrated circuits, weather satellites, child-safety seats, Spandex, GPS systems, oral contraceptive pills, biofeedback, communication satellites, glucose meters.

Kevlar, cordless phones, compact discs, calculators, virtual reality, Tasers, catalytic converters, post-it notes, acoustic microscopes, Ethernet, coolers, drilling rigs, gas centrifuges, air conditioning, autopilots, carburetors, carbon fibers, bulldozers, blenders, bobby pins, computer monitors, the computer mouse, crayons, debit cards, dehumidifiers, deodorant.

Dishwashers, electric knives, electric shavers, electric toothbrush, Fax machines, computing firewalls, flowcharts, fluorescent lamps, frozen foods, powered garage doors, gasoline pumps, road graders, hair dryers, hydraulic brakes, industrial robots, mace, light guns, keypunches, kerosene, jukeboxes, jet injectors, JavaScript, magnetic storage, masking tape, cloud seeding, meat slicers, microphones, nail guns.

Neoprene, power steering, polygraph, pipe cutters, pagers, radio telescopes, revolvers, Rogallo wing, rotary dial, roto-rooters, safety razors, salt and pepper shakers, semi-trailer trucks, metal arc-welding, shopping carts, silly putty, silica gel, skateboards, smoke detectors, soldering guns, soundbars, slide-away beds, staplers, storyboards, supercomputers, televisions, tea bags, supermarkets, windowed envelopes, wireless keyboards, workstations, and the telegraph.

Anybody reading this listing will find it amazing. Americans reading it will find it a source of pride. It is the author's hope that someone reading this will find that adding to human knowledge and capabilities is a worthy goal in life and that someday he or she will add to this list.

About the Author

The author, Russ Goodenough, was both a military and civilian pilot prior to concentrating on the writing of books. In the military, he flew the then-fastest operational fighter in the world, the F-4C Phantom II. He attended the United States Air Force Academy. During his wartime, he flew 148 combat missions over all of Southeast Asia, including North Vietnam, China, Laos and the Gulf of Tonkin.

In combat, he won the Distinguished Flying Cross (DFC), the Purple Heart, (9) Air Medals, the Air Force Commendation Medal, the Combat Readiness Medal, the Longevity Medal with Oak Leaf Cluster, the U.S. National Defense Service Medal, the Small Arms Marksmanship Medal, the Vietnam Service Medal with two Bronze Service Stars, the Republic of Vietnam awarded Civil Action Campaign Medal, the Republic of Vietnam awarded Civil Action Outstanding Unit Citation with Order of the Palm and the United States Air Force Outstanding Unit Award with an Oak Leaf Cluster.

Additionally, he wore the U.S. Army Paratrooper Wings as a jump-qualified Forward Air Controller. He was an F-4 Aircraft Commander, F-4 Combat Flight Leader, F-4 Instructor Pilot and Maintenance Test Pilot. While flying the F-4 for NATO as part of the European War Plan, he was also a nuclear bomb commander in charge of five bombs. The Martin Baker Company of London, England, maker of the Phantom ejection seats, honored him as the only airman in the world to have ejected from both the front and back seats of the F-4 Phantom.

For 15 years, Goodenough flew for Continental Airlines, the last four of which were in the South Pacific. His destinations included Hawaii, Samoa, Fiji, New Zealand, Australia, Guam, Okinawa, Taiwan, and Hong Kong. He flew the inaugural flight for Continental in the South Pacific and retired as a Captain on the DC-10.

For 34 years, he owned and was President and CEO of Cal U-Rent and Cal Party Rent of Thousand Oaks, and Ventura, California. Cal U-Rent was a homeowner and contractor rental company featuring tools and equipment up to large-sized loaders, dozers, excavators, backhoes, and lifts. He rented many different types of trucks and trailers and was the largest retailer of propane in the tri-county region of Ventura, Santa Barbara and San Luis Obispo Counties.

He started his writing career in high school, when he wrote articles about the Fillmore High football team. He was team quarterback and would write a column after the completion of each game. While at the Air Academy, the USAF published an essay of his concerning immigration. While with Cal U-Rent, he was lead-writer and Editor of the *Conejo Business Times*, a Chamber of Commerce paper widely read in the Conejo Valley.

Russ is now retired with his wife Carolyn and busy writing books. This is his fifth book.

Books by the Author

The author began writing books late in life, after several careers involving piloting of aircraft and the running of a business. Starting in high school, he wrote columns for the local paper, the Fillmore Herald. At the United States Air Force Academy, an essay of his concerning immigration was published by the United States Air Force. While running his small business,

Cal U-Rent, he served as Editor and principle writer for the Conejo Business Times, a regional publication in Eastern Ventura County. He has found writing to be exciting, educational, and very rewarding.

CURRENT BOOKS:

His first book was an unpublished **History of Hangar 99**, which was about the fraternal organization known as the QBs or Quiet Birdmen. The challenge for him was to find out the truth about the blending of three different histories of the national QB organization. Birdmen include about 20,000 nationally and included President George Herbert Walker Bush.

The second book of the author was **Why Johnny Came Marching Home.** Johnny was published and is available on Amazon.com. It is the story of the clandestine air wars that were fought in the skies over Laos, North Vietnam, the Gulf of Tonkin, and China during the Vietnam War. He returned from fighting that war fully expecting that an author would write about what really happened. His wait took 45 years and he finally became convinced that, if it was to be written at all, he would have to write it. He wanted to tell why we lost the clandestine air wars, which led to our defeat in the Vietnamese War itself.

He wanted to convey to the American public what life was like for a combat pilot in Southeast Asia. He also wanted other pilots who had participated, to find out what happened in the years that they did not participate in such a long war. In that, he sometimes got into the technical.

It took three years to write as it involved many declassified reports from agencies such as the DOD, CIA, NSA, USN, and the Pacific Air Forces (PACAF).

A reader may be interested to find out what happened in the battles in the skies that included severe losses against the forces of China and Russia, in addition to those from North Vietnam. North Korea was also a participant. American fighter-bombers attacked the most sophisticated and heavily gunned and heavily missiled air defense in the history of aerial warfare.

His third book was also published and is available on Amazon.com. It is titled **Darkness @ Noon: Battling the Beast.** It is the story of the day-by-day fight against the Thomas Fire, which consumed so much of Southern California in December 2017 and January of 2018. Due to the hellacious winds, the fire's start was explosive. At the time, it was the largest, single wildfire in the history of California. It involved the greatest assemblage of fire-fighting equipment, including over a thousand fire engines, in the history of California. It also involved the greatest usage of airborne fire-fighting in the then-history of the world.

The fourth book is titled **Westward Wagons: An American Family Journey.** In it, the author portrays the life and travels of a family that emigrated from England and arrived to settle the Massachusetts Bay Colony. It details the many adventures of the family as it crossed the United States by railroad, stagecoach and finally, by covered wagon. It describes many first-published accounts of the many battles fought and atrocities committed by the settlers, by the militias, and by the Indian tribes. It tells of the huge families of the original Puritan settlers in what would become the state of Massachusetts. He also details American white slavery in its many forms.

His wife, Carolyn, helped him in his extensive research, which took over two and a half years to accomplish and write. The book shows an America never previously described and a history never taught in our high school classrooms.

Made in the USA
Columbia, SC
21 April 2023

15660004R00141